D1166017

THE WON CAUSE

CIVIL WAR AMERICA Gary W. Gallagher, editor

BARBARA A. GANNON

THE WON CAUSE

Black and White Comradeship in the

Grand Army of the Republic

The University of North Carolina Press Chapel Hill

© 2011 The University of North Carolina Press
All rights reserved. Manufactured in the United States of America
Designed by Courtney Leigh Baker and set in Minion Pro by Tseng Information
Systems, Inc. The paper in this book meets the guidelines for permanence and
durability of the Committee on Production Guidelines for Book Longevity of the
Council on Library Resources. The University of North Carolina Press has
been a member of the Green Press Initiative since 2003.

Library of Congress Cataloging-in-Publication Data
Gannon, Barbara A.
The won cause : black and white comradeship in the
Grand Army of the Republic / Barbara A. Gannon.
p. cm.
Includes bibliographical references and index.
ISBN 978-0-8078-3452-7 (cloth : alk. paper)
1. Grand Army of the Republic—History. 2. United States—History—Civil War,
1861–1865—Societies, etc. 3. United States—History—Civil War, 1861–1865—
Veterans. 4. United States—Race relations—History—19th century. I. Title.
E462.1.A7G36 2011
369′.15—dc22
2010045628

cloth   15 14 13 12 11   5 4 3 2 1

MIX
Paper from
responsible sources
FSC
www.fsc.org   FSC® C013483

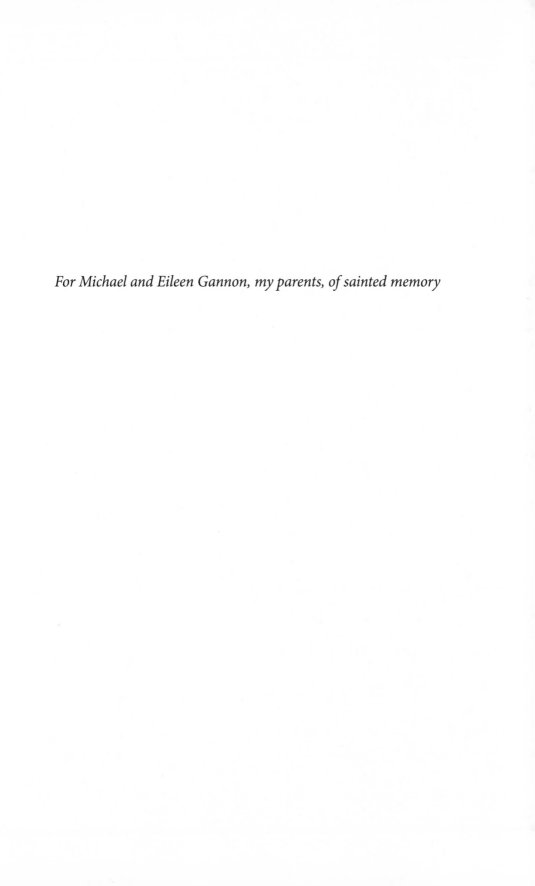

For Michael and Eileen Gannon, my parents, of sainted memory

In the darkness of despair we saw a vision,
We lit the light of hope, And it was not extinguished,
In the desert of discouragement we saw a vision,
We planted the tree of valour, And it blossomed.

★

In the winter of bondage we saw a vision,
We melted the snow of lethargy,
And the river of resurrection flowed from it.

★

We sent our vision aswim like a swan on the river,
The vision became a reality, Winter became summer,
Bondage became freedom, And this we left to
you as your inheritance.

★

O generations of freedom remember us,
The generations of the vision.

—LIAM MAC UISTIN,
"We Saw a Vision," from a plaque at
the Garden of Remembrance,
Dublin, Ireland, dedicated to those who
gave their lives for Irish freedom

Contents

Illustrations

Acknowledgments

Telling the story of the black and white members of the Grand Army of the Republic has been a great honor and privilege. Like most historians, I did not do this alone. While I worked with a number of fine scholars at Penn State, including Bill Blair, Wilson J. Moses, Bill Pencak, Carol Reardon, and Robert Harkavy, Mark Neely deserves special recognition. Every single comment he made, either on the overall direction of this project or on the manuscript, was right on the mark. I did what he told me to do right away, or I did it later, when I realized he was right.

During my graduate studies, the Richards Civil War Center at Penn State came into being, and I thank everyone affiliated with this organization for their support. In addition to scholars at Penn State, I owe a great debt to two historians I met at Penn State who are now at other institutions: Gary W. Gallagher of the University of Virginia and Thavolia Glymph of Duke University. Similarly, I must acknowledge the assistance of a number of scholars in the broader circle of Civil War or African American studies. Joseph T. Glatthaar, Kenneth W. Goings, Don Shaffer, Greg Urwin, and LeeAnn Whites offered valuable suggestions on specific aspects of this study. While I know all of these people and count them as friends, this book also materially benefited from the input of strangers, two anonymous readers. Ultimately, however, I am responsible for any errors of omission or commission in this work.

Within the academy I made a number of lifelong friends. Christine White, Penn State historian emeritus, befriended, housed, and fed me during my sojourn at Penn State. While all Civil War graduate students are comrades, I want to thank Bob Sandow, Mike Smith, and, most especially, Andrew Slap for their friendship and support. Penn State graduate students Tim Wilson and Lynne Fallwell were comrades who stood by me during my most difficult graduate school struggles. Thank you, too, to my new colleagues at the

★

University of Central Florida; their warmth and generosity helped ease my transition to academic life.

I owe debts outside the halls of academia. David Perry of UNC Press urged me on as I completed this project and provided invaluable guidance as I navigated the final stages of the writing process. In addition, I would also like to thank the staff at UNC Press for their patience with a first-time author. It was their hard work and expertise that made this book possible. Before a history book can be published it needs the help of men and women who are guardians of primary source material. I would like to thank the staff of the Library of Congress, archivists at the Iowa and Connecticut state archives and libraries, the Archives of Industrial Society at the University of Pittsburgh, and the staff of the Bentley Historical Library at the University of Michigan for their assistance in my research. I will never forget the kindness of the staff at the Mahoning Valley Historical Society in Youngstown, Ohio. My mother died suddenly during my visit to their archives, and they did everything they could do to support me on that terrible day. After I completed the research on this project, I returned to work at the United States Government Accountability Office (GAO). When all else failed, employment at GAO kept body and soul together and paid the bills. More important than material support, my colleagues at this agency provided emotional succor as I completed the book.

History is the homage the living owe the dead, and, in this spirit, I remember those who never lived to see this study completed. My mother and my father, as we Irish say, of sainted memory are always at my side. While I owe much to all of these men and women, the living and the dead, scholars and friends, my greatest debt is to my brother, Michael, and my sister, Mary, who always believed.

Introduction

The review of the Grand Army of the Republic passed down the broad avenues of Washington, D.C.: tens of thousands of veterans, black and white, marching together in commemoration of northern victory in the Civil War. One newspaper proclaimed, "The entire nation unites to celebrate the valor and patriotism of the brave soldiers who fought in defense of the Union." A group of African American veterans was singled out for praise: "They marched as they fought, nobly." The white and black spectators watching the parade recognized the "colored troops" with "hearty applause." This was not a description of the Grand Review of the victorious northern army in 1865; black soldiers had not participated in that parade. Instead, in 1892, twenty-seven years after Appomattox, aging former soldiers who belonged to the Union army's largest veterans' organization, the Grand Army of the Republic (GAR), reenacted this review and welcomed African Americans into its ranks.[1]

These men must have found this recognition particularly gratifying; black Americans had suffered many setbacks in their postwar struggle for equality. An African American veteran who marched in this parade had seen the end of Reconstruction — when the federal government removed troops from the South, it was "redeemed" by a Democratic Party dedicated to white supremacy. Black southerners in this procession who lived long enough would experience race-based de jure segregation — Jim Crow laws that relegated African Americans to separate, but never equal, accommodations. Similarly, southern states used poll taxes and other, more subtle attacks on the Fifteenth Amendment to end these men's, their children's, and their children's children's right to vote. African American veterans understood that their most precious liberty, their right to life, could be taken by white vigilantes without legal recourse. Southern racism, allied with northern indifference, led to the triumph of the three horsemen of the black apocalypse — segregation, disen-

★

Washington, Sept. 20th, 1892.

An unidentified African American post in the GAR's 1892 re-creation of the 1865 Grand Review, Washington, D.C. From author's collection.

franchisement, and lynching—making this era, as one of its most prominent chroniclers has called it, the nadir of black life in America.[2]

What was the Grand Army of the Republic, and why did it welcome African Americans at a time when so many American institutions excluded them? The GAR, the first nationwide veterans' organization, was the precursor to the American Legion, the Veterans of Foreign Wars, and the Iraq and Afghanistan Veterans of America. That we have needed so many different veterans' groups, for so many different wars, is an important part of this story. The GAR originated in the immediate aftermath of the Civil War when a handful of Union army veterans formed the first post, or local veterans' group, in Decatur, Illinois. From these small beginnings, the GAR grew until it enrolled hundreds of thousands of black and white members in posts all

across America. The GAR welcomed former soldiers and sailors who had received an honorable discharge from the U.S. Army or Navy during the Civil War. Posts were organized by state into departments—for example, the Department of Pennsylvania—that set policy and governed the local veterans' groups under its authority. In turn, representatives from GAR departments met yearly at conventions, which they called encampments, to elect the GAR's leadership and set national policy. During its heyday, the GAR was the nation's largest social and charitable organization, with all the political power inherent in representing such a large membership. Remarkably, the largest and most powerful social organization of the nineteenth century was an interracial group.[3]

Previous studies of the GAR have not emphasized the interracial nature of the organization. Instead, while acknowledging black membership, scholars have argued that this organization treated African American members poorly and that this treatment was somehow connected to the national retreat from black civil rights in the late nineteenth century. Stuart McConnell, who wrote the first modern study of this group, deems the 1865 Grand Review as emblematic of the racially biased treatment of black GAR members, which he links to broader civil rights issues. He argues that "where the black population was large, as in Philadelphia, black and white veterans maintained separate posts." "As in the Grand Review, as in the Union Army itself," McConnell continues, echoing the language of the Supreme Court's *Plessy v. Ferguson* (1896) decision that justified segregation, "black veterans were accorded separate and unequal status." More recently, Donald Shaffer acknowledges that black membership in the GAR represented an important victory for African Americans in their postwar struggle for manhood; however, he accepts the segregationist paradigm. Shaffer argues that since "most black veterans, northern and southern, attended segregated posts ... [and] most GAR activity took place locally, the racial separation of American society during the late nineteenth and early twentieth centuries tended to prevail." The GAR received partial credit for allowing African Americans to join; however, the fact that these men belonged to all-black organizations suggests that white veterans did not truly embrace their black comrades.[4]

These studies link the status of black veterans in this group to veterans' Civil War Memory. Memory (with a capital M) in this context refers not to an individual's personal memory but a group's, a generation's, or a nation's collective understanding of, or agreement on, a shared interpretation of its past. Memory is neither universal nor immutable. Memory is contested and, as a result of this struggle evolves, particularly from one generation to the next. Academics closely study the difference between Memory and History

because they view Memory as less accurate than History. To most nonacademics, however, there is little distinction between the two. McConnell argues that when white veterans remembered the war, "the Grand Army conception of the war was pivotal: because the members viewed the conflict primarily as a battle to preserve an existing Union rather than as a crusade to free slaves or establish social equality, they felt no compulsion to change their view of blacks once the war ended" and accept them in white posts. This study asserts that white veterans could remember the former, emancipation, without believing in the latter, equality. Shaffer found the same narrow view: "All that mattered [to white veterans] about the war was that the Union had been saved." Scholarly assessments of the GAR suggest that white veterans had a faulty Memory; they forgot the centrality of slavery and emancipation to the causes and consequences of the Civil War and that this partly explained black veterans' purported second-class status in this group.[5]

Amnesia about slavery and emancipation had consequences outside the GAR. David Blight, in *Race and Reunion: The Civil War in American Memory*, links the victory of the Lost Cause, southerners' perspective on the war's meaning, and Memory to the lost cause of black civil rights at the turn of the century. Almost as soon as the war ended, former Confederates reframed their failed national experiment and advocated an all-white version of the Civil War that had nothing to do with slaves or slavery. Southerners succeeded, and most Americans "remembered" the war that way for much of the twentieth century. Blight contends that defeat in the battle for Memory "was one part of the disaster that beset African Americans in the emerging age of Jim Crow." Blight indicts white Americans as much for their willingness to forgive as for their tendency to forget, arguing that Americans joined in an all-white sectional reunion at the end of the century and that reconciliation came at the expense of black Americans. According to Blight, "The problems of 'race' and 'reunion' were trapped in a tragic mutual dependence." If white northerners remembered emancipation and rejected reunion, he suggests, they might have aided African Americans in their civil rights battles. Instead, they abandoned former slaves and allowed white southerners to impose their own solution to the race question—segregation and disenfranchisement.[6]

To understand the profound nature of this abandonment, one must realize that the Civil War was the most brutal war ever fought on American soil. The American Civil War is our tragedy, and no degree of heroism, romance, or nobility of causes either won or lost mitigates the enormity of its horror. Lincoln argued in his second inaugural address that the judgment of the Lord may have required that "every drop of blood drawn with the lash [on the slaves' back] shall be paid by another drawn with the sword." He did not

exaggerate the price paid in four years of war for three centuries of slavery. The combination of low-velocity, rifled weapons made death more likely in battle and wounds more devastating. The failure to understand the germ theory of disease made wounds inflicted in battle more deadly due to infection, and the period between campaigns more dangerous. Disease killed more Civil War soldiers than bullets or shells. During the American Civil War, approximately 620,000 Americans died. The Confederate dead are included in these figures because soldiers from both sections redeemed the bondsmen's blood with their own. A war that incurred this level of casualties in the United States today would kill six million Americans; the per capita death toll for both sides equaled the losses experienced on September 11, 2001, every day, day in and day out, for four long years. We might expect northerners, who paid such a price for black freedom, to have more than a passing interest in black civil rights.[7]

The men who paid the price, the survivors of this horrific struggle who later joined the GAR, did not forget the bondsmen and the blood they shed at their side. Black and white veterans were able to create and sustain an interracial organization in a society rigidly divided on the color line because the northerners who fought and lived remembered African Americans' service in a war against slavery. While there were some controversies involving African American GAR membership in southern states, most white veterans accepted black Americans, and these men participated in the GAR's political life at the state level. At the local level, some black veterans created their own posts, and other members of the African American community helped sustain them; black women in the GAR's auxiliary organizations, for example, represented a critical element in a black GAR "circle." Despite poverty and illiteracy, African Americans maintained their all-black GAR posts well into the twentieth century, demonstrating the importance of these institutions to the entire community. In a nation in which black Americans, either male or female, had precious little autonomy, they had it in the world they made within this interracial organization.

While African Americans relished this sovereignty, they also understood that white southerners sought to define the Memory of the war and forget black soldiers. The Lost Cause version of the Civil War served the interest of southerners, and some northerners, who valued reunion and reconciliation over historical accuracy. The existence of African American posts directly challenged southerners' efforts, reminding white Americans of black service in a war for black emancipation. The African American GAR circle used its participation in commemorations such as Memorial Day to remind Americans of the central role played by slavery and slaves in the war's causes and consequences. African Americans created, maintained, and sustained their posts to shape Civil War Memory and not because the GAR forced them into separate and unequal organizations.

African Americans also belonged to integrated posts, challenging the notion that the GAR was segregated. Because it took only a handful of white members in a post to blackball an African American applicant, white posts sometimes rejected black applicants. Nevertheless, hundreds of GAR posts in cities and town across America welcomed black and white members. Although white veterans made up the majority and dominated these organizations, African Americans, while in the minority, fully participated in post life. All-black groups and their circle may have been more effective in reminding white Americans of black Civil War service, but black veterans also used their participation in interracial groups to contest Civil War Memory. Regardless, an interracial post represented GAR members' greatest aspirations, to create an organization where veterans of every race, creed, or ethnicity could come together as comrades.

One cannot exaggerate the importance of finding so many white Americans of this era willing to accept black veterans as their equals in their local social organizations. Black veterans were the political and social equals of white Americans in one of the most prestigious organizations in the United States. In an era in which race trumped virtually all other social identities, black and white veterans created an interracial organization at both the national and local levels. The first half of this book examines the involvement of black Americans in the GAR and how they made this a truly interracial organization. The second half examines the synergy of comradeship and cause that explains the status of black veterans in the GAR.

Ironically, previous studies were correct: Memory explained the relationship between black and white veterans. Veterans remembered that former slaves had suffered to achieve Union victory. The GAR's collective historical Memory included the wartime exploits of the approximately 200,000 African Americans who served in the army and navy; therefore, white GAR members considered black veterans their comrades. Moreover, many of these men could not forget their wartime suffering both on and off the battlefield—in hospitals, prisons, and military camps—and they felt a tremendous bond with those who experienced similar agonies, even if they had not served together in the same unit. Sadly, suffering was more than a memory for many veterans. Primitive medical practices in the decades after Appomattox meant that veterans lived with unhealed wounds and untreated physical and mental disorders. It was GAR members' memory of their wartime suffering and the reality of their postwar agony that created the interracial bond between black and white veterans.[8]

While northern veterans dealt with the physical and psychological toll of their wartime service, they also dealt with a more spiritual crisis—the struggle to find some larger meaning for their suffering. Just as these former soldiers found comfort in their comradeship, they found solace in their cause. The women who associated with the GAR joined black and white veterans in articulating the cause that they believed worthy of their generation's agony. Unlike southerners, these men and women never agreed to a single term to define their cause, though they had a definite idea of what they had achieved by their service and their sacrifice. I adopt the term "Won Cause," in apposition to the Lost Cause, which, ironically, won the battle for Civil War Memory for much of the twentieth century. These veterans and their associates acknowledged that, initially, Union soldiers had gone to war for Union—slavery and all—but they also understood the evolution of northern war aims and remembered that the war had ultimately both freed the slaves and preserved the Union. The men and the women who associated with the GAR articulated their understanding of the dual nature of their Won Cause as Liberty and Union, explicitly embracing emancipation—Liberty—if for no other reason than the end of slavery guaranteed the survival of the nation— Union. While they usually cited both Union and freedom as the reasons for which they fought, many GAR members interpreted the horrific price paid by their generation as part of God's plan to end slavery, quite literally echoing the refrain: "As he died to make men holy, let me die to make men free." Interracial comradeship epitomized the many layers and meanings of the Won Cause. White veterans embraced black veterans because their membership in the GAR demonstrated that their hard-won victory included the creation of a transcendent bond—comradeship—that overcame even the most pernicious social barrier of their era—race-based separation. Reinforcing the bonds of interracial comradeship, white veterans viewed the former slaves who sat with them in GAR meetings as living reminders of their wartime triumph, their Won Cause, which ended slavery and created a united nation of free men and women. Finally, interracial comradeship in the GAR represented a small victory, nineteenth-century African Americans' own won cause, for they achieved a level of political and social equality in the GAR that did not exist outside this group.[9]

Remembering a Won Cause that enshrined the centrality of slavery and emancipation to the causes and consequences of the Civil War may have allowed black Americans to achieve a level of political equality with the GAR;

however, it did not translate to civil rights victories outside the GAR, though black Americans hoped that it would aid them in their struggles. Even white veterans who passionately embraced the Memory of black freedom made no connection between freeing slaves in 1865 and protecting their civil rights in 1895. These men seemed willing to fight for the rights of their "Colored Comrades" but not for all men and women of color. Instead, racism shaped white veterans' response to attacks on black civil rights. When white veterans and their associates assessed the contemporary relevance of their Won Cause, they did not consider the failure at home to protect black civil rights as important as American success overseas in the Spanish-American War. When northerners and southerners united to bring freedom overseas to the remnants of the Spanish empire, white veterans interpreted these actions as validating the Won Cause of Union and Liberty. Moreover, victory in Cuba and the Philippines signaled the emergence of the United States as a world power. Only a united nation composed of freemen, made possible by northern victory in the Civil War, allowed the United States to achieve this premier status. Won Cause advocates embraced the fulfillment of what they believed to be America's national destiny to bring freedom to the world by example or, when necessary, by force of arms, as an outcome worthy of their generation's suffering and sacrifices. If Americans who had a clear personal memory of slavery saw no connection between fighting against slavery in 1865 and Jim Crow in 1895, then Memory was largely irrelevant to the progress or regress of African American civil rights.

The veterans who lived to see the rise of the United States at the beginning of the American Century would have been surprised that it was the Lost Cause, and not the Won Cause, that emerged victorious in American Memory. However, it was not the GAR or its associates who conceded; instead, it was their children and grandchildren who accepted the fundamental tenets of the Lost Cause to advance their own cause—reunion and reconciliation. Elderly veterans may have rejected this surrender; however, by the fiftieth anniversary of the battle of Gettysburg, they stood as silent bystanders. The next generation orchestrated the commemoration of this battle to create a useful Civil War Memory that glorified the military experience of the former Confederate states, recasting the Confederate national experience as an unfortunate, albeit heroic, example of American patriotism and valor. While scholars have emphasized amnesia regarding slavery, forgetting secession and disunion may have been more important to this nationalistic agenda. By the early twentieth century, white Americans' romantic notions of American slavery made the southern defense of this institution more acceptable; slavers, but not traitors, could be American heroes. The Memory of a Civil

War fought by heroic Americans inspired southern men and women—the generations of 1913, 1943, 1963, and 2003—in many future crusades for freedom overseas. That white Americans died for democracy around the world while denying it to African Americans at home reflected more the fundamental compatibility between the Won Cause and racism and less the victory of the Lost Cause in American Memory.

African Americans used their military service in these modern crusades for freedom overseas to advance their freedom struggle at home. Through the First and Second World Wars, black Americans struggled to become more equal members of the American community through their wartime sacrifices. In the aftermath of the first war fought by an integrated U.S. Army, the Korean War, the Supreme Court signaled the beginning of the end of segregation with the *Brown v. Board of Education* decision. In the decades that followed, the Civil Rights and Voting Rights Acts finally enforced the Fourteenth and Fifteenth Amendments, one hundred years after their passage.

While the battle for Civil War Memory continues into the twenty-first century, the first African American president has signaled that we may be ready for a truce in this struggle. Perhaps only the first black president could do so. On his first Memorial Day in office, President Obama sent wreaths to the monuments that honor both the unknown dead of American wars and to the Confederate dead at Arlington National Cemetery and to the monument in Washington, D.C., that immortalizes the African American soldiers who fought for the United States in the Civil War. If we truly want to remember the Civil War, it may be time to go beyond causes won and lost and remember the suffering and sacrifices of both the men who died and those who lived, including the black and white comrades of the GAR.

I DIFFER FROM MANY SCHOLARS who have studied the relationship between black and white veterans in the GAR because of the sources I used in this study and how I approached these documents. I began by studying black GAR members at the grassroots level, as described in African American newspapers, and their day-to-day life in the GAR. In contrast, previous studies have emphasized national records and documented the controversial, and less typical, involvement of black veterans in the GAR. Previous studies may have found re-creating this routine involvement difficult because GAR records are for the most part color-blind. Only black newspapers that chronicled the activities of African American organizations and GAR records that documented veterans' ranks and the units in which they served allowed me to identify African American involvement in this organization. I then examined the GAR at the state level. In state records, I found the evidence of integrated posts and veterans' ruminations on their comradeship and cause. My original intention had been to tell the story of the black members of the GAR; however, after examining both local and state records, I realized that I must include their white comrades, and the black and white women's auxiliary groups that seemed ever present, walking alongside the men of the GAR.[10]

As I read these sources, I listened to the black and white members of the GAR and their associates without expectation or judgment. The people of the past were neither saints nor sinners, merely men and women who lived, as we do, in both memory and reality and who attempted to make some kind of sense of their lives, particularly of their suffering and tragedies. Withholding judgment is particularly important when dealing with white veterans' racial attitudes. It may be hard to believe that racist white veterans considered black veterans their comrades, but they did. To explain why white veterans worked with black veterans to create and sustain an interracial organization, this study focuses less on how race separated Civil War veterans and more on what brought them together as members of the GAR.[11]

In addition to a keen awareness of nineteenth-century racial views, this study also benefits from the twenty-first-century science of personal memory—how individuals literally remember what happened in their own lives. Understanding the personal memory of the Civil War generation has been a missing element in discussion of the Civil War and collective Memory. Extensive research has been done on personal memory and trauma; scientists have concluded that the primary characteristic of trauma is how very hard it is to forget. Northern veterans' memories of wartime suffering defined much of their collective Civil War Memory. The searing nature of their personal memories explains veterans' sophisticated understanding of the tragedy that engulfed their generation; it would take academically trained historians until well into the twentieth century to articulate the same insight into the causes and consequences of the Civil War.

One reason that the personal memory and collective Memory of veterans may have been dismissed is the sentimental language that characterizes veterans' reminiscences. Twenty-first-century minds often scorn the heartfelt and sentimental pronouncements of nineteenth-century men and women. Today, the *Oxford English Dictionary* partly defines sentimentalism as "the tendency to excessive indulgence in or insincere display of sentiment." In our more jaded age, sentimentalism is, by definition, insincere. Ironically, the wars of the twentieth century, particularly World War I, created this modern discomfort with sentimental language. Paul Fussell identified sentimental remembrance as a casualty of World War I, noting that in this war's wake irony began to shape wartime recollections. Since most of the men and women associated with the GAR did not live to see the war to end all wars and witness this disillusionment, in this study, I assume that their sentimental language reflected their sincere devotion to their comrades and their cause.[12]

While Fussell found little glory in World War I, we have found it in the Civil War. Even the single movie made about black soldiers in the Civil War—the story of the Fifty-fourth Massachusetts (Colored) Infantry—is called *Glory*. In the last scene, Confederate soldiers throw the white commander and his black soldiers into a mass grave, leaving the impression that everyone in this unit died. Some of those men actually lived and later regaled their comrades at GAR posts all over America with the stories of their service and their sacrifice. This is the story of the survivors of this battle and so many others—the black and white members of the GAR.

PART I

The World African Americans Made in the Grand Army of the Republic

1

The Only Association Where Black Men and
White Men Mingle on a Foot of Equality

Comrade Jacob Hector, "a tall, fine-looking man, black as coal," was a popular speaker at Pennsylvania GAR gatherings. A Methodist minister from York, Hector described to his fellow Pennsylvanians the wartime service of black veterans at a state meeting in 1884. "He was here to remind his hearers that they had homes, churches and schools to fight for, while the dark-skinned people of his own race had neither flag nor country and a very poor home, nevertheless they went shoulder to shoulder with the white man" to war. According to Hector, comrades in war remained comrades in peace: "I greet you and you greet me as comrades of the Grand Army of the Republic—the only association this side of Heaven, where black men and white men mingle on a foot of equality." Similarly, Rev. William Butler, a Memorial Day speaker addressing an all-black GAR post in West Chester, Pennsylvania, understood the unique nature of the interracial GAR. African Americans, he explained, were "thankful for the G.A.R. as an organization, originating with the white man, which cannot shut its doors against the colored man. The Masons did that, the Oddfellows did that and the Knights of Pythias have done the same." The GAR was the only group that allowed Americans that were "as dark as coal" to stand on a foot of equality with their fellows.[1]

The GAR was an interracial social organization because its members, both black and white, thought it should be. Since black and white soldiers had served together in the Civil War, African American veterans joined this organization, and they were able to do so because most white veterans believed that their organization should include these men. African Americans participated in the political life of the organization at the state level. They spoke at annual meetings about matters profound and mundane and held elective office. No explanation is needed for why white veterans, who came of age in

★

a society that accepted race-based slavery, sometimes rejected black veterans. This study, therefore, examines why most white veterans accepted black soldiers as their political equals, a status that no other organization granted black Americans in this era.

The story of African Americans in the GAR began before the guns fell silent after Appomattox. Ironically, few Americans at the beginning of the war believed the United States would ever recruit black soldiers, so most Americans would have rejected the notion that African Americans would belong to an interracial veterans' group after the war. Most white northerners believed that African Americans had no place in a war fought to preserve the Union—slavery and all—and therefore the U.S. Army initially refused to recruit black soldiers. Some officers, such as David Hunter in South Carolina, armed slaves under laws written to facilitate the recruitment of laborers; officers who needed soldiers, particularly those opposed to slavery, refused to recognize a color line that excluded black troops. Ultimately, the Emancipation Proclamation allowed the U.S. Army to recruit and officially organize black regiments.[2]

It is no coincidence that Lincoln issued the Emancipation Proclamation after the battle of Antietam. Not only did he need a victory to announce his intention to free the slaves in rebellious states, but the battle made it clear to northerners that freeing and arming slaves was necessary. In one day, at Antietam Creek, Maryland, 24,000 northern and southern soldiers died or were wounded or missing. The only way modern Americans can appreciate this statistic is to extrapolate these figures based on the current population of the United States. If any battle incurred similar losses today, the United States would suffer more than 240,000 dead, wounded, or missing in a twenty-four-hour period. Antietam may have been the bloodiest single day in the war, but many other battles had equally appalling butchers' bills; the Gettysburg casualty list included more than 50,000 dead, missing, and wounded at the end of the three-day battle. Many northerners opposed slavery on principle, but most supported emancipation because the North needed more soldiers on the front line and fewer slaves behind the lines supporting the war; freeing slaves achieved both ends. Ultimately, 180,000 African Americans served in the Union army and approximately 18,000 served in the Union navy. During the war, the government recruited black soldiers and sailors because of the horrific nature of Civil War combat; in its aftermath, the cruel legacy of this struggle defined the comradeship of black and white veterans in the GAR.[3]

While both black and white soldiers and sailors served and died, they were not treated equally. African American soldiers served in predominantly black army units, under the command of white officers, and only a handful of African Americans received commissions. For much of the war, black soldiers earned less than their white counterparts; the government equalized pay only after black soldiers and their white officers protested this injustice. Moreover, many African American army units served in support roles, either guarding supply lines or performing manual labor. Given the racial attitudes of that era, it is not surprising that black soldiers were generally seen as inferior to white Americans, unworthy of an officer's rank, deserving less pay, and of questionable fighting value.[4]

African Americans who served in the Union navy were assigned to integrated ships. Ironically, because black Americans sailed and fought alongside white Americans, they are less visible in the GAR and Civil War Memory. Because the GAR did not officially label either individuals or posts as "Colored," I relied on the GAR's recording an individual's wartime service to determine a member's race. For example, a death record that lists John Smith, former private, Fifth United States Colored Troops (USCT), obviously refers to an African American member, but the race of John Smith of the USS *Vermont* cannot be determined. Fortunately, I was able to identify the race some of these sailors—such as James Wolff and John Bond of Massachusetts—and tell their story. Overall, the black and white sailors who served together at great hazard seem to have been forgotten, and it is their land-based comrades who have received the most attention. Even black Americans who struggled to remind Americans of black wartime service emphasized black soldiers at the expense of black sailors. Perhaps the heroism of African American sailors on an integrated ship received less attention because it reflected individual sailors' character and not, as would be the case with an all-black unit, the martial virtues of the race.[5]

When Joseph T. Wilson, a black official of the Virginia GAR and a former sailor who had served in the navy and in one of the earliest black regiments officially recruited into U.S. service in Louisiana, wrote the story of his African American comrades, he emphasized their land campaigns. He described the first major test of African American troops—the 1863 assault at Port Hudson, a critical bastion that guarded an important section of the Mississippi River. According to Wilson, the assault, which included both black and white regiments, had little chance of success. "Never was fighting more heroic than that of the federal army and especially that of the [black] Phalanx regiments," he wrote. "If valor could have triumphed over such odds, the assaulting force would have carried the works, but only abject cowardice or pitiable imbecility could have lost such a position." Despite the failure of this attack, Wilson argued, "the battle was lost to all except black soldiers;

they, with their terrible loss, had won and conquered a much greater and stronger battery than that upon the bluff. Nature seems to have selected the place and appointed the time for the Negro to prove his manhood." Service in black regiments allowed these men to demonstrate the manly qualities of their race in a way that service on integrated ships did not.[6]

Understanding the place of black veterans, both soldiers and sailors, in the interracial GAR requires a brief review of the black military experience in the Civil War. The second major engagement involving black soldiers, the attack on Fort Wagner, South Carolina, by the Fifty-fourth Massachusetts Infantry is better known today than Port Hudson because of the movie *Glory*. George Washington Williams, a pioneering African American historian who rose to the position of adjutant general of the Ohio GAR, chronicled the attack on this "strongly mounted and thoroughly garrisoned earthworks," observing that such a desperate charge was worthwhile because "the reduction of this fortress . . . [would allow] siege guns [to] be brought within one mile of Fort Sumter, and the city of Charleston, the heart of the rebellion[,] would be within extreme shelling distance." "From a purely military standpoint," Williams continued, "the assault upon Fort Wagner was a failure, but it furnished the severest test of Negro valor and soldiership. It was a mournful satisfaction to the advocates of Negro soldiers to point the doubting, sneering, stay-at-home Negro-haters to the murderous trenches of Wagner." As discussed in later chapters, Wilson and Williams, like their less literary African American compatriots, used their membership in the GAR to challenge those who doubted and scoffed at their service and who tried to erase African American soldiers' service from Civil War Memory.[7]

The Fifty-fourth Massachusetts and two other all-black units, the Thirty-fifth and the Eighth USCT fought alongside a number of white regiments in a failed expedition to Olustee, Florida. According to Joseph Wilson, who had transferred to the Fifty-fourth Massachusetts and was wounded in this engagement, "The rout was complete; the army was not only defeated but demoralized. The enemy has succeeded in drawing it into a trap for the purpose of annihilating it." He blamed the failure on the "miserable mismanagement of the advance into the enemy's country. The troops were marched into an [ambush], where they were slaughtered by the enemy at will." In the end, as Wilson explained, "the battle and the retreat had destroyed every vestige of distinction based upon color. The troops during the battle had fought together, as during the stampede they had endured its horrors together." How the horror of war destroyed, or at least damaged, distinctions based on color is an essential element in understanding the interracial GAR.[8]

While the Fifty-fourth Massachusetts, a state regiment, has received the lion's share of what glory has been allowed to black units, most black soldiers served in units organized by the federal government—the U.S. Colored Troops, such as the Eighth and the Thirty-fifth. In addition to the Fifty-fourth, Massachusetts organized two other African American units that kept their identity as state regiments throughout the war, the Fifty-fifth Massachusetts Infantry and the Fifth Massachusetts Cavalry. Only one other state, Connecticut, formed black regiments that did not transfer to federal authority, and only one of these units, the Twenty-ninth Connecticut, saw any action. William Fox's *Regimental Losses in the American Civil War*, published in 1889, documented the entire spectrum of black military service, which included USCT regiments. According to Fox, "Before the war closed the colored troops embraced 145 regiments of infantry, 7 of cavalry, 12 of heavy artillery, 1 of light artillery, 1 of engineers; [for a] total [of] 166" regiments. Three black regiments, the Fifty-fourth Massachusetts, the Eighth USCT, and the Kansas-based Seventy-ninth USCT, made Fox's list of the elite 300 Fighting Regiments. He listed all of the separate engagements and skirmishes involving black soldiers across the country from Wilmington, North Carolina, to Poison Spring, Arkansas. White GAR members who read Fox's book would have been aware that black Americans' Civil War service encompassed more than one attack by a single Massachusetts regiment that ended in glory. While historians have emphasized segregation in the Civil War, the existence of well over a hundred regiments with the word "Colored" in their name kept alive the story of black service and sacrifice in this struggle.[9]

Of all the battles of the Civil War, those that relied most heavily on black combat troops involved the final campaigns against Richmond and Petersburg. Williams maintained that "by the spring of 1864 a numerous force of Negro troops had been added to [the] army, and an active and brilliant military career opened up to them." These campaigns are not as well known today as are the earlier battles in the East, such as those at Antietam and Gettysburg. Neglect of these later campaigns may be due to their grim character. Much of the time, soldiers lived in trenches with only a few pitched battles to break the stalemate, similar to the battles in World War I, with its static warfare and none of the "romance" of the war's earlier battles. Unfortunately, when historians and others slight these campaigns, they reinforce the historical amnesia that wrote black soldiers out of the all-white brothers' war. Just when African American soldiers arrived on the center stage of Civil War history, much of the audience had left the theater.[10]

Fox's study would have reminded Americans of black Americans' service in the engagements around Richmond and Petersburg if they consulted Fox's study. An attack by African American soldiers on Petersburg on June 15,

The Twenty-second USCT advancing against the Confederate lines at Petersburg.
From *Frank Leslie's Illustrated Newspaper*, 1896, in author's collection.

1864, was, according to Fox, "a brilliant success, [which resulted in the capture of] the line of works in its front and seven pieces of artillery." He maintained that "had the Army of the Potomac arrived in time to follow up the
success of the colored troops, Petersburg would have been taken then." Later
in that campaign, a mine exploded underneath the Confederate line and
created a large "Crater," the name given to another battle involving black
troops. Fox contended that the black division that had been selected to lead
the charge was "sent in last. It was not ordered forward until the assault was
a bloody failure, and although it did all that men could do, it was unable to
retrieve the disaster." He cited fifteen black units for their service in the various battles around Petersburg and Richmond, including lesser-known engagements at Chafin's Farm and New Market Heights. Even though black
and white soldiers served in segregated units in these crucial final battles,
they later shared a common fellowship as members of the GAR.[11]

One year after Richmond fell, a handful of battered survivors of the Union
army formed the first GAR post in Illinois. While in theory the GAR was
born in 1866 and died in 1956, the life of the organization had two distinct
phases. During phase one, the first decade of its existence, the GAR flourished, but accusations of partisanship and the institution of an unpopular

new ritual that re-created military ranks and hierarchies led to the GAR's decline. Mary R. Dearing, in the first modern study of the GAR, *Veterans in Politics*, characterized the GAR and its local posts as "efficient cogs in the Republican [political] machine." Membership dropped so precipitously that in some states the GAR disappeared; by 1876, the organization had about twenty-seven thousand members.[12]

The GAR was reborn in the 1880s when it remade itself into an organization that emphasized charity, patriotism, and good fellowship among veterans of all political stripes. As Stuart McConnell has argued, "the overt involvement of the order in electoral politics . . . did not long survive Grant's first term. Instead, the GAR after 1872 wore several masks: fraternal lodge, charitable society, special-interest lobby, patriotic group, political club." Mary Dearing's study documents not so much the GAR as partisan political phenomenon but as the first major political interest group and lobbying organization—similar to its modern counterparts, the AARP (formerly known as American Association for Retired People). She also rightly emphasizes veterans' pensions as its overriding political interest. During the late 1880s, the GAR lobbied hard to ensure that all veterans received a pension based on their wartime service. (Previously, veterans had to prove a service-related disability to get this monthly payment.) The GAR's advocacy of veterans' pensions appears to have had a direct influence on its size. The same year it reached its peak in membership of more than four hundred thousand members, the service pension passed for all former soldiers. From this peak, the GAR began its long decline until it passed into history the day its last member died, in 1956; its last black member died in 1951. The GAR managed to maintain an interracial organization through the era of Jim Crow until three years before *Brown v. Board of Education*, which rejected race-based segregation.[13]

While the last GAR member lived to see segregation repudiated, integration in this organization was rooted in the nineteenth century and the shared Civil War service of black and white Americans. A New York official in the earliest years of the GAR's existence contended that any man "who honorably wore the Union-blue, on the sea or on land, of whatever rank, of whatever color, rich or poor, may enter and stand in line and answer to the glorious title *comrade*" in the GAR. Decades later, in the last year of the First World War, the Indiana commander maintained that Civil War military service was the primary qualification for membership in this group. The GAR welcomed all men regardless of "who he is, or who he was, or what color his skin may have been, *who gave his strength, his life, his services*, it matters not how humble those services may have been." From the earliest days of the GAR to its declining years, veterans remembered that both black and white Americans had served in the Civil War; therefore, the GAR defined itself as an interracial organization. White veterans seemed proud of the racial makeup of the GAR. The Missouri state commander wanted "every old soldier and sailor in Missouri [to] know that in the Grand Army of the Republic there are no generals or privates, no distinction of race, but all are comrades." The state commander in Arkansas maintained that the interracial nature of the GAR explained his devotion to this group. "I love the G.A.R.," he explained, because "when I meet a man wearing the G.A.R. button I do not stop to see if he is dressed in broadcloth or if he has on a pair of overalls, neither do I care whether he is BLACK or WHITE. I only see back of the button the man who had the courage to enlist as a soldier and risk his life in defense of our glorious country." From East to West and from the free states of the North to the former slave states, veterans explicitly asserted that the GAR included all races.[14]

Once accepted into the GAR, African American veterans belonged to local posts chartered and governed by GAR departments. The standing of Comrade Hector, who spoke to the yearly department-level meeting in Pennsylvania, rested on the political equality of black and white veterans at state meetings. The mechanics of equality were simple; state organizations apportioned voting delegates to the annual encampments, based on post size. The all-black Robert Bryan Post of Philadelphia, for example, included 288 members in 1892 and was allotted 6 representatives to the state convention. The state GAR apportioned 3 representatives to a smaller African American post in the same city for its 79 members. All Pennsylvania posts had at least two delegates, including the post commander, regardless of their size. Other states' organizations had slightly different rules regarding representation, but they always applied them to black and white posts equally. Moreover, black veterans sometimes represented their integrated posts at state meetings. As representatives of either African American or mixed-race posts, black veterans spoke at these gatherings, nominated their colleagues for office, and ran for public office themselves. Nowhere else during this era did African Americans stand as political equals to white Americans.[15]

Black veterans addressed their state encampments on a wide variety of issues. Comrade George W. Bryant of the all-black post in St. Louis asked for the status of a "resolution introduced concerning a Soldier's Home in Missouri." Later in that same meeting, he made a routine motion to suspend the meeting and allow a ladies' auxiliary group to visit the meeting. This seemingly mundane type of action was usually performed by a delegate tasked to ensure that the meeting proceeded smoothly. Less routine was a resolution by a member of Newark's all-black post to honor President McKinley upon his death. More practically, members of Boston's African American Bell Post urged the encampment to change the state meeting from January to July because "during [January], the weather is generally inclement, being a detriment to the old veteran." This measure failed, but it is noteworthy that an African American felt comfortable asking the encampment to change its meeting time by six months.[16]

Nominating a colleague for state office, what might have been a routine matter for a white veteran, represented a black veteran's assertion of political equality. Although members of the Bell Post may have failed to change the yearly meeting date, they succeeded when one of them nominated John Parker for the position of junior vice-commander, third in command of the Massachusetts GAR, and Parker won. Comrade Little nominated Joseph W. Kay for department commander. In his nominating speech he endorsed Kay as "a man who will do charity to a comrade who is as black as night." He pointed out to his comrades that he had "spoken on this platform several times for my own color; you have never heard me say a word for a white man." Little must have believed that biracial support was a plus for candidates, demonstrating that black veterans had a modicum of political power in this organization. While in his plea for this white candidate Little identified his own race and that of the nominee, not all black veterans invoked race when they spoke, making it difficult to determine the extent to which these men participated in the political life of the GAR. Comrade Hullett of a Chicago-based black post rose to second the nomination of a candidate for senior vice-commander. He argued that the nominee knew "thoroughly the work of the Grand Army; he has been on the staff a number of times, and if elevated he would hold up the hands of the Department Commander." Hullett did not identify either his race or that of the nominee. Because speakers did not always remark on their race or those of others, it is difficult to identify all instances in which black veterans spoke on the encampment floor. How often they spoke is not important; the fact these men were able to speak at all is the critical issue.[17]

African Americans did not merely support others for office; they were also nominated for state office themselves. Comrade Brown, an African American veteran, nominated Andrew James of an all-black post in Philadelphia to serve as junior vice-commander in Pennsylvania. "[This] nomination belongs to our side . . . ," he stated. "I think one of the department chairs belongs to us." Race is not mentioned, but this was the only "side" a black veteran might invoke when nominating another African American for office. His appeal failed, and Comrade James lost. Comrade McKie, commander of an all-black New York City post, supported an African American veteran,

Andrew James, an unsuccessful candidate for Pennsylvania junior vice-commander. Courtesy of the Daniel A. P. Murray Collection, Library of Congress.

Robert Hurley, for state chaplain. He explained that the candidate "was one of the first men to enlist after Lincoln called the sable sons of America to go to the front." Hurley lost the election that year but won the next. Even when they lost their election bids, their candidacies reminded their white associates that sable sons had answered Lincoln's call.[18]

Hurley was not the only black veteran to win elective office. A veteran nominating a white colleague to oppose Hurley argued that he would have been "loathe indeed to oppose any candidate whose color was a little darker than mine." He believed that he could in this instance because "this encampment had . . . for two years given its suffrages to a worthy colored comrade for chaplain." Comrade Smith, the worthy comrade, had expressed his appreciation to the GAR when he was initially elected as chaplain: "You preach that in our order there is no color line; and to-day you have demonstrated the fact by your actions, which I hail as the harbinger of the good times to come to men of my race; not only for the State of New York, but throughout the entire United States." While Smith's comments were a bit too sanguine a view of the effect that political equality in the GAR had on race relations outside the organization, they demonstrate that African Americans appreciated their status in this group. In the same year that Comrade Smith was elected to office, black veterans in New Jersey decided that they, too, wanted representation on the state staff. Comrade Johnson of Newark maintained that "there has never been a colored comrade elected to any departmental office." To remedy this omission, he nominated a black veteran. It appears that white veterans agreed that African Americans were due this recognition because Wells, a black man, won the election.[19]

Most states chose, at one time or another, a black representative to the national encampment. Andrew James and Wesley Price represented black Pennsylvanians and their race at the national meeting. Isaac Mullen and Burrell Smith, black veterans from Massachusetts, were sometimes part of the Bay State's delegation. William Murrell of New Jersey, Charles Douglass (Frederick Douglass's son) of Washington, D.C., and Rhode Island's Stephen West all took their places as African American delegates to the national encampment. Often, African Americans ran for election but did not receive enough votes to be a delegate and instead acted as alternate representatives. Black veterans seemed to have lost more than they won; however, participating in these contests represented a type of victory to men with no political standing outside the GAR. African Americans were often successful when they ran for a seat on the Council of Administration, an elective office with little authority. Members of the council did not serve in the department's chain of command. Black veterans in public offices that did not involve commanding white veterans may have been more acceptable to white GAR members.[20]

White veterans obviously believed that black veterans deserved a seat at the table, but usually not at the head. African American veterans in northern states only occasionally served in one of the three positions in the departmental chain of command, and, even then, they almost always served in the third-highest position in their department. At one point, an African American veteran served as junior vice-commander, or third in command, at each of the Illinois, Ohio, Pennsylvania, and Indiana posts. When a black member was elected at a given post, it was usually the only time a black veteran achieved this rank. While rare, these elections represented an important validation of the interracial nature of the GAR. Charles Brown, an African American veteran and Indiana's junior vice-commander, reported to his Hoosier comrades on his year in office: "[It was] the greatest honor that could come to me. Above all, it was an assurance that the Grand Army of the Republic is the one organization which ignores the prejudice of race

James W. Wolff, Massachusetts department commander. From a publication of the Grand Army of the Republic, Massachusetts encampment, 1906.

and regards as equally worthy all those who rendered the country service." African Americans' ability to compete for public office, and sometimes win, represented a remarkable achievement for the interracial GAR—more important than white members' racism and their failure to elect these men to higher office.[21]

When an African American became a state commander in Massachusetts, it was not a one-time, token appointment. James Wolff, a black sailor, served as junior vice-commander one year, second in command the next year, and finally, department commander. Moreover, Massachusetts was an overwhelmingly white department, so Wolff's election to these positions required the support of many white colleagues. Commander in Chief Blackmar, a white veteran, visited the Massachusetts GAR and hailed Wolff's election. When the post elected Wolff, he observed that members "recognized true manhood," and asked Wolff not to "try to be anything, because of your race and color. Put in on the score of manhood, and let us forget the color." The audience responded with applause to this remark, though it was likely impossible for Comrade Wolff or any of his comrades, white or black, to "forget the color." It is not surprising that the GAR in Massachusetts, a hotbed of abolitionism before the war, treated black veterans well after the war. In former slave states, the GAR faced greater challenges creating an interracial organization.[22]

2

Comradeship Tried

The GAR in the South

A surprising exchange at a Tennessee encampment revealed much about white veterans in the South and their relationship with their black comrades. Comrade Weaver, a black delegate, protested that after an annual election black members had "no representative on the entire list, and I think we are entitled to a representative on the Council of Administration." Comrade Gagahan, the new department commander, replied to this complaint: "I desire to go on record in favor of a colored representative. A colored man's body was as good a material as a white man's to be shot at, and it is just that at least he be given one member of the Council of Administration." A white comrade withdrew from the election, and a member of a black post joined the list of nominees and was elected to this post. It may seem strange that the largest northern veterans' organization had branches in Tennessee and other states in the South; however, former Union soldiers lived in this region. Most black veterans had been born in the southern states, and many returned home after the war to former Confederate states. Some white Union veterans had moved to this region after the war, while other native-born southerners had remained loyal to the federal government and fought in the U.S. Army. The latter group lived in areas like northern Alabama and East Tennessee.[1]

The status of black veterans in the Tennessee GAR would surprise scholars who have studied the GAR in the South. Scholars who have documented race-based controversies in the southern GAR, including some involving debate over a southern organization excluding black veterans, have deemed them as indicative of the GAR's, at best, ambiguous relationship with black veterans or, at worst, its acceptance of segregation in its organization. In contrast, this study contends that the fact that excluding black veterans was considered controversial reflected most white veterans' commitment to maintaining an

★

interracial organization. In virtually all nineteenth-century organizations, the participation of black Americans was not a subject of debate simply because they were barred from membership in white organizations. The reader will have to decide if white veterans' desire to maintain an interracial organization in most instances was more important than their occasional failure to do so.[2]

When white veterans in the South resisted black veterans' efforts to join the GAR, the national GAR took notice. In the late 1880s and 1890s it confronted several of its southern organizations over race-based discrimination. When Texans and Alabamans rejected the comradeship of black veterans, the national GAR challenged these racial policies. Texans had strongly opposed the creation of an all-black post in their state and resolved that "the best interests of this department would not be attained by the muster of a colored post, and [we] would recommend that our colored brothers be recommended to apply to the Department of Louisiana, where a number of colored Posts already exist." However, these officials understood that this was in direct contravention of the rules of the national GAR. At the next annual meeting in Texas, this resolution was rescinded because it was in "conflict with the regular rules of the order." Texans understood that barring black veterans was contrary to GAR policy. Similarly, white Alabamans also opposed black posts in their state. The state's senior vice-commander claimed that he had examined the "advisability of organizing 'Negro Posts,' of the GAR, in Mobile" and had not "deemed such [action] best to the interest of our Order, as such organization would be productive of a disbandment of the white Post [in this city], and doubtless that of those in other towns in the State." This official believed that Alabamans could not extend membership to African Americans because "such close comradeship as our order inspires, will not permit the introduction of this element into our ranks—at least, here in the South where the question of race enters so largely into the subject affecting man's happiness and success." It is not surprising that some veterans living in the South feared the social stigma of belonging to an interracial group more than they feared defying the GAR's race-blind membership policy.[3]

Southern officials recognized that the national GAR advocated color-blind admissions, though they often refused to enforce these policies. If challenged, state officials told the national GAR that black veterans were rejected for reasons other than race. When the GAR's national meeting addressed this controversy, an Alabaman argued that black applicants "had not shown any proof of eligibility to membership, and no color line had been drawn." Subsequently, Alabamans changed their story and contended that the city of

Mobile could not support two posts. When the Texas GAR refused to charter a black post in Austin, it claimed that the applicants did not have the proper paperwork. The GAR's national commander thought the situation in Texas was serious enough to send a representative to Austin to investigate the matter; however, his representative agreed with the Texas GAR that black veterans failed to document their membership eligibility. Interest in this issue was so great that the national commander discussed the controversy in his keynote address at the annual meeting. He explained that if the applicants had been "worthy of membership in our order, the post would have been mustered." Despite the rejection of a post in Austin, the commander maintained that he would never "forget that the only men who aided and shielded me in my escape from a rebel prison had black faces." Because of this memory, he argued that "no honorably discharged veteran shall be discriminated against on account of the color of his skin." Despite these protestations, however, national officials never required the Texas and Alabama GAR to accept African American members.[4]

Texas and Alabama were the exception and not the rule. In other southern states, white veterans failed in their attempts to stop black veterans from joining the GAR. Before the Department of Georgia and South Carolina officially joined the GAR and had provisional status, a petition was "referred to [their state meeting] by [a white post, the] Hancock Post No. 3, [to form] a colored post and verbal requests [were] made through comrades to that end." Despite the willingness of some white Georgians to welcome their black comrades, other veterans attending the meeting decided that "it was inexpedient to take action now [and form black posts], and the matter was laid on the table." After Georgia and South Carolina became an official GAR department, African American veterans established their own posts with the approval of white state officials. At the first annual meeting of the new department, black delegates demanded recognition and the right to attend the meeting as voting members. In the ensuing debate, the representative of one white post offered the black veterans "fifty dollars for the purpose of reimbursing them their expenses of the trip to the [meeting] on the condition that they withdraw." Black veterans refused this bribe and stood their ground.[5]

White veterans came to their black comrades' defense. According to the record, the black veterans were "strongly supported by a number of comrades, some of whom preferred an exclusively white department, but contended that these representatives had the same right there as any, and could not be excluded without a gross violation of the rules and regulations." One white veteran, Comrade Gleason of Savannah, explained his support for the black posts. "He had opposed the formation of a colored post in his city at first, as had all the members of his post, . . . [but] he finally gave his reluctant consent and was forced to testify that, contrary to his expectations, he could not see that the organization of [a black post] had affected them injuriously, either socially or in a business way but, on the contrary, his post had mustered more new members during the last quarter than for a long time past." The vast majority of the delegates present—twenty of twenty-four—agreed with Gleason, and African American posts joined the department. In the aftermath of this decision, one white post from Macon withdrew from the meeting and demanded that black members form their own department; however, the Georgia GAR remained an interracial organization. By 1894, three black posts belonged to the GAR in Georgia and South Carolina; the largest post, in Savannah, had seventy-six members. Despite their focus on race-based controversies, scholars never fully chronicled the satisfying outcome of the debate over black membership in Georgia.[6]

In contrast, scholars have thoroughly documented the best-known controversy involving a group of white veterans from the Department of Louisiana and Mississippi who, at a national encampment, proposed creating racially segregated departments in these states. Most previous studies of the GAR have devoted several pages to this incident and described it as indicative of black veterans' second-class status in this group. However, many black and white veterans at this gathering voiced their opposition to segregation and rejected the notion that race-based separation was, or ever should be, acceptable in the GAR and cited the more typical interracial makeup of the GAR. Comrade Johnson, a black veteran from Washington, D.C., addressed the national encampment on this issue. Because of his status as a delegate in this group, he was able to say "a word for [his] brethren in black." "We have always been one department," he argued, echoing Comrade Hector's view, "and of all the institutions that we belong to no other institution has brought us so near together as the Grand Army of the Republic." To dispute the notion that the GAR in the South could not have a single department where black and white veterans met as equals, another black GAR official, Comrade Richey, described his state, Kentucky, as "composed of about one hundred and eighty-two Posts, and twenty-seven of them are colored." Comrade Northcott, a white veteran from West Virginia, rejected segregation at both the state and the local levels. He proclaimed his willingness to welcome black veterans in his post: "[I] plowed many a day beside a nigger boy when I was a boy, and in the evening we would go swimming together," he commented. ". . . I am willing to meet him on equality in our post." Naturally, white veterans who accepted black veterans in their local posts rejected segregation at the state level as well.[7]

Many other white veterans rejected segregation as well, citing both their shared comradeship and the shared cause they believed worthy of their wartime sacrifice. Writers of the majority report that was submitted to the delegates before the debate condemned segregation in the gulf states explicitly cited Civil War military service as the basis for the interracial nature of the GAR. "During that fierce struggle for the life of the nation," they wrote, "we stood shoulder to shoulder as comrades tried. It is too late to divide now on the color line. A man who is good enough to stand between the flag and those who would destroy it when the fate of the nation was trembling in the balance is good enough to be a comrade in any Department of the Grand Army of the Republic. . . . No Department should be established for any color or nationality." Another white veteran connected the status of black Americans in peacetime to what Union soldiers fought for in wartime. Comrade Warner asserted that if these veterans abandoned their comrades, if the GAR adopted a color line, members "had better bury the old flag—comrades, you had better tear the badge from your breasts—than now, as our heads are silvering o'er with the frost of years, to go back upon the principles for which we fought and for which we bled." White veterans joined their black colleagues in opposing race-based separation because black veterans' membership in the GAR symbolized something fundamental about what they had achieved by their suffering and sacrifice in the Civil War.[8]

Since the status of black veterans was so pivotal to these men, it is not surprising that veterans rejected segregation in Louisiana and Mississippi by a voice vote, that is, there was not enough support for this measure to require a formal vote. Moreover, the men in the gallery indicated their emotional approval for this repudiation of segregation. According to one newspaper report, "The applause was simply deafening: veterans threw up their hats, shook hands with the comrades sitting next to them and shouted until they were hoarse." This action was not merely the work of a small number of politically conscious elite GAR men but instead reflected the views of many GAR members. Since only Texas and Alabama prohibited black members, and African Americans belonged to the GAR in all of the other southern states, then the GAR and its black and white members succeeded in creating interracial organizations in this region more often than they failed to do so.[9]

Given the controversial nature of black membership in southern departments, it is surprising that African Americans in former slave states had more success achieving public office than their counterparts in antebellum

Philip White, third in command, Kentucky GAR. From a publication of the Grand Army of the Republic, Kentucky encampment, 1915.

free states. In the Department of Louisiana and Mississippi, at least one African American rose to the rank of department commander. Moreover, African Americans generally occupied the third-in-command position and other key staff positions in this department. An African American veteran almost always occupied the position of junior vice-commander in Kentucky. Similarly, in Delaware, Georgia, and South Carolina, a black veteran often acted as third in command; and an African American usually sat on the Council of Administration. In addition, the GAR in these states usually sent black delegates to the national encampment. Robert Smalls—former congressman, slave, and Civil War ship's pilot—often served in one of these positions. In Maryland, black veterans always served on the Council of Administration and sometimes as state junior vice-commander. A writer to the black-owned *New York Freeman* explained that black veterans held a number of offices in Virginia. "For sixteen years," he observed, "we have had one or more department officers (colored). Our present junior vice department commander and chaplain are colored comrades, and the past department encampment of this state elected a colored comrade as delegate-at-large to the next national encampment." While emphasizing the initial challenges and sometimes the GAR's failure to create interracial organizations in the South, scholars have failed to document their successes. The GAR created and maintained interracial organizations and elected black veterans in states where African Americans were, by law, segregated and disenfranchised.[10]

Demographics explain some of the political success of African American veterans in former slave states. While black veterans constituted the majority of members in the Departments of Louisiana/Mississippi and Georgia/South Carolina, in the other southern states, they were often a minority. When Comrade Richey described the Kentucky GAR posts in 1891, he revealed that 15 percent of this border state's posts were all-black organizations. Even if they had been in the majority, the number of all-black posts and African American members in a state did not always translate into voting power at the state meeting. When African American veterans made up slightly more than half of the GAR membership in Georgia and South Carolina, only six of the twenty delegates present at the annual encampment represented black posts. Poor African American posts may not have been able to afford to send all of their representatives to the annual meeting. In most instances, when black veterans won an election in the South, white veterans likely voted for them and agreed with Comrade Gagahan, who asserted that these men deserved these positions because of their wartime service.[11]

To nineteenth-century black Americans, particularly those who had been slaves like Comrade Hector, white veterans' willingness to accept them in their group and elect them to office must have been tremendously gratifying; however, none of this would have been possible if black veterans had not asserted their rights and joined the GAR. While black veterans belonged to an interracial organization, they also created their own world within the GAR: the African American post.

3

The African American Post

A visitor to the meetings of Grand Army of the Republic Post 206 in Pittsburgh would have found them little different from the thousands of other GAR meetings held in the villages and hamlets, small towns and large cities of nineteenth-century America. Guided by the customs and rituals of the GAR and demonstrating its allegiance to the organization's three cardinal principles—fraternity, charity, and loyalty—Post 206 met twice a month. Fraternity bound these men to other GAR units in the three-river city; comrades from these posts frequented 206's meetings. At one particularly well-attended gathering, comrades from visiting posts made speeches, read poetry, and sang songs to commemorate their wartime experiences. The speakers included state and national GAR officials. In return, 206's members regularly visited the other posts in Pittsburgh; for example, a comrade from 206 spoke at the James C. Hull Post's meeting about his naval service.[1]

Fraternity also involved entertainment that recalled members' shared military service. Post 41 invited Post 206 to a "bean bake," a nostalgic recreation, albeit a freshly cooked and lavish version, of military fare. Posts outside of Pittsburgh welcomed Post 206 to their activities; Post 4, in Latrobe, Pennsylvania, received Post 206 at its "campfire." These events, rarely held around campfires or even outdoors, involved storytelling, songs, speeches—both serious and humorous—and other reminiscences of the joys and anguish of military life. Fairs encouraged fraternal feelings among Pittsburgh posts, including 206, which "turn[ed] out in a body to . . . attend the fair organized by Post 157." Post 206 also held bean bakes, picnics, and campfires and invited other veterans' units to these activities. Women's auxiliary units hosted their own social affairs. In 1900, the ladies of Post 206 organized an oyster supper for the men's group. Proceeds from these social activities provided funds for the post's charitable activities.[2]

The second cardinal principle, charity, may have been even more impor-

★

tant to the members of Post 206 than to veterans who belonged to wealthier posts. One of the very first actions at each meeting was to identify sick comrades. Post members qualified for two dollars a week in sick benefits. If members succumbed to their infirmities, the post's charitable works continued; comrades buried their own. When Comrade Therson died, each member contributed fifty cents to pay for his funeral. Death ended life, but not fraternity and charity among Pittsburgh's GAR posts. When Comrade Adams of Post 206 died, Post 157 attended his final rites. Similarly, Post 206 "resolved to attend the funeral of Comrade Nagle of Post 230." Post 206 also protected the dependents of deceased comrades. For example, veterans of the post engaged in a fierce battle to remove the orphaned daughter of a former soldier from a neglectful guardian's custody. They succeeded, and she moved to the highly regarded home for soldiers' orphans in Pennsylvania. Pittsburgh veterans believed that protecting the dependents of former soldiers was part of the debt owed these men for their loyalty and service.[3]

GAR members constantly reminded the nation of their cohort's fidelity and strived to inculcate patriotic sentiments in rising generations. Memorial Day observances represented the most important patriotic GAR activity. In 1892 and 1898, Post 206 took charge of Memorial Day ceremonies at the Allegheny National Cemetery. In 1901, the post presented an American flag to the Grace Memorial Church. In that same year, the post members denounced the assassination of President McKinley. While they expressed their "surprise at [the] dastardly deed," they believed that "restriction and careful legislation in regard to foreign immigration" would forestall a recurrence of such a tragedy. A sense of loyalty may have prompted these men to table, without action, a communication from the United Confederate Veterans (UCV), asking for funds to aid indigent Rebel soldiers.[4]

Post 206 was an odd place to appeal for such assistance. Apparently, the Confederate veterans were unaware that this post included men such as the Reverend Lafayette, whose most vivid memory of the war was that in the battles "around Dutch Gap, Deep Bottom, and Richmond," the "colored" troops were "determined to show the Jonies [sic] no quarter." Post 206, named for Robert Gould Shaw and composed entirely of former "colored troops," rejected the appeal to "brotherhood" with white southern soldiers.[5]

The Shaw Post and other all-black units existed because African Americans created these organizations and not because they were forced into all-black organizations by their white counterparts. Black posts were established for the most part in urban areas with a significant number of black veterans, demonstrating the African American community's enthusiasm for these

African American veterans at a GAR reunion in Norfolk, Virginia.
Courtesy Special Collections, University of Virginia Library.

groups. Historians have described these units as evidence of segregation, but, like the all-black church, they were organizations created and maintained by African Americans for their own purposes. Despite their poverty and their illiteracy, African Americans maintained their all-black posts through the Spanish-American War, the Great War, and into the fourth decade of the twentieth century, demonstrating their devotion to the GAR. While the world of the black post was made by African Americans, racial exclusivity did not mean isolation. Just as the Shaw Post and its counterparts in Pittsburgh celebrated together and mourned together, so did other black and white posts in other cities. While African Americans appreciated their fellowship with white veterans, they consciously created, maintained, and sustained autonomous, racially exclusive organizations as worlds that black Americans made within the larger, interracial GAR.

The world of GAR members, black and white, revolved around their hometown organizations. Posts formed in thousands of small towns and cities across the United States. A small town likely had a single post; while a large city like Philadelphia had around three dozen. A small-town post might never have more than twenty or thirty members, and posts in larger cities might have welcomed hundreds of former soldiers. Former soldiers who had served in all types of units—as foot soldiers, horse soldiers (cavalry), artillerymen, and even sailors—came together and shared a common fellowship in a GAR post room. The Shaw Post was fairly typical. It sponsored social events, participated in relief efforts for veterans and their families, and engaged in rituals and observances that encouraged national loyalty and patriotism. If it differed from other posts, it may have been because it represented the deepest aspirations of the African American community: political and civil equality within a larger, predominantly white, society.

Ironically, the political equality of black and white posts in the GAR may have hampered scholars' efforts to understand these all-black organizations; for all intents and purposes, GAR records are color-blind. The Shaw Post, No. 206, is listed in Pennsylvania GAR records between two white posts: the Loomis Post, No. 205, of Clarion, Pennsylvania, and the Griffin Post, No. 207, of Homestead, Pennsylvania. Only a study of anecdotal references in GAR records, a review of GAR death records and muster rolls, and a careful examination of black newspapers in this era revealed the identity of African American posts.[6]

Race-conscious black-owned newspapers have made re-creating the world of the African American GAR post in this book possible. Nineteenth-century African Americans created their own journals that chronicled life in their community. In the late 1940s, the Library of Congress and the Council of Negro Scholars gathered and microfilmed extant African American periodicals. Despite their best efforts, most black newspapers have disappeared. However, a number of important newspapers have survived. The *New York Age/Freeman/Globe*, for example, the same paper under different owners, was read by African Americans around the nation. To serve this nationwide audience, the *Age* had correspondents in cities up and down the East Coast and in the Midwest. W. E. B. Du Bois, the pioneering black historian who did so much to remind Americans of the importance of the struggle for freedom both during and after the Civil War, served as a correspondent in Connecticut. Correspondents reported the activities of the Shaw Post in Pittsburgh, the Bell Post in Boston, and the post in Jacksonville, Florida, for this New York–based weekly. While correspondents outside New York were not as faithful in recording post activity as we would like, the *Age* featured a weekly GAR column that chronicled the activities of African American posts in that city. It would have been impossible to piece together the life of black posts solely based on the Shaw Post records. It is the combination of GAR records and the evidence of all-black newspapers that permit the re-creation of the world African Americans made in the GAR and to share, if only in our imagination, the fellowship of their post rooms.[7]

Black newspapers and GAR records together allowed this study not only to re-create post life at the local level but also to identify how many of these posts existed and where they were located across the nation. If this macroanalysis found only a handful of all-black units, then these groups would be of limited historical interest; however, research revealed more than two hundred posts located in twenty-four states and the District of Columbia. (For a list of these all-black posts, see the appendix.) Maryland and Pennsylvania together accounted for more than forty racially exclusive units. Illinois, home of the first GAR post of any type, recognized at least eleven African American posts. All-black posts flourished in large cities such as Chicago, New York, and Charleston. "Colored Comrades" also established posts in small towns such as Chestertown, Maryland, and Brownsville, Pennsylvania. African American posts in small towns often claimed only a few members, such as the Pulaski, Tennessee, unit, which welcomed fifteen members in 1892. Larger cities usually meant larger posts. It was common for African American posts in big cities to have more than one hundred members, as did the Robert Bell Post in Boston, and the Bryan Post in Philadelphia, with more than two hundred and fifty veterans in its ranks.[8]

While the African American posts identified in this study make up only a small percentage of all GAR posts, their numbers do correlate strongly with the distribution and concentration of black veterans in nineteenth-century America. Almost all cities with at least 25,000 residents in 1890 that recorded at least 50 black veterans in the census had at least one African American unit; for example, Baltimore, Maryland, listed 1,093 African American veterans and hosted six all-black posts. Cincinnati supported one African American unit for its 216 black veterans. Overall, thirty-eight of the forty cities with a population of at least 25,000 that claimed more than 50 black veterans hosted African American posts. Fifty is an important threshold. A careful assessment of GAR records suggests that it was difficult to maintain a local post when fewer than 50 veterans lived in the area. The all-black post in Wilkes-Barre, Pennsylvania, survived only a few years—not surprising, given that only 21 black veterans were recorded in the city's 1890 census. Black posts also existed in cities with fewer than 25,000 people. Mound City, Illinois, for example, may have had enough black veterans to sustain its local post because the city was located near Cairo, Illinois, a staging point for wartime naval operations that involved African American sailors.[9]

The existence of all-black posts in cities like Baltimore prompted historians to describe the GAR as segregated, implying that African Americans were assigned to these posts because of their race; however, black veterans, not white GAR officials, formed these units. A GAR post, regardless of its racial makeup, was formed when veterans from a locality petitioned the state GAR for a charter. A state official in Illinois, for example, responded "at once" to a request by "ex-soldiers of Pulaski (colored)" who had applied for a charter and "mustered a small post of fourteen members." The GAR made no effort to mandate the racial composition of GAR posts; rather, the founding members of this group, and those who subsequently joined the post, determined its racial makeup. All-black GAR posts were similar to black churches. African Americans established these religious organizations to meet their own community's spiritual needs and further their own freedom struggle and not merely to accommodate society's racial mores. Similarly, African Americans created all-black GAR posts within a larger predominantly white organization to serve their local community and as part of a broader agenda: to challenge the notion of an all-white Civil War.[10]

While race did not seem to have been an impediment to creating a post, class may have made it hard to sustain it. African Americans in the nineteenth century were desperately poor, and the GAR required its members to pay dues. Even if all-black organizations wanted to welcome indigent veterans, they still had to pay their bills and send a certain amount to the state to retain their charter. Membership fees prevented some veterans, black and white, from joining this organization. The GAR commander in Indiana explained that "some who are not [members] want to join the Grand Army . . . [but] have little of the world's goods and cannot pay their dues." Dues represented only one expense incurred by GAR members. First, veterans paid a muster fee to join the organization. New Yorkers paid as much as $25.00·or as little as $1.25; most posts charged between $1.00 and $2.00. One black post in New York City, the John A. Andrew Post, charged a $4.00 muster fee and $3.00 a year in dues. Poor veterans struggled, and did not always succeed, in paying these fees. Post 206's officers read the names of delinquent members at meetings to encourage these men to pay their debts. The all-black post in Keokuk, Iowa, charged $1.00 a year in dues. Veterans in this small river town may have struggled to pay this relatively modest fee. Regardless of their racial makeup, GAR posts frequently dropped from their rolls members who had not paid their fees out of either indifference or indigence.[11]

Veterans cited class more than race as an impediment to joining the GAR. A New Yorker described Post 251 as a small post with only "thirteen in number, [and] with only the little they can earn as laborers, they find it hard to pay their dues." The inspecting officers explained how these men sustained their organization: "So strong is the desire to keep up the organization that if a member cannot get his, the more fortunate 'chip in and pay for him.'" The official did not identify this post's racial composition. Dues were necessary because posts paid the taxes owed to the state GAR from these funds.

A veteran in Massachusetts asked the state to lower its taxes because "it was a heavy burden on some posts to pay the tax on members whose dues were remitted." When the New Jersey GAR proposed an increase in this tax, an African American veteran explained how poverty affected black comrades' membership: "There is a class of comrades, your colored contingent, who wish to remain with you, but many of us have grown too old to occupy lucrative positions and we consider the . . . tax of ten cents as much as we can pay." The New Jersey encampment may have been influenced by this appeal since it did not raise this levy.[12]

Not all black posts were poor or all white posts rich. The wealthiest post in Philadelphia, an all-white post, reported assets of thirty thousand dollars in 1891. While not as well-off, the all-black Bryan Post of Philadelphia owned one thousand dollars in property and securities. The all-white Capt. M. L. Stone Post in Conneautville, Pennsylvania, on the other hand, was poor; its assets amounted to only thirty-one dollars. In the southern states, white Unionists may have been as economically disadvantaged as their black counterparts. Most posts in Tennessee possessed less than one hundred dollars in property. Poor veterans, black or white, formed poor posts.[13]

Despite their poverty, African Americans appear to have been as dedicated as their white counterparts, if not more so, to following GAR guidelines; for example, black GAR men seemed to have been more likely to own and wear their GAR uniforms. Uniforms were not free. The men of the all-black Fribley Post in Williamsport, Pennsylvania, would have paid around $6.25. White veterans cited and applauded black GAR members for their uniform dress. The department inspector for the District of Columbia commended the African American veterans in the O. P. Morton Post and the Charles Sumner Post because most of the members owned GAR uniforms. All members of the Sumner Post in Maryland owned uniforms as did those of the Sumner Post in Lexington, Kentucky. A department inspector in New Jersey described the all-black Post 65, the I. M. Tucker Post, as "composed entirely of colored comrades, fully uniformed, and thoroughly imbued with a desire to progress." GAR members interpreted a post's willingness to buy and wear uniforms as a sign of their commitment to the organization. Given the poverty of black veterans, purchasing a uniform required great sacrifice and indicated their devotion to the GAR.[14]

Post inspections, officer elections, Memorial Day ceremonies, and funerals all followed a prescribed format. The close adherence to GAR rituals by members of all-black posts demonstrates that these men valued this organization's traditions and their membership in this group. A GAR member followed the prescribed rituals of the GAR from his first day in the organization, his mustering ceremony, to his last day, his burial. Induction in this organization was formal and involved a ceremony that both welcomed and obligated the new member to the organization. A state inspector complimented "the membership of the John Brown Post, No. 50" of Chicago who "with one exception were all slaves." "The proficiency with which they conducted the work in the Post room," asserted, "is said to be truly wonderful." The local GAR columnist in Philadelphia wrote that "as usual . . . post attendance on Tuesday night was good, [and] a record number of visiting comrades were present" at the all-black Robert Bryan Post. The reporter gave one reason why these guests might have attended this meeting: "Few posts go through the [mustering] ceremony in a better manner." One week later, the same columnist reiterated this sentiment, proclaiming, "If you want to see a good muster go to [Post] 80." Southern posts received similar recognition. Four of the five black posts in Tennessee received high marks for their facility with the ritual, while overall only one of ten Tennessee posts of any racial composition achieved this high grade. One African American post's execution of GAR rites was legendary. The Robert Gould Shaw Post of New Orleans frequently demonstrated the mustering ceremony at the national encampment. Even the GAR's junior vice-commander who hailed from Texas, a state that refused to charter African American posts, praised this unit. The Shaw Post, he explained, "exemplified the work of the Grand Army in a masterly manner." White GAR men demanded that these men meet the same standards they required of themselves, indicating that they believed that these posts were no different from their white counterparts. If white veterans deemed all-black posts as separate and unequal organizations, they likely would not have cared if these posts followed GAR protocol.[15]

Record-keeping requirements represented a more daunting challenge to African American posts than the GAR's rituals. All state organizations demanded quarterly reports based on personnel and financial records kept at the post level, but few African American veterans had received enough formal education to maintain these records properly. Officials discussed these difficulties in their inspection reports. An inspector of the Chestertown-based Sumner Post of Maryland found "very good material" to build a post among its black members, but he had to "explain the proper mode of keeping books." Similarly, the John Brown Post in Cambridge, Maryland, was described as "active and in earnest. Books badly kept." All-black posts struggled to keep up with their paperwork in other states as well. Tennessee department officials had "grave doubts as to the propriety of organizing [a black] post owing to the difficulty of getting persons who are able to keep the records." Eventually Tennessee organized the all-black Blaine Post, but only after they found someone willing to maintain the unit's records. These concerns can be judged as racist or realistic; record keeping required literacy. When the all-black post in Circleville, Ohio, was formed, sixteen of the twenty-eight founding members signed the charter of this post with an X. Since over half of this post's members could not even sign their own names, recording meeting minutes and keeping financial ledgers might well have been challenging. Some African American posts kept their records in good condition, particularly those in large northern cities. Chicago's John Brown Post also received high marks in this area when an inspector reported its "meetings well attended, comrades in good spirits, books well kept." This last must have been difficult because the post was composed of former slaves, who likely had little formal education. Most black posts in Illinois received only fair marks, as did many white posts.[16]

The best evidence of how black posts kept their books is the records themselves. The Shaw Post's records in Pittsburgh, while written by individuals whose poor penmanship indicates a limited formal education, are legible. The surviving documents are, in format and content, similar to those of other GAR posts that were not racially exclusive. Many Pennsylvania natives are on Shaw Post's membership lists, and some of these men may have been educated in the antebellum era. The African American officials of the William Anderson Post in Washington Courthouse, Ohio, managed to keep minutes that contain the type of information recorded by other GAR posts, though the entries are terse and sometimes misspelled and not as complete as the Shaw Post's records. In contrast, the few surviving proceedings of the Pratt Post in Keokuk, Iowa, illustrate the type of poor record-keeping practices of some African American units. Unlike in the Shaw and Anderson Posts' journals, where meeting events were recorded, Pratt Post records only list dues received and bills paid. Whether well or poorly kept, these records represent a remarkable tribute to black veterans who maintained these organizations despite the challenges created by their poverty and illiteracy.[17]

Undaunted by poverty and illiteracy, black veterans maintained their posts for an extraordinarily long time. While no master record exists that chronicles the life cycle of black GAR posts, or for any other type of GAR post, African American units appear to have been extremely resilient. An all-black post in Christiana, Pennsylvania, tenaciously clung to life in the 1920s with only a handful of aged members. This post and three other African American posts in the Keystone State survived until the Great Depression. Occasionally, a black post would disband, but later, phoenixlike, another African American association would rise from its ashes. The Fort Wagner Post of Evansville, Indiana, replaced the John Gill Post, just as the Frederick Doug-

Edward F. Harris, commander, Post 27, Philadelphia. Courtesy of the Daniel A. P. Murray Collection, Library of Congress.

lass Post succeeded the John Brown Post in Memphis. The John Brown Post in Chicago surrendered its charter in 1934 — during Franklin Roosevelt's first presidential term. African American posts were among the senior posts in their respective states; when these posts finally succumbed to the ravages of time, they had been in existence for at least seven decades. Baltimore's all-black Lincoln Post received its charter in the immediate postwar era and was still in existence in 1929, as were four other African American units in Maryland. Black posts in Florida seemed more resilient than white posts. Of the six African American units that had formed in this state by 1903 only one had disbanded, while seven of the other twenty-four posts in the state had surrendered their charters. A Florida official recognized the efforts of black veterans to maintain their organizations when he described a meeting of the all-black Gabriel Post in Jacksonville: "The meeting was fully attended and the officers seemed anxious to do their whole duty. Of course, they lack money and the advantages possessed by officers of white posts." Although African American veterans lacked money or a formal education, they managed to maintain their black associations sometimes longer than their more advantaged white colleagues.[18]

African American posts may have formed and prospered because they provided opportunities for leadership. The Gabriel Post may have been disadvantaged, but it did have black officers. The Shaw Post in Savannah, Georgia, listed a commander, a senior vice-commander, a junior vice-commander, an adjutant, a quartermaster, a surgeon, a chaplain, an officer of the day, an officer of the guard, a sergeant major, and a quartermaster sergeant on its muster roll. Since these positions rotated, many of the post's seventy-six members might expect to hold these positions during their lifetime. These men likely valued the social autonomy inherent in an all-black organization and the opportunity for leadership in a world that provided few opportunities for black authority figures.[19]

While black groups had autonomy, they were not isolated; white veterans were familiar figures at black post meetings. The commander of the GAR in Delaware described his "visits to [his] colored comrades, especially Charles Sumner, No. 4, they do much good work and are having better attendance than the white posts." During this visit, he observed that "colored comrades [have] a feeling that they are required to be more exact in their work, and I know that they do live up to the requirement of the law a little closer than many white posts." Given this statement, one could draw the conclusion that racist white GAR members scrutinized the behavior of black members. However, the fact that the department commander visited this all-black post regularly and cared enough about its treatment to discuss his concerns with his colleagues indicates otherwise.[20]

The minority press described similar integrated social gatherings at other posts. The New York Age reported on the installation of a GAR post composed of white veterans, the John Rawlins Post, because "[black] Grand Army veterans were largely represented." The GAR column chronicled this function as part of the interracial world African Americans made in the GAR. Similarly, the New York Freeman reported that comrades of "Naval Post, 516, spliced the main brace [drank] with their ship mates of the Thaddeus Stevens and John A. Andrew Posts." And when the Lafayette Post in New York welcomed the commander in chief of the GAR to its hall in 1888, black GAR members attended the gathering. Likewise, white veterans visited African American posts. The John Andrew Post's installation benefited from the presence of "visiting comrades from many posts [who] were present to do honor by their fraternal assistance." These integrated events represented a measure of social and political equality in an era of increasing race-based discrimination and segregation.[21]

Black and white veterans often gathered together under more solemn circumstances. When Joseph Walker died, for example, the Age described a funeral in which "the church was packed to the doors with friends and acquaintances of the deceased, Grand Army veterans to little children." Twenty organizations were present to honor Walker, and while the paper did not mention Walker's race, it noted with pride that among these were "thirteen different posts of the G.A.R., both white and colored, representing states as far South as Virginia." The Bethel Church celebrated a more joyous event, "the centennial of African Methodism." During this "extraordinary" celebration, the *Age* explained, "a beautiful sight presented itself, in the commingling of the Grand Army of the Republic and navy of both races upon the stage and in the ranks which filled the auditorium of the church."[22]

Letters from journalists in the cities and towns served by the *Age* included more accounts of interracial GAR gatherings. The Providence-based correspondent described the all-black Ives Post's fair as a "centre of attraction for this city. The Governor, his staff and State officials, the Mayor and city officers, together with the magnates of the G.A.R. of Rhode Island" attended. A letter from New Jersey chronicled "the re-union and reception of the [all-black] I. M. Tucker Post, No. 65, G. A. R." The posts in attendance were "Philip Kearney, No. 1, Lincoln, No. 11, Garfield, No. 4, Hexamer, No. 34, and a great many others," which were likely all-white posts. The Boston correspondent reported with pride that "Commander Isaac S. Mullen of the Robt. A. Bell Post, 134 G.A.R., was most agreeably surprised on Tuesday evening, the 5th, while on a visit to Benjamin Stone, Jr., Post 68, located at Dorchester, with an order for a chandelier to be placed in the Robert A. Bell Post's hall." The Stone Post welcomed both black and white veterans as members. While these local correspondents discussed many aspects of these posts' activities, they took special pride in reporting interracial social events. Perhaps these journalists considered the interracial GAR as a beacon of hope in the dismal landscape of nineteenth-century race relations.[23]

While the world of an African American post was not all black, neither was it all male; women and other members of the black community also shaped the world that black veterans made in the GAR. While African American post life centered on regular gatherings held in its meeting rooms, an all-black post was not confined to a single geographical space. Instead it acted on a larger stage that encompassed disparate elements of the black and white communities—a circle that included nonveterans, women, children, and veterans' sons and daughters.

4

The Black GAR Circle

An African American post commander held a housewarming for his post, and according to a *New York Freeman* article, "Comrade Lee took occasion also to present his bride, who is also a comrade." An odd choice of words, since GAR members addressed brothers-in-arms, and usually not sisters of any sort, as comrades. His bride probably belonged to one of the two major ladies' auxiliaries of the GAR—the Woman's Relief Corps (WRC) or the Ladies of the GAR (LGAR). Just as the GAR included black and white members, black women and white women belonged to affiliated women's groups.[1]

The existence of these ladies' auxiliary organizations demonstrated that the world of black Americans included more than male Civil War veterans. African American GAR posts stood at the center of a nexus of relationships, a circle that included other members of the black community: women, veterans' sons and daughters, children, and other nonveterans. While the *Freeman* article about Comrade Lee concerned one post, it illustrated a broader phenomenon—the close relationship between black women's auxiliaries and African American GAR posts. African American women belonged to a national interracial women's organization not because of their shared sisterhood with white women but because of their comradeship (for lack of a better word) with members of all-black posts. Race mattered more than gender in an organization devoted to remembering a war that shattered the bonds that held African American men and women as slaves and destroyed an institution that called into question the civil and political status of all African Americans, even those born free. Not surprisingly, a sense of gratitude and pride tied black veterans' posts to the rest of the black community. The black post, its auxiliaries, and other elements of the African American GAR circle prospered because they met the needs of black society, either as a center of local social life or as a source of charitable relief. Finally, the all-black circle allowed the African American community to experience the social

★

autonomy inherent in racially exclusive social organizations and the status inherent in its association with the larger, interracial GAR circle.[2]

Any re-creation of the world African Americans made in the GAR would be incomplete without an examination of its ladies' auxiliaries: the Woman's Relief Corps, the official auxiliary of the national GAR, as well as the largest and most well-known, and the Ladies of the GAR (LGAR). Membership qualifications differed between these two organizations. The LGAR required a tie of blood or marriage to a Civil War veteran. In contrast, the ladies of the WRC needed only to demonstrate that they were "loyal" women, devoted to both the northern cause and veterans' welfare. A recent study has emphasized the WRC's patriotic and nationalistic activities, which may be because of the organization's emphasis on loyalty and not blood ties. The loyal women of the WRC organized in units called "corps," which usually bore the name of the GAR post with which they were affiliated; for example, the Shaw Corps affiliated with the Shaw Post. The LGARs organized in "circles" that chose their own name. The Charles Sumner and Martin Delany circles of the LGAR associated with the Shaw Post of Pittsburgh.[3]

Historians have suggested that African American membership in these auxiliaries, particularly the WRC, indicates a failure of interracial "sisterhood" and that southern white women segregated all-black WRC corps. However, scholars have failed to explain what happened in the southern states after segregation and ignored black women's auxiliaries in northern states. More important, these scholars have examined African American women's groups solely to discern their relationship with white women and not their connection to African American men. Earlier studies have also failed to recognize that, through trials and struggles, African American women created and maintained these organizations for their own purposes. Providing charity to members of the African American community in an era with no social welfare net may have been quite literally a matter of life or death for impoverished African Americans. Finally, in a world so closely defined by race-based separation, women and other members of the black GAR circle belonged to a larger interracial GAR circle that allowed them to contest and shape Civil War Memory.[4]

The first step to reclaiming the history of black women's auxiliaries is to complete the story of these organizations in the southern states. In contrast to their male counterparts, most southern organizations segregated their African American WRC. White women faced the same type of social pressures as men in the southern states and had not shared the same kind of wartime comradeship as veterans. Only such a powerful bond could overcome the color line. Practically, this separation involved requiring some units to report to the national WRC headquarters, while other corps formed the official state organization. Previous studies have emphasized the instances in which state organizations detached their black corps; for example, Kentucky mandated this type of separation. In some instances, segregation was accomplished by detaching a white corps, and the state organization became an all-black, autonomous unit. The Virginia-based WRC consisted of all-black organizations; the single white organization separated from the state organization and reported to the national headquarters. African American women's groups in Louisiana and Mississippi constituted the official state organization, and white women operated as a detached unit. The national WRC designated Virginia, Louisiana, and Mississippi "provisional departments" as opposed to permanent departments, one way they slighted all-black state organizations. Despite their provisional status, African American women likely welcomed the autonomy they achieved with segregation, particularly when they became the official state WRC.[5]

The prosperity and longevity of black corps in the South suggest that black women were relatively untroubled by racial separation. African American organizations continued to exist in 1933 despite their separation from white units. Five all-black corps still survived in Virginia. In Florida, one such all-black detachment remained, as did two each in North Carolina and South Carolina. Five African American detached corps operated in Kentucky in 1933—thirty-three years without the aid or approbation of their white counterparts. The white organizations in this state recognized their activities and prosperity. While the historian of the state organization maintained that white Kentucky women were in "entire sympathy with the Lincoln proclamation," she justified segregation by explaining that "white women of the Southland do not associate so closely with the colored race. . . . Never in the first place should they have been intermingled with the department." Despite this woman's advocacy of racial separation, she believed that "much work was accomplished by the Colored Corps and they are a great asset to our organization." In the same year that Kentucky cited the contribution of its black ladies' corps, twenty-six African American corps still operated in Louisiana and Mississippi, and they constituted the whole of the WRC in these states. Black women's groups did not wither and die after their segregation because their association with their white counterparts was less important than their affiliation with black posts.[6]

Similarly, all-black ladies' auxiliaries formed in northern states to support their African American men. African American women created organizations in northern states as far east as Boston and as far west as Topeka, Kansas. Just as the men in Pulaski, Illinois, established their own post, the women in Cairo, Illinois, instituted their auxiliary under the auspices of the Illinois state organization. Large cities like Indianapolis hosted these units, as did small towns like Jeffersonville, Indiana. Black women were among the pioneering members of these organizations. The first WRC unit formed in Chicago, either white or black, associated with the all-black John Brown Post, indicating that black women moved more quickly than their white counterparts to affiliate with their GAR posts.[7]

Black women also appeared to be more likely to affiliate with their own all-black posts than white women were to white ones. We have already met the men of the Shaw post; this post allied with three ladies' organizations. This wealth of female associates remains unmatched by any other post identified in this study, suggesting that black women had a special relationship with the Shaw Post. Overall, thirteen of nineteen African American posts in the state of Pennsylvania associated with a women's group, while only about one in three predominantly white Pennsylvania posts associated with female organizations. In 1895, all but one extant African American posts in New Jersey affiliated with a women's group. Of the 115 posts of any type in New Jersey, only 41, or a little more than one-third of all posts, reported such a link. Black and white posts in southern states demonstrated a more dramatic divergence. In Tennessee, 9 of the 53 posts inspected by state officials in 1893 associated with women groups, and 5 of these women's organizations affiliated with African American posts. Loyalty may partly explain this divergence. Southern women may not have supported the northern cause, the primary criteria for membership in the WRC; however, race played a more important role. Southern men belonged to the interracial GAR because they shared a wartime bond of comradeship; black and white women had no such bond, and many white women in the South refused to join an interracial group. While race separated white and black women, it also tied black men and women more closely together in the GAR circle. African American women, many of whom were freed slaves, may have wanted to do whatever they could to aid the men who had freed them, black GAR members. Focusing on black women as part of interracial women's groups and examining their interactions with white women may have obscured this more important relationship with black men.[8]

Contemporary observers noted these close ties. The national junior vice-commander in chief of the GAR explained that "it would be impossible to retain a colored post in Richmond [the Custer Post] without the auxiliary they have," demonstrating that the prosperity and survival of the all-black post may have been the primary focus of African American women's auxiliaries. The chief inspector of the South Carolina and Georgia GAR described

Mrs. Mary J. Berry, president of a Woman's Relief Corps unit in Philadelphia. Courtesy of the Daniel A. P. Murray Collection, Library of Congress.

some of his visits to three African American posts. He noted, "Although they have been more or less deeply depressed by . . . recent hard times, they are all now inspired by the renewed hopes for the future. . . . In this they are ably supported by the several Woman's Relief Corps, which has rendered efficient aid in the past, and have pledged themselves to still greater effort" in the future. African American posts in northern states also valued their ladies' auxiliaries. A wrc official chronicled the trials of the all-black David Birney Post auxiliary. The wrc suspended and later reinstated this group. She described the newly rejuvenated Birney Corps as "a band of earnest workers in the interest of the GAR . . . an auxiliary of whom the officers and members of Post 95 are exceedingly proud." African American posts in Philadelphia published a pamphlet welcoming "Colored veterans" to the 1899 national convention held in that city. This souvenir guide to the convention features pictures of the African American women who led Philadelphia's ladies' associations alongside portraits of prominent black GAR members. This place of honor illustrates the importance of women in the GAR circle.[9]

Mrs. Maggie J. Harris, prominent member of the Woman's Relief Corps in Philadelphia. Courtesy of the Daniel A. P. Murray Collection, Library of Congress.

African American newspapers, such as the *New York Age*, evinced the black community's own notion of the universe these men and women made in the GAR. The *New York Age* and its predecessors, the *Globe* and the *Freeman*, provide the most systematic record of the all-black GAR circles' activities. This newspaper covered the activities of the all-male posts, their ladies' auxiliaries, and diverse elements of the African American community considered part of their milieu. The *New York Age*'s "Grand Army Notes" column reported equally on the election of officers in GAR posts and of those in their auxiliaries; for example, it reported the names of GAR members and women auxiliary members who had been elected to represent New York at their respective 1886 national meetings. Similarly, it regularly reported the result of elections in the local posts and auxiliaries.

Correspondents in cities and towns outside New York wrote letters describing local ladies' auxiliaries. In Trenton, New Jersey, the local correspondent noted that the all-black Thomas Hamilton Post "celebrated the silver jubilee" of the GAR in 1891 and that "the Ladies Relief Corps were well represented." The correspondent for Red Bank, New Jersey, provided a sketch of the local African American community: "Red Bank contains only about 400 colored inhabitants, yet it affords 5 organizations; namely, D. Birney post, G.A.R., Woman's Relief Corps, Rising Sons of Monmouth, Ladies' Monmouth Circle." An article headlined "Race Doings at the Hub" discussed the formation of a Boston WRC. A report from the *Age*'s Norfolk correspondent is indicative of African American attitudes toward these women's organizations: He described the Virginia state GAR as having "twenty posts . . . who have labored long and faithfully for the organization." "Recently," he added, "we have added to the different posts relief corps. . . . Every veteran must feel proud to see the change made since their introduction with us." The black community was the "us," an essential element that shaped the world African Americans made in the GAR.[10]

Black newspapers in other states also described African American GAR posts and their auxiliaries as partners. The Washington *Bee* reported that the local Sumner Post held a joint installation with its ladies' auxiliary and listed the names of the officers for both organizations. The *Republican Courier* of New Orleans announced that the Shaw Post of New Orleans held a joint installation with its LGAR circle. On the same page, the newspaper described a WRC ceremony officiated by a GAR post commander in Thibodeaux, Louisiana. A notice in the *Leavenworth [Kansas] Advocate* announced that entertainment would be provided by the local Shaw Post and its relief corps, noting, "We have of our comrades to care for, that are not able to care for themselves; also widows and orphans who need our assistance." In Leavenworth, as in Norfolk, the posts and their auxiliaries were considered part of the community.[11]

Woman's Relief Corps members repeatedly invoked charity, or relief, as their most important duty, a mission that has been slighted by modern studies more interested in their political and cultural activities. Twenty-first-century Americans cannot imagine nineteenth-century poverty; a well-cooked meal, a helping hand for the sick, or a dollar to aid a family in distress meant the difference between life and death in an era with virtually no social welfare system. The WRC's relief work may explain, in part, the organization's value to its post and its community. The president of the Connecticut WRC maintained, "Too much emphasis cannot be placed upon our relief work. Place this first and foremost in our efforts to carry out the principles of our order." The charitable aspect of the all-black associations' work is one important reason that white women supported them. "As this class have their needy and crippled ones and their widows and orphans, who should have aid," the national WRC president explained in 1890, "I can see no reason why respectable, loyal, colored women cannot be organized into Woman's Relief Corps." In 1891, Elizabeth Turner, a national WRC official, praised the all-black corps in St. Augustine, Florida. Although she reported that "they do little ritualistic work as so few read," she maintained that "they exemplify our greatest good, charity." Turner complimented "another good corps," the African American unit in Elizabeth City, North Carolina. "They take good care of their sick and needy ones and walk in perfect harmony with their post." While these reports represent the views of white observers, that does not make them inaccurate. Women who cared enough about black WRC members to visit their organizations likely characterized accurately the activities and contribution of these groups.[12]

African American women also recognized the importance of their relief work. The John Brown Corps in Chicago reported sending "3 quilts, 6 handkerchiefs, 2 night shirts, 1 pin cushion, several books and pictures" to the Soldiers Home in Illinois. The Fort Pillow Corps of Topeka related its extensive child welfare activities to Kansas officials well into the twentieth century. This "Colored Corps" cared "for four babies at members expense, bought $25 worth of toys, gave 56 baskets of food and fruit, secured homes for 2 orphan children, gave $1.04 in cash, . . . secured homes for 8 children; gave stove, rug and 12 garments to needy families." When the WRC of New York needed more members, it cited charity as its primary function. According to the *New York Age*, these organizations needed "a loyal addition of new members to make them flourish, as the posts to which they are auxiliary need their assistance now more than ever before. Orphan children and widows are being left as wards of the post and money and clothes are needed to keep them from being dependent upon public charity." This notice, found in the GAR column of the *New York Age*, represents the best evidence of black Americans' appreciation of the relief provided by ladies' auxiliaries.[13]

While the women's auxiliary seemed to be the most important group in the GAR circle, the all-black GAR post interacted with a whole host of community organizations. GAR posts also allied with the Sons of Veterans and the Daughters of Veterans, organizations composed of the lineal descendants of northern soldiers. The fourth anniversary of the Bell Post's auxiliary in Boston was, like all important milestones, celebrated with the African American men and women who shared their affiliation with the GAR. The *Age*'s Boston correspondent reported that "members of the G.A.R. and the Sons of Veterans appeared in full uniform, lending a pleasant effect to the occasion." These organizations also hosted benefits for their parent posts, as did the New York–based "John A. Andrew Post Sons and Daughters," who gave a "concert for the Posts benefit." The Stevens Post and its ladies' auxiliary buried John H. Gall, a member of their affiliated Sons of Veterans. When the Stevens Post formed its Sons of Veterans unit, the *Age* proclaimed that "this will be the beginning of a new era in colored G.A.R. circles." The African American community understood that the GAR circle extended beyond the narrow confines of the all-black post.[14]

The younger members of the black community participated in the circle as well. When the John A. Andrew Post presented a flag to the Bethel Sabbath School, "the Woman's Relief Corps turned out in force," and a group of teenaged girls who performed a military drill reportedly "received storms of applause." According to this account, about six hundred people turned out for this event. Most GAR posts seemed to have organized a drum corps made up of young boys and teenagers who provided music for GAR parades and participated in ceremonies memorializing the war. The *Age*'s Providence correspondent described a service attended by GAR members, commenting that the Ives Post "drum corps made a fine appearance in their new uniforms." Baltimore's all-black Lincoln Post, the senior post in the state, the New York–based John A. Andrew Post, the Stevens Post, and the William Lloyd Garrison posts had both drum and fife corps.

These youth groups were not trouble-free. At one point, the *Age* claimed that, contrary to rumor, the Stevens Drum Corps had not disbanded. Later, the same newspaper reported that this unit had reorganized, indicating that it must have experienced some difficulties. The Garrison Post announced that it "has organized a new drum corps of boys, and they expect a better and more perfect work in the future." The announcement implied that their past performance was less than perfect. The Shaw Post in Pittsburgh endured an ongoing battle to maintain a drum corps. In 1882 it appointed a committee to deal with its "insubordinate" members. While these sources do not explain posts' difficulties with these groups, it is likely that the boys resisted the discipline of a semi-military organization.[15]

All-black posts also served the African American community by providing entertainment. The Stevens Post of New York City hosted a "Full Dress Reception" with music by "Walter F. Craig's Celebrated Orchestra." The Garrison Post in Brooklyn filled the house with "a concert given them by the Ideal Opera Company." When the African American Sons of Veterans group in New York gave a social, the *Freeman* described the event and the "rousing good time the boys had." African American posts outside New York City played a similar role in their local communities. The John Brown WRC planned a lawn party in Chicago, and the Old John Brown Post of Oxford, Ohio, held a "grand entertainment." The Ives Post in Rhode Island organized a masquerade ball.[16]

While African Americans appreciated the GAR because it provided so-cial outlets, they also realized the important role played by these all-black posts and their circles in the battle for Civil War Memory. Black veterans and their circle reminded white Americans that African Americans had served and sacrificed in a war for their own freedom, a message that northern and southern apologists for the Lost Cause wanted erased from the nation's col-lective Memory. The men of the Shaw Post in Pittsburgh explained the role of African American posts, their ladies' auxiliaries, their sons and daughters, and even their somewhat recalcitrant drum corps in the struggle to shape Civil War Memory. Sitting in their post rooms, likely admiring the portrait of the post's namesake, who was born in Boston and buried in a mass grave in South Carolina, they wrote in their personal war sketches their hope that their "Children and [their] Children's Children . . . cherish the memories of those comrades names which are written in this book when the great cause for which they Suffered and Died will be known only in history."[17]

5

Heirs of These Dead Heroes

African Americans and the Battle for Memory

Speaking to the New York GAR encampment of 1898, Mrs. William Scott, a former slave, teacher, and missionary, explained that she was "glad to stand before you as one redeemed by your blood." With this opening she managed both to compliment her audience members and to remind them that they had liberated her race. Mrs. Scott's speech recalled incidents from her life as a slave. She repeatedly used the word "remember"; in some ways her speech seems like a prose poem because of this literary device. Mrs. Scott hoped that these men would "remember when four millions were made free—when the chains were struck off four millions of human beings." She wanted these men to remember how slavery destroyed families by recalling her mother's agony. She "remember[ed], early in the sixties, when a band of black men and women were passing by [her] home after an auction, on their way to Texas. In the front of the rank was [her] mother's husband. . . . [She] never forgot how [her mother] prayed the night before when she heard he had been sold." The Missourian told these men that her mother was not allowed to approach him and how her mother "went back to the cabin and lay there all day, mourning and mourning as if her heart would break." After describing this heartrending scene, Mrs. Scott asked her predominantly white audience, "Aren't you glad that you made such a scene as that impossible again, and that you wiped out that dark stain of slavery?" This speech, transcribed in the encampment record, represents the longest address made by a woman, white or black, to any state GAR examined in this study. Mrs. Scott may or may not have been welcomed by everyone at this gathering because she was a woman, especially an African American woman, but she used this opportunity to make sure they remembered.[1]

African American veterans' associations, their auxiliaries, their sons and

★

Mrs. William Scott, African American speaker at a New York GAR encampment. From Richings, *Evidence of Progress among the Colored People.*

daughters, and other elements of the African American GAR circle fought the efforts of those who would forget slavery and the black military experience in the Civil War. Black veterans and their associates used their membership in the GAR to contest Civil War Memory on the local, state, and national stages. Locally, the African American GAR circle participated in a number of activities that commemorated various aspects of the black freedom struggle, such as Emancipation Day celebrations and Fifteenth Amendment commemorations. Nationally, African American posts took part in patriotic celebrations such as Fourth of July observances, centennial celebrations, and integrated parades at annual GAR meetings. But black veterans and their associates did more than march at these gatherings; they also addressed their colleagues and reminded them that they had fought together in a war against slavery. While African Americans may not have fully succeeded in their efforts to shape Civil War Memory, their efforts to do so may have sown the seeds for later victory. Today we remember black soldiers and their struggle for freedom, and this may be the triumph of those who kept this version of history alive within the African American community.[2]

African Americans began their struggle for Memory as soon as they created their own posts. The state GAR assigned numbers to posts, but the founding members chose their names. As one might expect, African Americans chose names that emphasized their own Civil War experiences. A local Woman's Relief Corps usually shared its post's name, while LGAR circles usually did not. We have already met the men and women of the Robert Gould Shaw Post and Shaw Corps and their associated LGAR circles, named for Charles Sumner and Martin Delany. Charles Sumner fought for the Civil Rights Act of 1876, and black veterans in Delaware, Pennsylvania, and Maryland paid tribute to his memory in Sumner posts. Similarly the Delany posts in Georgia, Illinois, and Indiana memorialized the black nationalist and major, 114th USCT. Other posts, corps, and circles were named after individuals prominent in the African American freedom struggle. John Brown was such a popular name that in Ohio there was a John Brown Post and an Old John Brown Post. In this way, two groups of black Americans honored the hero of "Bleeding Kansas" and Harper's Ferry and evaded the general prohibition against naming two posts in a single state for the same person. Black Ohioans and New Yorkers, among others, honored Thaddeus Stevens, who, at his own instruction, was buried in a mixed-race graveyard, making his last statement on human equality. Frederick Douglass posts formed in Tennessee and Washington, D.C. African Americans also named posts for lesser-known black heroes, such as Robert A. Bell, a sailor killed at Fort Fisher. Bell's mother was a member of the WRC affiliated with the Boston post named after him. Veterans in Lancaster, Pennsylvania, honored a sergeant killed in action with the Third USCT by forming the Joel Benn Post. The Keith Post in Wilkes-Barre, Pennsylvania, memorialized the first black veteran who died in peacetime. The local white-owned and -edited paper described Keith as "a colored veteran who was killed some 17 years ago in this city . . . and who, when he was in the Army, was a brave soldier." Iowans honored one of their officers, who died with the Sixtieth USCT, out of Iowa, by organizing the all-black Pratt Post in Keokuk. While most posts were named for individuals, other African Americans named their posts for important battles fought by black troops, such as Fort Wagner.[3]

White veterans recognized and approved of black veterans' naming practices. The commander in chief of the GAR commented favorably on the membership record of the Charles Sumner Post of Washington, D.C. This post, he explained, had "sustained no loss by death, by transfer, or by suspension, but has gained two, and now has a membership of 117." When he was told that this was an African American post, the national commander replied that he was "glad to know that. They could not have selected a better name than Charles Sumner; never was there a man in this country that made [a] stronger defense of the rights of the slave." While the commander thought Sumner an appropriate choice, naming the post remained the prerogative of its black members.[4]

Black GAR posts sometimes chose names of white individuals or battles that were not related to the African American experience. Black veterans in Chattanooga, for example, named their post for the battle of Chickamauga, though no African American units fought in this engagement. Lieutenant Robert Ives, who was killed at Antietam before Lincoln announced the Emancipation Proclamation, was honored by African American veterans in Providence. A Maryland department official described his visit to the all-black John Logan Post, named for the volunteer general and founder of Memorial Day: The African American members felt "proud of their name Logan and their post." While the selection of Logan, Chickamauga, or Ives as the name for an all-black post may seem incongruous, these men demanded by their actions that "Colored Troops" be integrated into the larger history of the Civil War and asserted that their all-black associations were appropriate memorials for these individuals and battles.[5]

An all-black Logan Post was the exception; most black post members chose names like Sumner or Shaw that recalled some aspect of the Civil War they wanted memorialized. Members of the Shaw Post in Pittsburgh asserted that they established the post "to perpetuate [Shaw's] Memory and to cherish his bravery and loyalty to his country and flag" and to honor his allegiance "to his loyal colored regiment the 54th Mass. Vol. For he fell with scores of them leading the desperate charge on Ft. Wagner." By remembering the leader, they memorialized those he led. Shaw Post members' sentiments likely reflected those of other black veterans who named their posts for Charles Fribley, the late commander of the Eighth USCT, or for Robert Bryan, a black hero of the Roanoke Island campaign. Naming a post represented black GAR members' first opportunity to memorialize their experience in the Civil War. For as long as they were able, black men and women used these institutions to contest Civil War Memory.[6]

African American posts and their circles sponsored activities that reminded their community, black and white, of the centrality of slavery to the Civil War's causes and consequences. Some posts commemorated the life of individuals who had fought against slavery; for example, the African American women of the John Brown Circle celebrated the 105th anniversary of their namesake's birth in 1905. In 1887, the *New York Freeman* reported that "a lecture on the life of Thaddeus Stevens and presentation of a portrait of the 'Old Commoner' to the Thaddeus Stevens Post occurred at the Bethel Church" in New York in 1887. The WRC joined the festivities, as did members of the all-white Admiral Reynolds Post, who presented a "magnificent steel engraving of Thaddeus Stevens" to his namesake post. The gift demonstrates that white veterans recognized their black counterparts as appropriate guardians of Civil War Memory.[7]

But this was not the first time members of the two posts assembled together. Members of the New York–based Stevens Post visited Lancaster, Pennsylvania, home of the Reynolds Post and the last resting place of Thaddeus Stevens, "friend of the colored race," to make sure he was properly honored on Memorial Day. In 1886, a representative of the Stevens Post, Mr. Henderson, went to Lancaster to place a wreath on his grave. According to a newspaper report, representatives from the local white posts met him at the train: "He was at once escorted to the cemetery, where they assembled about the graves of Thaddeus Stevens and his nephew. Mr. Henderson then gave the command to uncover, which all obeyed." Rarely in this era did African Americans either command the actions of white Americans or force them to literally remove their hats to honor either a man or an idea that black Americans cherished. Henderson then eulogized Stevens: "It is right and proper that at least once a year the representatives of the people for whom he fought with tongue and pen through long years of opposition at a great personal risk, should assemble to honor his memory and drop a tear on his sod." This was not the end of Lancaster's relationship with this African American organization. The entire Stevens Post traveled to Lancaster for the 1890 Memorial Day parade and marched in the parade's vanguard, in front of local white posts. It was only after the Stevens Post's visit that local black veterans formed their own post honoring Sergeant Joel Benn.[8]

African American posts and their associates also participated in a variety of activities to memorialize African American military achievements. In Jeffersonville, Indiana, "Post 351, G.A.R., colored, held a reunion. . . . The main features of the evening were the sham battle, skirmish, drill, etc." The lieutenant governor of Indiana attended the event, and according to a correspondent, "the town was full of strangers, both white and colored, who attended the great reunion." In Kansas, the Shaw Post sponsored a "reunion of the first and the second volunteer regiment [Kansas, Colored] afterwards known as the Seventy-eighth and the Eighty-third U.S. Troops." The reunion celebrated the "twenty seventh anniversary of the day in which colored troops were mustered into the service of the Union." In New York, the *Age* joined with local African American posts to sell copies of a "picture of the charge of the Fifty-fourth Massachusetts Regiment on Fort Wagner on the 18th July 1864 [*sic*]." Subscribers could purchase this image for one dollar. Since "the supply [was] limited," the *Age* advised, "orders should be sent in without delay."[9]

GAR men commemorated other battles involving black soldiers. Black veterans frequently recited "The Black Regiment," a poem honoring the "dusky line of soldiers" that charged the vital fortifications at Port Hudson, Louisiana. With their "bright bayonets bristled and firmly set," the poem goes, the soldiers were "Glad to breathe a free breath, though on the lips of death." In places where one might expect more interest in eastern battles, such as the Shaw Post in Pittsburgh, veterans recited this paean to the heroism of western soldiers. African American post members in New York frequently recited this poem at their meetings. At one such gathering, the commander in chief of the national GAR was an honored guest. A little more than seventy miles from Fort Wagner, a speaker at Beaufort, South Carolina's, Memorial Day ceremonies read this salute to black Louisianans' gallantry. While today the charge at Fort Wagner might be the most famous engagement involving black soldiers, African Americans also honored the sacrifice of the black troops who stormed Port Hudson.[10]

All-black posts hosted lectures on a variety of topics that concerned African American history. The William Lloyd Garrison Post in New York City, named after the famous abolitionist, heard the state's African American chaplain speak on "the Boys in Blue." "Our Fallen Heroes" was the subject of another lecture; according to the New York Freeman's "Grand Army Notes," the audience included "the veterans . . . Sons of Veterans, the Ladies of the Relief Corps, and the drum corps." At the Fort Pillow Post in Topeka, Kansas, a lecturer "referred with much feeling to the inestimable service of the Negro soldiers in all the wars of his country. His talk was replete with glowing tributes to Negro heroism and sacrifice." The black GAR circle wanted Americans to remember African American heroism in all the nation's wars.[11]

Speeches or poetry readings likely were featured at the most popular GAR activities, the "Campfire." These social events harkened back to veterans' military experience when their primary entertainment involved singing songs and telling stories around a fire. At these events, which were usually held in a hall or theater, former soldiers regaled their comrades and the general public with songs, poetry, and stories recalling their military service. GAR campfires could be part of informal post-level gatherings organized to entertain the local community or larger, more formal gatherings at state and national encampments. African American newspapers frequently reported on these events. In Jeffersonville, Indiana; Topeka, Kansas; and many points in between, the African American community organized these events to entertain and to inform. The Charles Sumner Post of Wilmington, Delaware, held "an open campfire . . . to which all ex-soldiers and sailors [were] invited." A Rhode Island correspondent emphasized that a local gathering was interracial and welcomed men and women. The all-black Ives Post "lighted one of their pleasant campfires, at which their ladies were present." Several senior white officials of the state GAR joined the black GAR circle for this event.[12]

African American veterans expected white veterans to attend their campfires and acknowledge their military service, demonstrated by their response to an incident in which they felt they had been slighted by a white veteran. The *New York Freeman* reported in 1885 that the Keith Post of Wilkes-Barre, Pennsylvania, held a campfire; however, "the big guns, white Republican generals, failed to come and do the speaking." One of these generals, W. H. McCartney, was running for attorney general. The *Freeman* attributed the general's absence to his racist views: reportedly, the general exclaimed that "he was not going to . . . speak for them d—n niggers." McCartney's failure to appear may have been worthy of comment because it was unusual; white veterans' attendance at these events was routine. McCartney's remarks at a later Keith Post campfire support this interpretation. At this meeting, the general "eulogized the bravery of the colored soldiers, and said that they fought like the devil." He denounced the *Freeman*'s earlier report as a lie, the product of "a miserable cur," and denied that he ever used "scurrilous language towards" black veterans. McCartney's political aspirations may have inspired his appearance at the second campfire and his reply to newspaper's charges, but, regardless of his motives, the African American community insisted that he attend their campfire to celebrate their sacrifice, and he complied.[13]

African Americans never forgot their military service and never forgot that this duty occurred in a war that freed their race and made them citizens. Celebrating Emancipation Day was another important activity for all-black posts and their circles. According to the *Age*, Emancipation Day activities "under the auspices of Col Shaw Post 206" demonstrated that "our people did not forget that 22 years ago . . . our people were freed from the chains of bondage." In Virginia, the celebration of freedom involved a broad segment of the black community. A parade included "mounted men, wearing different society emblems and uniforms[,] . . . the militia and members of the civic societies arrayed in the garb of the respective organizations," and members of the hod carriers (unskilled laborers) union. The all-black Cailloux and Shaw posts of the Virginia GAR marched with the other groups. The African American posts of New York City took an active part in the Emancipation Day parade in Jamaica, Long Island. Some of them recognized emancipation as a worldwide phenomenon; the Thaddeus Stevens and John Andrew posts, for example, acted "as escorts to the Cuban Society who . . . celebrate[d] the emancipation of the slave on the isle of Cuba."

African Americans celebrated postemancipation accomplishments that increased their political rights as well. The Custer Post, based in Richmond, marched with the black militia, the "First Colored Battalion of Virginia Volunteers," in a celebration of the Fifteenth Amendment, which gave African Americans the right to vote. The Garrison Post of New York also celebrated this milestone. Contemporary concerns frequently preoccupied the men and women at these celebrations. According to the *Age*, the speakers at the Garrison Post's celebration "dwelt upon the duties of citizenship and deplored the shocking absence among us of race pride and business effort." Since "the Women's Vigilance Committee" organized this commemoration, it is clear that women in the black GAR circle felt comfortable asserting their right to lead these efforts.[14]

African American posts and their female allies also held events honoring Ulysses S. Grant, who was president when the Fifteenth Amendment was ratified. In New York in 1885, the Andrews WRC resolved that "while it has pleased the almighty to visit our illustrious Gen. U. S. Grant with sore and stressing illness and unit death," they did "hereby offer our sympathy . . . and pray to the Father of all to send strength and comfort to the sufferer to enable him to fight the battle with heroism so worthy a great man." The ladies presented this resolution and flowers to the general's son, Frederick Grant. When the general lost his battle with cancer, the GAR and the entire African American community mourned his death. Black churches held memorial services. The *New York Freeman* not only featured a large woodcut of Grant on page one, but it also placed black borders around each article on the front page to mark his passing. In Newark, New Jersey, the "Isaac Tucker Post commander, Henry Johnson, took a very prominent part in the Grant Memorial Service at the Grand Opera House." Black veterans in the nation's capital consciously connected this major Civil War figure with their own efforts to memorialize the African American Civil War experience. Two years after Grant's death, the Morton Post commemorated "the birthday of the great commander." This event was "intended not only as a tribute to the life and the services of Gen. Grant, but to recall the heroism and the valor of the colored soldiers and sailors in the late war." GAR men discussed plans for a tangible reminder of black military service at this meeting, "a National monument in the capital in their honor." (This effort succeeded, 111 years later.) Membership in the interracial GAR allowed these men and women to use the Morton Post commemoration to shape Civil War Memory and honor the man who, in the words of an African American poet, "broke the fetters of the slave."[15]

Because they were members of a powerful, interracial organization, black GAR members marched in patriotic parades that may not have welcomed other all-black organizations. These impressive spectacles may have been one of black veterans' most valuable weapons in the struggle for Memory. At the centennial of the United States, two African American posts participated in the Philadelphia parade celebrating this milestone. Six years later, the Sumner Post of Wilmington, Delaware, marched in the City of Brotherly Love's bicentennial parade. The Keith Post of Wilkes-Barre went to Scranton, Pennsylvania "upon invitation . . . [to take] part in the parade which came off there in honor of the glorious fourth [of July]." The John Brown Post of Chicago welcomed General Grant to Chicago in 1879, marching alongside the city's other posts. Black Baltimore residents joined their white counterparts in celebrating the inauguration of Maryland's governor in 1896. "One hundred and twenty-five uniformed men from Dushane Post, No. 3, joined Lincoln Post, No. 7" in this procession. The drum corps of the all-black Lincoln Post marched with their elders and, according to Maryland officials, "furnished [them] with a most creditable appearance." Representatives from three New York–based black posts visited the Antietam National Cemetery in 1886 to attend ceremonies commemorating the twenty-fourth anniversary of the battle. According to the *Age*, "Forty thousands people crowded the walks." The New Yorkers marched in the lead group. "As the dusky veterans led the way," the *Age* reported, "the populace seemed to realize that they must have done something worthy or they would not have the post of honor. The applause gradually broke forth, until it was caught up by the entire line, and with continuous ovation from the beginning to the close of the march, the colored veterans the great centre of attraction." The New Yorkers had made the long journey to Maryland, a former slave state, knowing that they could play a prominent role in this GAR-sponsored event and become "the great centre of attraction."[16]

The parades held at the GAR's national encampment were the most important showcases for African American veterans in this era. The audience at these parades numbered in the tens of thousands; sometimes, more than one hundred thousand people observed the spectacle. When Boston welcomed the GAR in 1890, the all-black Shaw Post of St. Louis marched in the procession, as did the African American members of the Morton Post of Washington, D.C., and the Ives Post of Providence. Fourteen years later, the national encampment met again in Boston. African Americans from Louisville, Kentucky's, Delany Post joined Ives Post members at this event. The time and expense required to make the trip to these encampments likely prevented many black and white GAR posts' from attending. The African Americans members of Kansas's Shaw Post, for example, attended the Denver encampment in 1905 but did not attend either Boston meeting. But the all-black Delany Post of Indianapolis made the relatively short trip to Chicago for the

1900 encampment, where it received a banner from the citizens' committee honoring it as the "post representing the best appearance in line" at the main procession.[17]

The largest and most memorable parade held at an encampment was the reenactment of the 1865 Grand Review of the Northern Armies; in 1892, the GAR, at least fifty thousand strong, marched again through Washington, D.C. Reporters commented on the participation of many black units in the procession. The *Philadelphia Inquirer* described the parade in detail, including the appearance of black veterans: "The first colored [post] then appeared, [the] Lewis Post. . . . Other colored troops were seen later, and came along at odd intervals, just as popular as any other sections of the columns, and just as proud." African American veterans marching in this parade came from all over the nation, and, according to the *Inquirer*, "colored soldiers . . . constituted the majority of the Southern representation." The entire Delaware contingent was "led by the Charles Sumner Post (colored) No. 4, of Wilmington." The presence of black veterans from this nearby state may not have been a surprise; however, the Mississippi delegation, who the *Inquirer* reporter noted "number[ed] nearly two hundred, every man as black as the ace of spades," traveled a great distance to march in this procession. Despite his use of what we consider racially offensive language, the presence of these southern men, so far from home, prompted this observer to comment on the heroics of black soldiers in a war for freedom: The Mississippians, "colored soldiers who fought nobly, . . . marched with the mien of men who had earned their freedom through fire and blood." He also reported overhearing the comments of an "old bent Negro veteran . . . honest but poverty stricken" describing the sacrifice required to attend this event: "I had to sell my stove to get here, but dare ain't no winter cold enough to chill dis ole body if can only see Washuntun and de old sojers again." The *Inquirer*'s commentary demonstrates that white Americans saw no contradiction between their racial views and remembering black soldiers' military service in a war for black freedom. Regardless of their racial attitudes, reporters and other white Americans could not completely erase the memory of black American Civil War service as long as African Americans marched in GAR parades.[18]

While the veterans marched, the black community did not stand by idly. An "arch erected by the colored citizens" welcoming the national encampment to Buffalo in 1897 highlights the involvement of the entire black community in the struggle for Civil War Memory. A stereograph sold by Griffith and Griffith, a prominent purveyor of such images, captured this short-lived Civil War monument, which spanned an unnamed broad avenue. "They fought for the liberty we now enjoy," the words engraved at the top of the

The arch erected by African American citizens in Buffalo, New York,
to welcome the GAR's 1897 national encampment and to remind them of black
service in a war for black freedom. From author's collection.

arch, established liberty as the most important outcome of the war, the cul-
mination of the GAR's service and sacrifice. Portraits of Grant and Lincoln
occupied the left and right flanks of the epitaph. The right supporting column listed some of the black soldiers' most important engagements: Fort
Wagner, Olustee, and Petersburg. The left column indicates that the "Colored
Citizens" of the city erected the arch to honor the GAR. Left unsaid was its
second purpose: to remind observers of black Americans' active role in this
conflict.[19]

Just as national encampments allowed African American GAR men and
their circles a national audience, black men and their female allies exploited
their status as members of state organizations to fight for their version of

Civil War Memory. An African American clergyman speaking at an event commemorating the Fifteenth Amendment described the role of black veterans at state annual meetings: "Their presence has been conspicuous. . . . Thus may it ever be, until the last of the glorious army shall have crossed the river and their tents be pitched on fame's eternal ground. . . . Take pride in the deeds and doings of your race. Recount them." Black men and their female allies exploited their status as members of state organizations to fight for their version of Civil War Memory.[20]

African Americans frequently reminded their colleagues of black military service while conducting state encampment business, for example, when black GAR men made nominating speeches for their white colleagues. Comrade Little, commander of an all-black post, seconded the nomination of T. K. Beecher for department chaplain in New York not only because "Henry Ward Beecher, his brother, did great good for our people," but also because "Colonel Beecher served in the brigade two years and five months and led the colored troops bravely." The person recording the meeting minutes noted that the audience cheered. Across the country, Comrade Bryant, a black Missourian, nominated Comrade Leo Rassieur for state commander. Bryant endorsed Rassieur for high office as the representative of "the survivors of [the] 180,000 men . . . [who were] proud of the honor of being named among Grand Army men." At the same gathering, Bryant requested funds to send home the body of an all-black post's commander who died at the meeting. He described the post commander as "eighty years of age . . . old, decrepit, . . . his face black; . . . he was at Ft. Pillow when a hundred soldiers were murdered for their flag." The encampment raised the necessary funds.[21]

The veterans of Fort Pillow and other USCT battles served in federal regiments, and GAR members fought to ensure that they received the same recognition as soldiers who served in state regiments. According to Comrade McKie, commander of a black post in New York City, "None were more loyal, faithful and brave than the nation's sable heroes" who had served in the USCT. McKie asked that New York's African American veterans receive the same treatment as soldiers in other states: "Wherever, these sable citizens were mustered into the service of the United States Army, the State in which they were raised, with one exception, gave credit in its quota of men and regiments, regardless of color, race, or previous condition." The one exception was New York. The state had "rejected [the] records of the two regiments (colored), the Twentieth and the Twenty-sixth United States Colored Troops [mobilized in New York] on the grounds that they were raised by a special order from the immortal Lincoln, then President of the United States," not the governor of New York. McKie demanded that the men of these units be placed on the same muster rolls that recorded the service of volunteers in New York state regiments. The resolution lost, as it was deemed "impracticable, if not impossible, that men enlisting in United States regiments be taken as New York soldiers." Though this effort failed, African Americans had reminded their New York colleagues of their service. Recognizing USCT regiments raised in northern states as equal to state regiments appeared to be common practice, as McKie's comments suggest. Black veterans in New Jersey, in fact, obtained recognition for their federal service because of an effort spearheaded by a white colleague. This former department commander requested that the state organization ensure that the "hundreds of veterans of the state of New Jersey who were accredited to New Jersey who served in U.S. colored regiments" receive the state medal given to those who served in other state units; the encampment agreed.[22]

Another practical measure to equalize USCT and state units involved an effort to preserve the colors of black regiments raised in northern states. The men of the all-black Stephens Post in Harrisburg complained to the encampment that, although the regimental colors of Pennsylvania state regiments were honored in the state flag room, "there were ten regiments of soldiers who served as the portion of the quota of the state whose flags are not preserved by the state." The petitioners asked that the encampment urge the legislature to "have the flags of the colored troops placed in the Flag Room of the state of Pennsylvania." The encampment agreed to support the proposal. Saving the regimental colors represented no small victory for these men; preserving relics of black units shaped Civil War Memory.[23]

Other black GAR posts endeavored to preserve old relics and create new monuments commemorating their military service. The five black posts in Baltimore argued that "every nationality has a monument erected to their soldier dead but the colored soldier." The men proposed to the Maryland GAR that a monument to African American soldiers be placed in Baltimore's national cemetery. The resolution, adopted on a rising vote of members, encountered little or no opposition. Such unanimity may have been easy to obtain since this proposal did not ask for funds, merely assistance in securing resources for this project. The black GAR circle in Philadelphia also wanted to erect "a suitable monument commemorative of the valor of our comrades who gave their lives in defense of the flag of our country." The three black posts in Philadelphia, their Woman's Relief Corps, the Sons of Veterans, and a local black militia unit signed this petition and requested "as a matter of equal rights and even-handed justice an appropriation similar to those granted the Pennsylvania State Regiment Monument Association." The state rejected this plea because the money appropriated by the state had been for units that fought at Gettysburg only. Maryland veterans may have succeeded and Pennsylvanians failed because the resolution regarding the Baltimore monument asked only for support while the Philadelphians asked for public funding.[24]

A desire to build a national monument to the USCT prompted black veterans to ask for the assistance of their comrades at annual encampments. In 1891, members of the "Colored National Monument Association of Brooklyn" proposed a memorial "to commemorate the memory of the colored soldiers who freely gave their lives, together with their white comrades, during the rebellion, so that the nation might live." The petitioners, including churchmen and GAR officials, argued that there is no "such monument to teach the rising generation, and also the naturalized citizens (who have become such since the close of the rebellion), that citizens of color had taken active part in helping to preserve the Union." Black Chicagoans also wanted a national memorial to African American soldiers and asked the state GAR to support a motion in Congress to appropriate one hundred thousand dollars for this purpose. The Chicago-based Brown Post in turn appealed to the state for assistance, explaining that African Americans served "with scant hope of honor or promotion" and in the face of an "inhuman threat of 'No Quarter' which the enemy declared against them." While these men fully supported a national monument, they also wanted their fellow Illinoisans to assist them in changing the location of this monument from Washington, D.C., to Chicago. Illinois officials did not endorse this bit of parochialism. Other black veterans solicited support of white women. George W. Bryant, the black Missourian so active at the Missouri encampment, traveled to the WRC annual meeting in New Jersey to ask for their help in building a monument to black soldiers. Despite "all the thousands of colored soldiers who fell in defense of the flag," Bryant explained to the women, "not one 5 cents have ever been appropriated by the people to erect a monument to their memory." The predominantly white audience "responded liberally," although the amount contributed to this cause was not specified in the meeting minutes. Today a memorial in Washington, D.C., at last, honors the African American soldiers of the Civil War.[25]

Reminding their comrades of black service was not enough; black veterans also reminded these men of black slavery. Comrade Hector stood on his "foot of equality" at a Pennsylvania encampment campfire and "referred feelingly to the shackles struck from the limbs of 4,000,000 slaves and said that he was a slave until the army set him free." At a New Jersey encampment, William Murrell argued that Lincoln's birthday should be a state holiday because "the name of Lincoln, with the Negroes of America, will never die; we love his name; we love his memory. We ask you to receive from us this holiday." Lincoln deserved this holiday, he explained, because he "struck the shackles from four million of human beings, I was one from whom the shackles fell." James Wolff, who occupied the highest position held by an African American veteran, department commander, reminded members of the Massachusetts GAR that they "made it possible that the old flag should ever fly triumphant over every inch of soil, and beneath which . . . we live today a nation of freemen and not the footprint of a slave desecrates the land." The GAR accepted Hector, Murrell, and Wolff into its fellowship, and as such these men were able to wage an effective campaign in the battle for Civil War Memory.[26]

While the GAR no longer marches, the most effective platform the black circle used in its struggle for Memory still exists today: Memorial Day. In an address to a black GAR circle on Memorial Day, 1884, W. H. Banks described the group as a fitting guardian of Civil War Memory: "We are related to the dead as the son is to the father—the son is the heir to all the father leaves behind. So we are the heirs of the dead heroes. . . . They died for us, and their dying was the cost of all the benefits we enjoy today, be they political, civil, or social. It requires us to guard their names from defamers and oblivion, and though the whole nation is bound to do this, it is fitting that we, the partners of their toil, should be the foremost in commemorating their sacred deeds." How African Americans in the GAR circle used Memorial Day to save black veterans from "defamers and oblivion" is the subject of the next chapter.[27]

6

Memorial Day in Black and White

The Memorial Day of today is not celebrated in the same way that the GAR observed it. On the last Monday in May, we honor the dead of all American wars with long weekend getaways that signal the beginning of summer. In contrast, by order of General Logan, the commander in chief of the GAR, a specific day each year, May 30, was set aside to honor the Union army's war dead. General Logan explicitly cited emancipation as a reason for this commemoration. Northern "soldiers' lives," he explained, "were the reveille of freedom to a race in chains." The black GAR post and its associates enthusiastically participated in Memorial Day activities, such as church services, graveside ceremonies, and parades. Segregated observances allowed the African American GAR circle, particularly women, to shape the message of Memorial Day. When African Americans controlled the Memorial Day message, they had an invaluable tool to construct their own version of Civil War Memory. Members of the black GAR circle also participated in interracial commemorations, although these did not always allow them to define the meaning and Memory of the Civil War. However, interracial Memorial Day commemorations, particularly parades, had large mixed-race audiences. The mere presence of a black post and its associates at these observances challenged the Civil War Memory that hailed white soldiers and forgot black soldiers.[1]

Interracial observances were not always possible. African Americans often held Memorial Day observances at their churches. Mainstream newspapers frequently reported on the sermons given at black churches on this day. Some chose a few quotes, while others printed the minister's remarks in their entirety, suggesting that their audience included whites. Black posts held Memorial Day services at African Methodist Episcopal (AME) churches. The Garrison Post of New York City "listened to a sermon by the Rev. Wm H. Thomas at the Bridge Street A.M.E." The Sumner Post in Wilmington, Dela-

★

ware, heard the "Rev W. Brodie preach a most eloquent sermon at the Bethel A.M.E. church." Similarly the Charles Sumner Post in Chestertown, Maryland, attended its local Bethel AME's service. The African American Methodist church was not the only black denomination that welcomed the GAR. An "efficient and able pastor of the colored Presbyterian congregation" in Carlisle, Pennsylvania, spoke on "the GAR which was called upon to assist in liberating 4 million slaves" and extolled the virtues and "the valor of the colored soldiers at Ft. Wagner under Col. Shaw and at Ft. Fisher under General Butler." At a service in Wilkes-Barre, Pennsylvania, a "colored preacher," denomination unknown, who was described by a local paper as "one who fought to uphold the Union," reminded his listeners that the war did more than preserve the status quo. "The first gun at Sumter," the minister maintained, "echoed the death knell of slavery." Black churches had vigorously courted members of Pittsburgh's Shaw Post, sending their invitations to them more than two months before this service to ensure that they would have the opportunity to host this liturgy. While sermons may be forgotten, the Ives Post in Rhode Island left a permanent memorial to its comrades. The post, accompanied by white state officials, dedicated a window "in honor of the fallen heroes of the Civil War at the Peoples A.M.E. Zion Church." Black posts' involvement in churches allowed these important African American institutions to commemorate their own community's Civil War experience.[2]

Although the color line often meant that the black GAR circle performed ceremonies at all-black cemeteries to memorialize its honored dead, white newspapers took note of the proceedings. The all-black Stephens Post observed Memorial Day at the Lincoln Cemetery, the final resting place of Harrisburg, Pennsylvania's African American community. Most black veterans who died in Washington, Pennsylvania, were buried in the "Old Graveyard," and the local African American post held its annual ceremonies in this cemetery. Black posts and their circle decorated these graveyards because of their special obligation to their own comrades. African American posts in New York City sent "a special committee to all cemeteries to decorate their post's comrade's graves." The New Jersey–based all-black Roberson Post "decorated their soldier dead . . . strewing flowers in abundance upon the colored heroes," and the "Delany Post (colored) decorated the graves of their departed comrades" in Chambersburg, Pennsylvania. The newspaper reporting on these events identified both posts as "colored"—a detail northern newspapers usually omitted. Reporters who did reveal the posts' race may have wanted the public to understand that African American soldiers, both living and dead, were recognized on Memorial Day.[3]

Because of the sheer number of graveyards to be decorated, GAR posts sometimes visited a number of them, whether they were white or black, Catholic or Protestant. Members of the all-black post in York, Pennsylvania, honored the dead in the Lebanon cemetery, but they also decorated veterans' graves at the Alms House and Potter Field, the final resting place of the impoverished honored dead—likely both white and black. Detailed to care for the graves in the Catholic Cemetery, the all-black post in Washington, Pennsylvania, honored many white Catholic veterans. Philadelphia posts divided up the city's cemeteries to make sure all were visited on Decoration Day. The all-black Jackson Post regularly ornamented the graves at the Third German Baptist Church and Trinity Lutheran Church cemeteries, which were unlikely to be the resting place of many black veterans.[4]

In the South, the color line on this day was often the result of white southerners' indifference toward a holiday that honored northern war dead. Sometimes African Americans honored the Union army's dead of both races in the South because they were the only part of the local community that observed the day. The *Age* reported that the all-black "Fletcher post No. 20 GAR and the Afro-Americans generally" in Elizabeth City, North Carolina, observed Memorial Day. The local white Democratic paper in Chestertown, Maryland, reporting that memorial commemorations were led by "the colored G.A.R. post," seemed somewhat chagrined by white apathy on Memorial Day: "The sacred duty of honoring the memory of those who died in defense of our country . . . seems to devolve upon the colored people of the town. At least they are the only ones who observe the day in Chestertown." On the other hand, the local paper in Salisbury, Maryland, appeared untroubled by local apathy: "The graves of the Union dead whose ashes repose on our sacred soil were decorated with the national flag. In all other respects the day passed without observance." The writer of this article leaves the impression that the sacred soil of this city was outside the United States.[5]

While local Memorial Day ceremonies may have been manageable in the North, the large number of northern war dead in southern cemeteries represented a more daunting challenge and prompted southern GAR circles to hold racially separate ceremonies. The tens of thousands of war dead severely taxed the GAR in Georgia and South Carolina. As one department official explained in 1894, we are "one of the smallest departments as to numbers, having a membership of only 420." Responsibility for decorating the graves of thirty-six thousand Union soldiers rested upon this small group of black and white veterans living in "the very heart of the old confederacy." Black posts often took charge of the ceremonies at national cemeteries because they were the only GAR posts in the area. GAR officials, for example, directed that the "Beaufort, S.C. Cemetery will be under the charge of David Hunter

Post, No. 9, aided by the Robert G. Shaw Post, No. 8." Later, after the GAR expanded in this area, five all-black units supervised ceremonies at this cemetery—the final resting place of more than nine thousand U.S. soldiers.[6]

While interracial ceremonies seem more desirable, the broader African American community was better able to participate in black Memorial Day commemorations. A GAR chaplain described the large black GAR circle that participated in ceremonies at the Beaufort National Cemetery. One hundred and fifty black GAR men attended this ceremony accompanied by members of the WRC and the Sons of Veterans, as well as "ten militia companies, brass bands, school children, civic organizations, and citizens generally, from Beaufort and surrounding towns, aggregating an attendance over 12,000." In areas where there were no black posts, the African American community took charge on Memorial Day. The National Cemetery in Florence, South Carolina, was so isolated from the GAR that one department official complained that "for years the presence of only one comrade has been noted at exercises at this cemetery," so the GAR relied on "the persevering and devoted attention of a few faithful hearts—members of the Florence Memorial Association (colored)—to decorate the graves." Separate ceremonies allowed many elements of the African American community to commemorate their Civil War experience in a region where they had little social or political autonomy.[7]

Like their southern counterparts, African American posts in northern states supervised their own Memorial Day ceremonies, and these observances incorporated many elements of the black community. The Garrison Post of New York staged its Memorial Day service at the Lincoln statue in Prospect Park. The ceremony featured "singing by the Sunday schools," and "the U.S.S. of V. No. 36 (Sons of Veterans), the Woman's Relief Corps, No. 33, Knights of Pythias No. 11, and the Society of the Sons of North Carolina" participated. The ceremonies organized by the Philadelphia-based Bryan Post included the local African American militia unit, "the Gray Invincibles," their Sons of Veterans units, and their ladies' auxiliary units. White observers commented on the role the African American community played in these commemorations. In Steeltown, Pennsylvania, the ceremonies of the day were under the control of the all-black post from nearby Harrisburg. The *Harrisburg Patriot* complimented "the colored people" of Steeltown and not merely the all-black David Stephens Post for preparing "excellent memorial services." It is unclear whether white Americans participated in the black Pennsylvania observances, but it is likely they attended their own ceremonies.[8]

The *Patriot* reporter's reference to "colored *people*," a term that would have included both men and women, suggests that he observed the important role played by African American women at Memorial Day observances. The African Americans of the John Brown WRC of Chicago reported that they "attended memorial services in a body. . . . Flowers were contributed and [a] memorial prepared for the unknown dead." In Springfield, Illinois, the all-black Bross Corps prepared "a lovely floral design for the tomb of Abraham Lincoln." The Shaw Corps of Quincy, described as "colored," reported that it "strew[ed] flowers with profusion upon the fallen heroes, regardless of color." The reference to the corps' race may have been made to explain why their inclusive decoration practices deserved recognition. The decoration of white soldiers' graves represented more than a thoughtful gesture; it asserted these women's right to shape Memorial Day commemorations by honoring men of both races. Even when there were no all-black GAR posts in an area, women's groups participated in Memorial Day commemorations. In 1910, after the all-black Shaw Post of New Bedford, Massachusetts, disbanded, the LGAR organized the African American community's Memorial Day observances. According to the *New York Age*, the New Bedford–based Jane Jackson Circle sponsored "a patriotic concert in the A.M.E. Zion Church. . . . A vocal selection was given by the veterans of the Civil War, after which followed an exercise by a number of school children."

Black women's groups continued the struggle for Civil War Memory well into the twentieth century. In 1924, the WRC erected the only statue in Kentucky honoring African American Civil War service. Similarly, the WRC, together with their GAR posts and Spanish-American War veterans, built a memorial to African American veterans in Norfolk, Virginia, in the 1920s—a statue of Sergeant William Carney, a Norfolk native, Medal of Honor winner, and color-bearer of the Fifty-fourth Massachusetts.[9]

Women's groups sometimes formed during the Memorial Day period, demonstrating the connection between the black community's enthusiasm for ladies' auxiliaries and their role in Civil War commemorations. In 1896, the Joel Benn Post in Lancaster, one of the few black posts in Pennsylvania not yet affiliated with a ladies' organization, reported on Memorial Day the creation of a women's group. The Boston-based Robert A. Bell Post's announcement that it had "decided to form a ladies' auxiliary association" appears alongside its Memorial Day plans in the local newspaper. That women's auxiliaries were formed around this time of year suggests either that a post that had not yet affiliated with a women's group felt its absence more keenly during this period or that local women demanded inclusion in the day's activities and formed these units to assert their right to participate.[10]

A Memorial Day speaker at a black church in West Chester, Pennsylvania, explained women's role in Memorial Day commemorations. Professor

William H. Day reminded his audience that "during [the] war the colored soldier left a memory that will always be kept fresh and green in the hearts of those who love liberty, and he also left a name that will endure forever. It is for the members of the George F. Smith and other colored posts to make this fact apparent and keep it alive before the world." He also urged these men to "not forget the women. Those who stood nobly by you in the times of death and carnage, gather them together that they might stand by you in times of peace." Women needed no prompting to stand with veterans and remind Americans of the African American Civil War experience.[11]

The black GAR circle's choice of a Memorial Day speaker, like Professor Day, shaped the message of the day. George Washington Williams, the pioneering black historian and GAR member, addressed the all-black Bell Post on "the advent of the colored soldier." Williams reminded his audience of white Americans' initial reluctance to arm black soldiers. "Will the Negro fight?" Unionists asked. African American soldiers, Williams maintained, answered at "Port Hudson, Ft. Wagner, Ft. Pillow, Olustee, Honey Hill, Petersburg, Richmond, Appomattox and a hundred other well fought and well won battlefields." African Americans chose Rev. William Palmer, a classicist from the black South Carolina state college, to address the audience on Memorial Day at the Beaufort National Cemetery. Palmer compared African American soldiers to the famed warriors of antiquity and to more recent heroes. The "Black Phalanx" was as "brave as Leonidas at Thermopylae; as resolute as Hannibal crossing the Alps; as plucky as L'Overture then a match for the proud Napoleon, as daring as Meneleck of Abyssinia, the conqueror of Italy's Army." The Reverend Mahlon Van Horne spoke at Memorial Day proceedings organized by the Ives Post in Providence, Rhode Island. "The colored men in the South were the most loyal to the Union," Van Horne declared. While he described white icons of the conflict, such as Grant, Burnside, Sherman, and Sheridan, he argued that "no acts in the drama of patriotism, recorded in the history of the world illustrate more courage and soldierly quality than were exhibited by the Fifty-fourth and Fifty-fifth Massachusetts at Fort Wagner." Published privately, Williams's and Palmer's speeches have survived, but it is not known who listened to them or read them later. It is very likely that white Americans heard these speeches, for white GAR members would have felt duty bound to attend these important commemorations and to hear African Americans articulate their own version of Civil War Memory. Regardless of who heard their messages, these men used this platform to shape Civil War Memory, and they were able to do so because the African American community had its own separate observances.[12]

Segregation was not always the order of the day; most black posts participated in some type of integrated observance on Memorial Day. Churches may have been exclusively black or white, but the GAR overcame this barrier in common memorial liturgies. The all-white Post 201 announced in the Carlisle, Pennsylvania, newspaper that "in pursuance of an invitation from [the all-black] post 440, the members are requested [to] meet at Headquarters . . . and proceed in a body to the opera house to attend divine services to be held by Rev. Parker of the Baptist Church in Carlisle Pennsylvania." In Lancaster, Pennsylvania, "200 members of the Thomas No. 84, Reynolds No. 405, and the [all-black] Benn Post 607 listened to a Memorial Service at the Duke Street M.E." In Washington, Pennsylvania, the all-white post, No. 120, and the all-black post, No. 577, usually attended two services together, one at a black church and another at a white church: "The Grand Army of the Republic posts together with all old soldiers in the city were asked to meet . . . for the purpose of attending services at the A.M.E. church from whence they will be escorted . . . [to] the M.P. church." Another year, both posts heard a sermon at the local AME church that was "principally of historical character and referred to the important place that the colored race had played in American wars." Shared liturgies celebrated in black churches represented a rare opportunity for a black post to shape a message given to an interracial audience.[13]

Interracial unity did not end when the posts left their churches; they also held joint ceremonies at local cemeteries. In Carlisle, Pennsylvania, the black and white GAR posts held joint ceremonies; according to one account, "at both public and colored graveyards salutes of three shots were fired." The all-black Pratt Post of Keokuk, Iowa, and its white counterparts participated in joint Memorial Day ceremonies. The local newspaper reported that "a dozen little colored girls assisted in the ceremonies." The all-black Ives Post regularly held joint Memorial Day ceremonies with other Providence posts and later decorated other cemeteries alone. New Bedford GAR posts observed the day with both separate and joint commemorations. "At the Bethel last Sunday afternoon," the Age reported, "the memorial sermon to R. G. Shaw Post, 146, G.A.R., was delivered by Rev. J. C. Brock. . . . The closing exercises of Memorial Day were held in Liberty Hall." That the orator of the evening was a former state commander suggests that this was an integrated commemoration. Similarly, in Newark, New Jersey, the chaplain reported that a "union service" brought together all the posts of the city, including the African American members of the Tucker Post, to hear the state commander address his comrades.[14]

Observances at national cemeteries, where the dead of both races slept, prompted the living to hold interracial ceremonies, even in former slave states. More than fifty-seven thousand Union soldiers rested in national cemeteries near the Chattanooga and Stones River battlefields in Tennessee. Black and white posts frequently celebrated Memorial Day together in these graveyards. The all-black Chickamauga post worked with an all-white post on observances at the National Cemetery in that city. "Special thanks are due to P. H. Sheridan 67 and the [all-black] Lincoln Post 4, Nashville, who went to the Stones River Cemetery and carried out an excellent program," a department official noted in 1899. GAR men and their female associates in Baltimore decorated the "Laurel, Sharpe and other colored cemeteries" in the morning, and in the afternoon, all city posts, black and white, participated in an interracial ceremony at the city's national cemetery. In western Maryland, at the Antietam National Cemetery, the local all-black post participated in ceremonies with its white counterpart. The Hagerstown veterans' groups from Martinsburg and Harpers Ferry participated in the procession to the cemetery. The Lyon Post joined these West Virginia units and marched in front of Sharpsburg's local organization, the Antietam Post.[15]

On rare occasions, African American posts commanded interracial observances as well. Grand Army posts in Pittsburgh took turns leading the ceremony at the Allegheny National Cemetery. In 1892 and 1898, the Shaw Post supplied the commander of the day and the orator. The *Pittsburgh Press* published the address of Commander M. J. Barks, who spoke before an enormous crowd. Barks's eloquent address lauded "the brave men [who] came forth from every hill side, from every vale, from every city, town, and village, offering their breast as a living shield in defense of their country." While Barks did not specifically remind the audience of black military service, his presence and status at this observance represented powerful and undeniable evidence that African Americans had been among those brave men.[16]

Memorial Day parades were the most common and visible integrated activity on Memorial Day. Religious services often separated not only the races but also believers from nonbelievers. Further, the somber nature of graveside ceremonies may have limited participation. Parades, on the other hand, provided both patriotic inspiration and entertainment, particularly in small towns lacking other diversions. African American posts in many cities marched with their white comrades on Memorial Day, and they were not relegated to the back of the parade. At an 1887 parade in New Jersey, the all-black Post 51 of Camden, New Jersey, marched in the middle of the procession, between Post 5 and Post 102, both white posts. The all-black Shaw Post, No. 146, marched behind the Rodman Post, No. 1, New Bedford's white post. An African American post's position in these processions generally reflected its seniority in the state GAR, usually indicated by its number; lower num-

Dedication of the memorial to Robert Gould Shaw and the
Fifty-fourth Massachusetts Regiment, Boston, May 31, 1897. Albumen
print, James H. Smith and William J. Miller (fl. 1897) © Massachusetts
Historical Society, Boston, Mass., USA, The Bridgeman Art Library.

bered posts were more senior. The all-black Post 51, for example, marched
in front of the less senior white Post 5. Sometimes a less senior white post
marched in front of a more senior black one. In a Memorial Day parade in
Keokuk, Iowa, for example, the local all-black Pratt Post, No. 413, marched in
between a white post, No. 515, which led the procession, and the most senior
post, No. 2, which brought up the rear. While this marching order was not
explained, it may well have been the tradition in this town that more senior
posts marched behind more junior units. Since the Pratt Post's less senior
white counterpart marched in front of it, then the Pratt Post's position in this
parade reflected its status in the GAR and not its racial composition.[17]

Although race-based discrimination was rare, the placement of an all-
black post in the rear of a 1898 parade demonstrates that it did occur. The
Uniontown, Pennsylvania, Democratic paper complained that at the Memorial Day parade, the marshal had "directly and intentionally insulted the
colored Grand Army organization . . . [by] ordering them to [march at] the
rear of the line behind the Boys Brigade." Consequently, "the colored Grand
Army boys dropped out of the parade." The next Memorial Day parade may
have been designed to apologize for this slight. In the 1899 procession, the
all-black post, No. 593, marched in front of the white post, No. 180. In other
years these posts paraded in numerical order. In the Uniontown incident,

the parade marshal's order was such a dramatic departure from the accepted treatment of African American GAR members that the local Democratic newspaper, representing a party that generally refused to support black civil and political rights, repudiated this action. Mixed-race processions were an effective tool against those who portrayed the Civil War as an all-white war, particularly when these events rejected nineteenth-century notions of a racial hierarchy that would have demanded that black veterans march behind their white comrades.[18]

In Iowa, black veterans rarely paraded with all-black posts on Memorial Day since most black veterans belonged to mixed-race posts—the world that black and white veterans made together.

PART II

The World Black and White Veterans Made Together

7

Where Separate Grand Army Posts Are Unknown, As Colored and White Are United

The Integrated Post

The *Cleveland Gazette* published a letter from an "Attorney at Law and Notary Public and Real Estate Agent," "Robert A. Pinn, Commander, Hart Post, No. 134, Department of Ohio," who objected to plans "on the part of the colored ex-soldiers of your city to organize a G.A.R. exclusively for colored soldiers in 1886." He considered this action an insult to his comrades and hoped that he would "hear no more about colored posts." In contrast, the *Gazette* also reported an example of interracial amity: "Upon the corner of Cross and Orange streets is an old soldier, a *colored man*, who is dying for a little attention and a doctor's care, John Smith by name. . . . All the attention, money, food, and everything given him thus far has been tendered by his *white* comrades of the G.A.R." When Smith died, he was buried by his GAR post. While of disparate economic origins, Smith and Pinn had a great deal in common: both men had served as enlisted men in the Fifth USCT and both were "Colored Comrades" in predominantly white GAR posts.[1]

Like Smith and Pinn, many black veterans shared their fellowship with white veterans in hundreds of integrated posts in cities and towns across the United States. (For a list of the posts identified in this study, see the appendix.) African Americans enrolled in predominantly white posts in large cities such as Denver, Colorado, and Hartford, Connecticut, and in small towns such as Piqua, Ohio; Peoria, Illinois; and, most improbably, Maryville, Tennessee. The prewar social structure of states, slave or free, and the disparate nature of veterans' Civil War experiences explain why some states had more integrated posts than others. More integrated posts existed in free states than in former slave states. White soldiers who had served with black troops in wartime appeared to be more open to sharing their fellowship in

★

peacetime than those who did not. While GAR officials encouraged inter-racial posts, it was not always easy for a black veteran to join a predominantly white post since a post could reject a black applicant even if only a handful of white members desired to do so. And integration often occurred only after rank-and-file white veterans made a stand against racial discrimination. That hundreds of integrated grassroots organizations existed, defying so many nineteenth-century race-based social norms, demonstrates the strength of interracial comradeship in the GAR.

Previous studies of the GAR may have failed to report the existence of integrated units because they are so hard to find. Even black newspapers, and their race-conscious correspondents, so helpful in identifying African American posts, rarely labeled these units as interracial. The *New York Freeman*, for example, published a letter from a member of the Twenty-fifth Infantry, one of the predominantly black regiments that served in the post–Civil War U.S. Army. He wrote as a member of a GAR post that included members of his unit and the all-white Seventh Cavalry, both assigned to Fort Meade, Dakota Territory. Since this soldier did not identify the racial composition of these regiments, only a knowledgeable reader understood that this was an integrated post. The same paper reported the death of Solomon Tierce, a "soldier of the late war, having enlisted in the 29th Connecticut Colored Regiment; he was wounded at Deep Bottom, Virginia, and was in other engagements. He was a member of the Ward B. Burnett Post, G.A.R. the members of which attended him while sick. They also attended his funeral in a body and buried him with all the honors." Tierce's military service as an enlisted man in a black regiment revealed his race, but what about his GAR comrades? Only the death of a white veteran, a former captain of the Thirty-second New York Volunteers, reported by the Burnett Post revealed that during Tierce's final days, he was likely comforted by both black and white comrades.[2]

While the living remained silent, it was the evidence of the dead that often revealed interracial fellowship. Many, though not all, state organizations recorded the name, ranks, and regiments of veterans who had died in a particular year. If Captain Smith of the Twenty-fifth Ohio Infantry and Private Jones of the Fifth USCT died as members of the same post, we know that this was an integrated post. The same record that confirmed that Comrades Tierce and Jones belonged to an integrated post also listed four deceased members of the Watson Post in Catskill, New York. Three of these men served as privates in white units, and the fourth served as a private in the Thirty-first USCT. That same year, four Michigan posts reported the deaths of black and white members to the state; for example, a post in St. Joseph mourned a former member of the Forty-third USCT, and a white comrade. The Sol Meredith Post of Richmond, Indiana, reported the death of at least six African Americans over an eight-year period, just as they reported the death of their white comrades.[3]

Supplementing the evidence of death records, some states published rosters listing all of their posts and their members, ranks, and regiments. Even these more comprehensive records had their limits. Black sailors remain invisible in both death records and state rosters because their wartime affiliation with an integrated ship, as opposed to a segregated regiment, makes it impossible to identify their race. Despite the difficulties in identifying individual black soldiers or sailors, GAR state records that documented the living and the dead demonstrated that veterans overcame the nineteenth-century color line and formed interracial veterans groups.

State records both identify individual interracial posts and reveal broader patterns in states and regions. Scattered in the cities and towns of the western states, black veterans joined integrated posts. In southern states, in contrast, antebellum social structures and postwar racial attitudes made forming an integrated post almost impossible. Differences in levels of integration in free states—Connecticut versus Pennsylvania, for example—suggest that integration at the local level often reflected the wartime experiences of black and white veterans rather than the prewar social structure of the region.

It is not surprising that the West and the South were at the opposite ends of the spectrum. First, in the West, not enough African American veterans lived in a particular city or town to form their own posts. In Omaha, Nebraska, the thirty black veterans listed as living in that city in 1890 would have been hard-pressed to maintain a viable GAR post, so these men joined their white comrades in an integrated post. Similarly, the few black veterans who lived in Oklahoma City, Minneapolis, and Marysville, California, belonged to integrated posts. The Colorado GAR left the most thorough records: rosters of all its posts and members. In 1890, 112 black veterans lived in that state, and 35 of these men lived in Denver—too few to maintain a post. However, black veterans were members of at least five of the eight posts in Denver, indicating that these posts were integrated. While, in general, records of integrated posts do not explain why white veterans welcomed blacks into their ranks, Colorado GAR records do provide a clue: most members of this state organization, white and black, came from other states; few had served in Colorado regiments. As strangers in a strange land, these men may have been more willing to embrace all veterans, regardless of their race, who had shared their wartime experiences.[4]

In southern states, on the other hand, only a handful of African American veterans belonged to integrated posts. But it was also the case that the GAR in southern states had relatively few members and little money and published less information on their state organizations than their northern counterparts. For example, it is impossible to deduce from the few records from the Virginia and North Carolina GAR that survive whether any racially mixed posts existed in these states. More extensive records in Louisiana and Mississippi are similarly silent on this issue. In 1894, Georgia and South Carolina published a roster of their posts and members; the list reveals that the posts in these states were either all black or all white. Racial attitudes and social customs likely made interracial social organizations unacceptable in former slave states. Given the challenges of establishing interracial state organizations in this region, creating integrated local organizations may have been impossible.[5]

The level of integration in the South varied from state to state; the border states of Kentucky and Tennessee had more than one integrated post. Levant Dodge, the Kentucky state commander, revealed in a speech to his encampment that his state had a small number of mixed-race posts: "In my travels I have found a half dozen posts which, while chiefly white, admit on equal terms the few colored soldiers who live in the neighborhood. My own home post is one of these." At least twelve integrated posts were formed in Tennessee—all in eastern Tennessee, the Unionist stronghold in this Confederate state. Because East Tennessee Unionists suffered at the hands of the Confederate government, they may have been more willing to accept "loyal" black veterans in their home posts than to reject these men to satisfy southern racial customs. The existence of even a handful of integrated posts in former slave states may be one of the most remarkable findings in this study.[6]

The racial composition of local posts may have reflected the antebellum social structure in Missouri and Kansas. Missouri, a slave state, stayed in the Union during the war; however, pro-Confederate Missourians participated in an insurgency against the U.S. government. Kansas joined the Union as a free state after a bloody struggle between pro- and antislavery settlers. Because both states published a roster of all of their posts and their members at about the same time, it is possible to compare these geographically conjoined states in terms of their different prewar social structures. Given what we know about the GAR in the South, it is not surprising that only four predominantly white posts in Missouri welcomed a handful of black members in 1895. In 1894, over 40 percent of black GAR members in Kansas belonged to integrated posts. The Kansans who fought slavery more than a decade before the war began may have been more willing to accept African Americans in their posts than the men who had grown up in a state that accepted race-based slavery. A Missourian described the challenges of forming any type of GAR post in Missouri: "It is almost impossible to sever the issues of the present from the past. The extension of the privileges of citizenship to the previously down-trodden race has been antagonized for the beginning in Missouri." Despite these challenges, the GAR grew to include about 300 posts, though most would not accept black members.[7]

While the prewar agitation against slavery may have made white Kansans more willing to accept former slaves into their post, the wartime experience of Kansas, as well as other states, may have shaped the peacetime composition of the GAR. Kansans formed all-black state regiments during the war; one of these units was recognized as one of hardest-fighting regiments in the U.S. Army, the First Kansas Colored, later known as the Seventy-ninth USCT. Similarly, antebellum attitudes toward slavery may partially explain the large number of integrated posts in that hotbed of abolitionism, Massachusetts; but the state's Civil War military experience also may have been a factor. During the war, Massachusetts officials also organized all-black volunteer regiments. After the war, 60 percent of all African American soldiers who enrolled in the Massachusetts GAR affiliated with racially integrated posts. While the Fifty-fourth Massachusetts (Colored) Infantry is the best-known regiment, two other black regiments formed in the state: the Fifty-fifth Massachusetts Infantry and the Fifth Massachusetts Cavalry. In contrast, most other African American regiments in the Union army served as federal units. White veterans in Kansas and Massachusetts who had served in state regiments may have been more likely to assume that black veterans' military service was comparable to their own experience, which may have made it easier for them to accept black veterans in their local posts.[8]

Connecticut's situation was similar. As the local correspondent for the *New York Age* explained, "We have no separate posts here as colored and white are united." Black veterans in Connecticut never formed their own posts, even in cities like New Haven, where there were enough veterans—eighty-nine in 1890—to create their own, racially exclusive units. Like Massachusetts, Connecticut fielded an all-black regiment—the Twenty-ninth Connecticut (Colored) Infantry—but it is likely the unusual military history of Connecticut's white Civil War regiments is the reason for the unique racial composition of its GAR posts. Many white Connecticut soldiers who joined integrated posts had fought their battles alongside black troops. The Seventh Connecticut was designated one of the three hundred exemplary regiments in the Union army because of its conduct at Fort Wagner and Olustee—a battle involving black troops. The Sixth Connecticut served in the same brigade as the Fifty-fourth Massachusetts and supported its assault on

Fort Wagner. Other Connecticut regiments fought at Port Hudson, a critical bastion that guarded an important section of the Mississippi River, the first major battle involving black troops. Charles Puffer, formerly of the Twenty-fifth Connecticut and a member of an integrated post in Hartford, characterized his "duty in the rifle pits" at Port Hudson as "the most important event of my military history." His comrades in the Connecticut GAR likely agreed.[9]

A comparison of the prewar free states in the Midwest and the Middle Atlantic region better illustrates the effect of white veterans' Civil War experience on integration in the GAR than an examination of any one state. Most, if not all, white Americans in antebellum free states were racist, and midwesterners appeared to be more virulent in its attitudes. According to one scholar, "On the eve of the Civil War except for the South the Middle West . . . was the region most firmly committed to white supremacy." After the war, however, midwesterners were surprisingly willing to accept black veterans in their local posts, at least according to death records. Based on my research in Massachusetts, death records are roughly representative of the racial composition of the GAR posts in a state. Over a seventeen-year period, integrated posts in this state reported about half of former black soldiers' deaths; the other half were reported by all-black posts. An examination of a fairly comprehensive list of GAR members revealed that about 60 percent of its black veterans belonged to integrated posts. According to the available death records for the Indiana GAR, for example, 100 African Americans were members of integrated posts while only 75 were members of all-black organizations. Similarly, death records in Illinois reveal that 186 black veterans were in integrated posts as opposed to 97 in all-black posts. Midwesterners' embrace of their "Colored Comrades" after the war represented a fairly significant departure from their hostility to black Americans before the war, suggesting that the wartime experience of these men shaped their response to African American veterans.[10]

Death records provide only partial evidence of interracial comradeship in midwestern states; however, Iowa preserved the names, regiments, and post numbers of almost all GAR members in the state, and from these records we can confirm the number of integrated posts. While Keokuk's African American veterans formed their own post in that city, the rest of the black veterans in the state belonged to integrated units. About forty racially mixed posts existed in Iowa, from Davenport in the east to Red Oak in the west. The state's black newspaper, the *Iowa Bystander*, noted the GAR's largely color-blind membership policy: "The GAR post in Newton continues to be the only one in the state which continues to refuse admission to colored soldiers. Such action would be expected in Texas or Louisiana, not proud Iowa."[11]

Joseph Ozier, integrated post member in Batavia, Illinois.
Courtesy of the Batavia Historical Society.

In contrast to the midwestern states, there seemed to be some resistance to integration in the Middle Atlantic states of New York, New Jersey, and Pennsylvania. While lack of data on the racial makeup of posts in these three states hampered the efforts to identify integrated groups, evidence suggests that the three were less likely than other northern states to have integrated posts. The New York GAR did not publish death records regularly, and when it did, it did not always include the deceased veteran's post in his obituary. When these albeit limited records were complete, they identified only a handful on integrated posts. In fact, at the annual meeting, a black veteran complained of race-based exclusion in the western part of state, suggesting that more than one post in this region refused to admit black members. The New Jersey GAR left better death records than New York; however, virtually all of the African Americans whose deaths were recorded by the state GAR belonged to all-black posts.[12]

Comparing the racial compositions of posts in Pennsylvania and Ohio demonstrates the difference between eastern and midwestern states. The Pennsylvania GAR seemed more similar to its eastern neighbors, New York and New Jersey, than to its western neighbor, Ohio. Just as in New York, a black veteran complained at the Pennsylvania state meeting that a white post excluded black members. The all-black post in Harrisburg, the state capital, was organized because of this exclusionary policy. An examination of Pennsylvania death records, which were more complete than those for either the New York or New Jersey GAR, revealed that the vast majority of black veterans in Pennsylvania lived and died as members of the state's all-black posts. In most years, 1 or 2 black veterans in Pennsylvania died as members of integrated posts. Though there were exceptions. In 1909, 4 of the 18 black veterans who died in Pennsylvania belonged to integrated posts. In contrast, all 20 African American Pennsylvanians who died in 1906 belonged to all-black posts. In Ohio, in contrast, over a nine-year period, almost 50 percent of black veterans' deaths were reported by their racially mixed posts. Robert Pinn reported that even in a large city like Cleveland, African Americans could join integrated posts. While a lack of the kind of statewide rosters that survive in Kansas or Colorado makes it hard to be sure the number of integrated posts in midwestern states, death records suggest that GAR members in the Midwest were more open to racial integration than those in eastern states.[13]

The differences in the number of integrated posts in these regions suggest that wartime experiences were critical to GAR members' attitudes. Most Middle Atlantic regiments (Pennsylvania, New Jersey, and New York) fought in eastern armies, the largest being the Army of the Potomac; midwesterners fought in western armies—the Army of the Cumberland or the Tennessee. These armies fought two very different wars. The largest and least successful northern army, the Army of the Potomac, fought in a geographically confined region between Richmond and Washington. Under a series of sometimes lackluster commanders, they fought a number of battles against the most successful southern army, the Army of Northern Virginia, and its iconic commander, Robert E. Lee. Soldiers in the Army of the Potomac, which only had a handful of black units, rarely fought with black soldiers. In the West, regiments raised in Ohio, Illinois, Indiana, and Iowa belonged to more successful armies that won more battles, usually against hapless southern generals, and occupied large swaths of the South: Tennessee, Mississippi, Georgia (Sherman's march), and the Carolinas. Robert Hunt's recent study of one of these western armies, the Army of the Cumberland, demonstrates that the memory of liberating slaves was central to men's understanding of what they had achieved during the Civil War. Though African American regiments that fought in the East were better known—for example, the Fifty-fourth Massachusetts—larger numbers of black soldiers served in the West. Veterans of the Army of the Potomac remembered one kind of war—the one most Americans remember today, a traditional military campaign that was more about strategy than slavery. A synergy of comradeship and cause, therefore, likely explains integrated posts in the heartland.[14]

Examining the number of mixed-race posts at the state level cannot adequately explain this phenomenon because integration only occurred when rank-and-file veterans decided to create these units at the local level. State officials certainly encouraged posts to integrate. When in 1882 the Massachusetts state commander briefed the annual meeting on the status of local posts, he pointed to the general prosperity of Massachusetts posts, though he also referred to one post that surrendered its charter during the year, the Robert Gould Shaw Post of New Bedford: "This post was composed of colored comrades and consequently had a small and limited membership, and against the odds they struggled manfully for existence, but without avail." The commander "express[ed] the wish of the mass of comrades of this department. . . . I hope that the *mother* Post of the department [Post 1, New Bedford] will take such as are worthy within her membership and thus illustrate the broad foundation stone on which our order rests." Similarly, the attempt of Comrade Lester, a black member of a mixed-race post, to force the New York GAR's white posts to accept black members illustrates the grassroots nature of a local post's decision to integrate. In 1887, Lester asked the New York GAR to resolve that posts "shall not abridge, on account of color, the rights of colored veterans who served as soldiers in the late rebellion, when they apply for membership in any post of the Grand Army of the Republic, when they are eligible for membership." When the encampment requested a clarification of this resolution, Lester maintained that "in the portion of the state where I reside, I know of men who have served their country with honor . . . but when they applied for admission to a Post [they] have been ignored because of their color. I ask you to stamp out such an act and seal your condemnation on it." A less binding substitute resolution was proposed and passed: "Resolved, that the Grand Army of the Republic, in annual encampment assembled in the state of New York, deprecates such action." The resolution reflected reality; the GAR could not control an individual's vote or force a white veteran to accept a black veteran in a post. Previously, in a case unrelated to race, the judge advocate of the GAR ruled that a member "cannot be restrained of his [voting] privilege. He must answer to his own conscience." As long as a post followed voting procedures, individuals could vote as they pleased and decide with whom they shared their fellowship. White and black veterans created integrated posts at the local level when they agreed to share each others' company, and not because the GAR at the state or national level mandated them.[15]

The decision to integrate the GAR was made at the local level and required a majority of white post members to accept black applicants. Veterans used an anonymous blackball system to accept or reject applicants; they cast their vote on a potential member's application by dropping either a white ball (yes vote) or a black ball (no vote) into a box. During the early and middle years of the GAR, two black balls in twenty votes led to an applicant's rejection. Later, as members aged and posts became smaller, the GAR changed the rule to two black balls in ten votes. Under this system, even if a majority of the members voted to accept a black veteran, he could be rejected. Given this voting system and the dismal state of race relations in this era, the existence of any integrated posts, let alone the existence of hundreds, is astonishing.[16]

Complicating our attempt to understand racial integration in the GAR is the fact that race was not the only reason that veterans blackballed applicants. When white posts rejected white veterans or black posts refused to admit black veterans, then something other than race was a factor in members' decisions. New York records list fifteen men rejected by state posts in 1884; only one of these applicants served as an enlisted member of an African American regiment. The other blacklisted veterans served in all-white units. The Wilcox Post in Springfield, Massachusetts, spurned a veteran of the Twenty-ninth Connecticut Infantry, that state's all-black regiment, and a veteran of the First Massachusetts Cavalry, a white unit. Since the Wilcox Post was integrated, racial bias likely was not a factor in this man's rejection.

Race certainly did not matter when black posts spurned African American recruits. The all-black Bell Post of Boston rejected a veteran of Massachusetts's only African American cavalry regiment. No state indicates the reasons for rejecting potential members.[17]

Newspapers documented some race-based rejections. The *Waterbury* [Conn.] *American*, for example, reported with disapproval that "Emerson Peters, a Negro living in Augusta, honorably discharged from the army where he served with credit, of good character and a Republican voter [was] blackballed for admission to the local G.A.R. post for no reason that anyone can discover save the blackness of his skin." A correspondent for the *Leavenworth* [Kans.] *Advocate* reported that he was "forced to confess that in Moberley [Missouri] the Grand Army Post refuses to receive the Negro soldier, that walked side by side with them in battle." The *Detroit Plaindealer*, an African American newspaper, reprinted a report that "a newly-established G.A.R. post at Anacostia refused the applications of two colored men. They said that it would necessitate social equality." (This report did not reveal the location of Anacostia, but it may have been the section of Washington, D.C., located east of the river of the same name.) Newspapers generally report unusual or noteworthy events, and not the day-to-day routine happenings, so the fact that these articles documented race-based exclusion suggests that this was neither an acceptable nor a customary practice in white GAR posts.[18]

When an African American tried to join a white post in Connecticut, newspapers chronicled the controversy that ensued. As far away as New Orleans, a local white newspaper, the *Times Democrat*, reported that the Lyon Post of Hartford, Connecticut, had "ordered a court-martial because of the forced withdrawal of the application for membership of a negro man named Hamilton and his rejection on the color line alone as unfit for comradeship with Grand Army men." While the Lyon Post had accepted black veterans in its early years, by the late 1880s it had no African American members. In the last year of that decade, Frank Hamilton, formerly an enlisted soldier in the Twenty-ninth Connecticut (Colored) applied for membership. The post received his application at its September 17 assembly. According to the minutes for the subsequent meeting, the "action on the application of Frank Hamilton was postponed until next meeting as the application cannot be found." In the many volumes of GAR meeting minutes examined for this study, no other post ever declared an application lost. By mid-October, the membership committee presented the application to the post; however, the committee had not signed this form. This unsigned document indicated either disapproval or cowardice on the part of this group; the record is unclear. Since the post commander was late for this meeting, another official stepped in to chair the meeting. He urged Hamilton to withdraw his application, which he did.[19]

Hamilton's exit did not signal the end of this controversy. At the following meeting, the official who asked Hamilton to pull his application resigned as chairman of the committee that investigated prospective members. The post then resolved that "hereafter the investigating committee would be appointed from the members present." The records do not indicate why this official resigned or why this new rule was necessary. At the next meeting, the crisis escalated. According to meeting minutes, the post "adjutant read charges against J.V.C. [third in command] A. J. Green pressed by another official and the post voted to sustain the charges." In December, the Lyons Post charged Comrade Ira Forbes with "violating his obligation"; the minutes did not specify the nature of this transgression. According to the *Detroit Plaindealer*, "One of the men to be court-martialled [i.e., Green] defended Hamilton's rights and made public the reprehensible conduct of those soldiers who refused to fraternize with him." The judicial actions started in February and were completed by April 1890. The minutes do not specify Green's punishment; however, Forbes was dropped from the post rolls and must have been discharged from the order. The seven months of upheaval in the Lyon Post support the notion that rejecting these comrades was not routine. Some white veterans believed that African American veterans should be allowed to join their fellowship, and these men took a stand against race separation.[20]

On the surface, this tale had an unsatisfying ending: an African American veteran barred from the GAR's fellowship. But what the minute books of Post 2 do not tell us is that, according to the *Plaindealer*, "another post in Hartford . . . elected him after knowing the action of the Nathaniel Lyon Post." Hamilton joined the Taylor Post, which, like most Connecticut posts, routinely and without controversy accepted black veterans. The Lyon Post's rejection of African American members made news because rejecting black applicants was not an accepted practice, particularly in Connecticut. The predominantly white Taylor Post welcomed black veterans, a common, but less newsworthy, practice.[21]

Other struggles over black applicants found their way into public view. William Dupree, formerly of the Fifty-fifth Massachusetts Infantry (Colored), had been one of a handful of black officers appointed by Governor Andrew to Massachusetts regiments. According to a profile in a black newspaper, he was of "free parentage. His mother was a mulatto and his father was of mixed Negro and French blood." After the war, he supervised all mail operations in South Boston. Despite his wartime accomplishments and his important government position, Dupree was rejected by the Charles Stevenson Post of Roxbury. According to the *New York Freeman*, "The colorphobia in the Charles Stevenson, Post 26, G.A.R. . . . exists only in five or six men [since] 70 took part in the balloting to admit Mr. Dupree [and] sixty-five of this number were in favor of receiving him as a member." "In censuring the Post, therefore, for drawing the color line," the *Freeman* continued, "care should be exercised that every veteran of which it is composed is not harshly and severely condemned." The newspaper pleaded with readers to excuse most members of this post since "the action of these five Negro-haters [was] unsparingly denounced by all Grand Army men who were present and absent. Several of them said they would leave the Post." While white veterans may or may not have left Post 26, William Dupree, like Hamilton, found a home in another predominantly white unit. He joined a post in Cambridge and eventually commanded this unit; his wife belonged to the post's Woman's Relief Corps. As was the case in Connecticut, the newspaper report on this incident reflected the rarity of race-based exclusion.[22]

White Iowans also struggled to form integrated posts. The Crocker Post of Des Moines received an application from "Robert Bruce (colored) late a private in Co G. 113th Regt. Colored Infantry." According to a letter to Iowa's assistant adjutant general, the application "was received and referred to a committee raised [to review the application], the committee reporting favorably, the ballot was [taken] which proving [unfavorable, the] applicant was rejected on second ballot [and] the applicant was declared firmly rejected." Someone must have demanded an explanation for this rejection because blackballing recruits did not require a special letter to state officials. This letter did not end the controversy; a white post member, Comrade Christy, protested Bruce's rejection. At the next meeting, Christy explained that "he had paid numerous bills when [he was] Post Commander amounting to more than $35 and that upon correct accounting the post would be found indebted to him, hence he believed that the action of the post last regular session should be reconsidered." Since Bruce's rejection constituted the only action of note at the previous meeting, it appears that Christy was using this debt to force the post to reconsider Bruce's application. Post members passed a resolution to review the books and credit Comrade Christy with any money he might be owed, but no other action was taken. While Christy's efforts failed in the short term, he and others succeeded in the long term. Bruce joined the Crocker Post in 1889, the same day two other black veterans joined the post. Crocker Post records do not explain this change in policy; however, most members must have believed that comradeship trumped race and lobbied their recalcitrant colleagues to accept black veterans. Later, other black veterans joined the Crocker Post without any difficulty.[23]

Similarly, Michigan veterans challenged their comrades who denied African American veterans a place in their post. The Welch Post of Ann Arbor, Michigan, an area with only a few African American veterans, enrolled a handful of black members. In 1886, the Welch Post accepted a transfer from another post, Stephen Jacob, an African American who had served in the Fifth Massachusetts Cavalry. The subsequent black applicant, John L. Cox, Fifth United States Colored Heavy Artillery (USCHA), received thirty white and three black balls and was rejected. According to the minutes of this meeting, Comrade Rivenaugh rose to his feet and demanded another vote because "the ballots were so near of a color that some of the comrades may have made a mistake." The minutes indicate that this "opinion was shared by many of the post. There being no opposition the motion was put and carried." The second ballot produced a more desirable result, twenty-five white balls and only one black, and Cox was elected. The incident did not conclude with the vote. Some members questioned the accuracy of the meeting minutes describing the first vote on Cox. Consequently, the post adjutant offered to resign, but his resignation was rejected. The next black applicant required two votes as well, but the second vote that accepted his application was unanimous.[24]

Controversy following the blackballing of African American applicants is one of the best indicators that many white veterans welcomed black veterans in their local fraternity. If racist white veterans unanimously agreed to segregate black veterans, then rejecting black veterans would have been routine. The uproar among white members in the wake of a black applicant's rejection suggests that race-based exclusion was not an accepted practice. While white veterans' willingness to share their fellowship with African American comrades was laudable, it cannot be taken at face value. Only a close examination of life in mixed-race posts reveals that this was a world that black and white veterans made together.

8

Community, Memory, and the Integrated Post

Readers of the *New York Times* in late January 1915 must have been surprised when they read the obituaries. Sandwiched between the death notices of a ninety-four-year-old woman from Brooklyn whose father had been a hero in the War of 1812 and an eighty-five-year-old man who had been the postmaster of Hackensack, New Jersey, was the announcement of the passing of an African American woman from a small town in Indiana. According to this notice, Lucy Nichols deserved this distinction because she was "the only negro woman honored with membership in the Grand Army of the Republic, and pensioned by the Government for her service in the civil war as a nurse." Nichols was affiliated with the predominantly white Sanderson Post in New Albany, Indiana. The *Times* made one mistake in this notice: she was not alone. At least two African American women associated with predominantly white GAR posts.[1]

We have met Robert Pinn, the Medal of Honor winner who became a lawyer after the war, and John Smith, who fought in the same regiment as Pinn and fell on hard times late in life—both members of integrated posts. However, Lucy Nichols's affiliation with a predominantly white post suggests that neither class (she was a housekeeper) nor military service (she was a nurse, not a soldier) were prerequisites for membership in a mixed-race post. Explaining the existence of integrated GAR posts requires an in-depth analysis of the white and black members, including their political views, ethnicity, class, and Civil War experiences. Moreover, a GAR post's acceptance of blacks into its circle was one thing; truly welcoming these men or women as comrades was another. Only a careful assessment of everyday life in a mixed-race post can determine if these were truly interracial organizations—in spirit as well as on paper. Finally, it has been suggested that integrated posts were somehow better, more "regular," than their all-black counterparts, implying that an assessment of the relative merits of black membership in these orga-

★

nizations may be needed. Were integrated posts somehow better or more historically significant than all-black posts and the world black Americans and their circle made in the GAR?[2]

An integrated post represented a world that black and white veterans with disparate political views, from varying social and economic groups and a wide variety of military backgrounds, made together. African Americans with all types of military service were welcomed. Some had seen a great deal of combat, while others had been garrison troops. White veterans who fought in battle and campaigns alongside black troops seemed more likely than others to embrace African American soldiers into their fellowship. White veterans, who were typically the majority, often dominated post affairs, but black veterans played an active role as officers and committee members. Despite their minority status, African Americans were able to use their membership in these groups to advance their own version of Civil War Memory. Regardless of their value in the struggle for Memory, integrated GAR posts represent an important chapter in the history of American race relations — an extraordinary accomplishment for the black and white members of the GAR.

While previous studies have emphasized the political nature of the GAR, partisanship appears to have played no role in the racial makeup of GAR posts. While the Veterans Post of Elgin, Illinois, included black veterans and Joseph Vallor, a "life long Republican [as] one of [its] most prominent members," the same organization welcomed veterans who rejected the Republican Party. Edward S. Joselyn, chairman of the district Democratic committee, for example, belonged to the Veterans Post. Joselyn was described as "a man of rare eloquence, remarkable personal magnetism, an exhaustless fund of general knowledge and a power for argumentative debate." Moreover, the local newspaper portrayed Patterson Sharp, another post member, as "quite a radical thinker in all political questions, and never averse to expressing his opinions. During the last presidential campaigning [1892,] he was a member of the people's (Populist's) party." If the GAR was a tool of the Republican Party, as some scholars have suggested, Joselyn and Sharp would have refused to affiliate with it, or as members would have blackballed African American recruits and hurt the Republican Party's reputation in the black community.[3]

Integrated posts outside Illinois embraced veterans who claimed varied political loyalties. When members of the Welch Post of Ann Arbor were giving speeches about their military experience, Comrade Soule described his wartime meeting with the governor of Michigan. The governor explained that he endorsed Soule's commission because "he would just as [soon] send a Democrat down there to get killed as anybody else." While Soule may not

Members of the Welch Post, an integrated post in Ann Arbor, Michigan, circa 1890. Courtesy of the Anne Abbrecht Collection, Bentley Historical Library, University of Michigan.

have remained a Democrat after the war, other mixed-race posts welcomed members of this party. Edward F. Thrall, "a well-known . . . and strong Democrat . . . a militant Democrat" who served in the Twenty-second Connecticut was a member of the integrated Taylor Post for over two decades. A Crocker Post meeting in Des Moines adjourned early because "each party in the election had a meeting and the members wished to hear rather than make speeches." Post members might have disagreed on political issues, but they all agreed to belong to an interracial social organization. Therefore, partisan politics cannot explain the existence of mixed-race posts.[4]

Integrated posts were diverse in terms of race, but they welcomed veterans from various economic classes as well. Henry Dean, wartime colonel, Twenty-second Michigan, president of the Ann Arbor Milling Company, regent of the University of Michigan, and state GAR commander, was a member of the Welch Post of Ann Arbor. The Taylor Post, "composed of a large number of the best citizens of Connecticut, the commonwealth having chosen from its ranks the present governor, an ex–Lieutenant Governor, three ex-mayors of the city, judges of the court and various city officers," included twenty-three African American veterans in its ranks. Integrated posts frequently accepted good citizens with little social standing. John Mullen, an Irish-born laborer and veteran of the Fifteenth Iowa, joined the Crocker Post, as did native-born laborer Thomas Starbuck. Many of the laborers in New Haven's Foote Post, including Patrick Cronin and Coleman Foley, claimed Ireland as their birthplace. The Foote Post welcomed a variety of unskilled and skilled crafts-men and professionals. Augustus Farmer was a coachman and a private in the Forty-second USCT. Muster rolls also list a merchant, a mechanic, a ma-chinist, a coal dealer, and a corset maker. Some posts included veterans with more of one profession than another; for example, many watchmakers from the Elgin Watch Company were members of the Veterans Post in Elgin, Illi-nois.[5]

Posts that accepted black members did not merely welcome lawyers such as Robert Pinn; instead, African Americans who joined integrated posts, like their white comrades, represented the skilled, the unskilled, and the profes-sional classes. The Tod Post in Youngstown included three black ministers in its ranks. Ministry was one of the highest-status professions in the African American community. However, most of the post's black members worked as laborers. Other African American members of this Youngstown-based post practiced skilled professions such as bricklaying, carpentry, and bar-bering. The Taylor Post of Hartford embraced African Americans of lesser social and economic standing: laborers like Frank Hamilton and janitors such as George A. Lattimer; only a few black members practiced skilled pro-fessions such as roofer. At least eight black veterans joined the Crocker Post in Des Moines; two of these men were laborers and three worked as bar-bers. The other three men listed their occupations as expressman (teamster), cook, and headwaiter. This group included more African American skilled workers than found in other posts; perhaps black veterans without skills had not migrated to Iowa. Black barbers or headwaiters, particularly those who served in the Union army, might find employment in a city with few black residents. The Pat McGuire Post in Tennessee included eight black mem-bers, seven of whom were farmers, as were most of the white veterans in this group. African American members of integrated posts reflected the diverse social and economic status of black veterans. Only a few of these men were professionals like Robert Pinn; many more labored for their daily wage; and a few, like John Smith, may have lived in abject poverty at the bottom rung of nineteenth-century American society.[6]

The presence of immigrants in racially mixed posts suggests that integrated veterans' groups embraced other types of diversity. At least 30 percent of the members of Elgin's integrated Veterans Post were immigrants, representing eight nations, and at least one-third were German. Just before the Crocker Post in Des Moines relented and accepted more black veterans in its ranks in 1889, its membership was about 10 percent foreign-born. The fact that the integrated post welcomed the foreign-born demonstrates that immigrants accepted African Americans as comrades. If these men rejected interracial comradeship, they could have blackballed African American applicants and maintained the racial exclusivity of their group.[7]

When the *New York Age* reported that in New Haven, Connecticut, "colored and white were united," it could also have said that the foreign- and native-born were united in at least two of the city's three posts. The Admiral Foote Post of that city at one point mustered approximately one thousand members, including about sixty-five black veterans. The Foote Post welcomed members from disparate social classes and ethnic groups. The same page that lists David Ferris, coachman, veteran of the Twentieth USCT, as a post member lists a banker born in New York state and an Irish-born mason, both veterans of Connecticut's white regiments. The same page that includes Virginia-born Moses Jones, a laborer and veteran of the all-black Twenty-ninth Connecticut, lists a music teacher from England who served as an officer in the Tenth Connecticut. Foote Post records list William Keyes, a noncommissioned officer in the Thirty-fifth USCT, beside two German-born men named Klein, formerly privates in the Sixth and Ninth Connecticut, and one Irish-born O'Keefe, a policeman and former second lieutenant in the Ninth Connecticut. New Haven's Merwin Post included at least twelve African Americans in its ranks, and most of its white members were foreign-born.[8]

In New Haven, the color line never materialized, and instead a language line separated veterans. The Von Steinwehr Post performed its rituals in German and likely never had any African American applicants. Like their African American counterparts, German veterans exercised their right to create their own ethnically exclusive veterans' organization. The desire for their own post might have been rooted in their shared wartime experience in German regiments. Like all-black posts, German post members may have wanted to remind Americans of their contributions to Union victory; for example, because they formed their own post they were able to name it for a German American hero, General Von Steinwehr.[9]

Since these were veterans' organizations, shared military service may explain the racial composition of these posts. We have already discussed how this may have affected the number of integrated posts at the state level; however, an integrated post required white members at the grassroots level to accept black veterans into their fellowship. The particular experiences of integrated post members may help explain this acceptance.

In some integrated posts, former officers and enlisted members of black regiments shared a postwar fellowship. Henry Harrison, an African American veteran of the Sixtieth USCT, joined the Crocker Post, as did a number of white officers of black regiments, men like Alexander St. Claire, second lieutenant of the Forty-third USCT, and Captain Frederick Cressy, formerly of the Fourteenth USCT. Colonel Thomas Jefferson Jackson, commander of the Eleventh USCT, the units massacred at Fort Pillow, belonged to an integrated post in Newton, Kansas. In 1910, the Major How Post of Haverhill mourned the loss of Wallace George, former first lieutenant, Thirty-seventh USCT, and William Aiken, a former private in the Fifty-fourth Massachusetts Infantry.[10]

White officers from black regiments did not always join their former enlisted comrades in GAR posts, nor did all integrated posts include men who commanded black troops. Two USCT officers were members of the all-white Torrence Post in Keokuk, Iowa; however, African American veterans in this city joined the all-black Pratt Post. The Veterans Post in Elgin, Illinois, was integrated, but none of the white members had been officers in black units. In Tennessee, mixed-race posts included the enlisted members of African American units but not their white officers. White posts in Tennessee cities like Memphis and Chattanooga included officers from African American units, but their subordinates affiliated with all-black posts. Since northern veterans in these cities tended to be newcomers, fear of being ostracized might have prompted these men to avoid any association with African Americans. Overall, in predominantly white posts, there appeared to be no correlation between the presence of white officers who served in black regiments and a post's acceptance of black veterans. White veterans of black regiments made up a very small percentage of the membership of any given post, so these men could not have overcome the objections of even a small minority of members if they blackballed black veterans.[11]

White Americans who welcomed African American veterans in their posts may not have served with them, but they certainly recognized that some of them belonged to distinguished all-black units. The president of the WRC of the predominantly white Rodman Post in New Bedford, Massachusetts, speaking at an annual meeting, declared, "We have Ft. Wagner's hero here, who round his body wound the flag he bore when wounded and 'it never touched the ground.'" She was referring to post member Sergeant William Carney, the soldier immortalized in Norfolk's African American

Civil War memorial who saved the colors at Fort Wagner. The Tod Post welcomed veterans of the Fifty-fourth Massachusetts and other hard-fighting black regiments, including Isaac Johnson, formerly of the Sixth USCT, who was wounded at Petersburg, and James Chenney, formerly of the Fifth United States Colored Cavalry (USCC), who was injured at the well-known raid in Saltville, Virginia. A post likely looked with favor upon the application of a black veteran who had been wounded in action or had served in a distinguished regiment.[12]

African Americans who served in lesser-known units were also accepted into integrated posts. The Crocker Post welcomed three former members of Iowa's own black regiment, the Sixtieth USCT. The other seven black members belonged to a variety of units, including the 110th USCT, a regiment that guarded railroads for most of the war. Both a veteran of the Fifty-fourth Massachusetts and a soldier of the lesser-known Fifth Massachusetts Cavalry (Colored) were members of Hartford's Taylor Post. Black veterans of the Thirty-first USCT, mustered in New York City, and the Thirty-fifth USCT, which was originally organized as the First North Carolina Colored Regiment, were also members of integrated posts.[13]

It was not so much military experience of black members of the post but rather the experience of its white members that may explain the existence of integrated posts. Black and white members of integrated posts did not always serve in the same units, but they often fought in the same battles. While posts, particularly large ones, included members who served in a number of different units, veterans of a handful of regiments often dominated local posts. The nature of recruiting during the war explains the composition of GAR posts after the war. Towns, cities, and counties across the North raised companies that formed volunteer regiments. In Cazenovia, New York, the local post accepted black members; the unit recruited in that city, the 114th New York, fought alongside black soldiers at Port Hudson. Similarly, the soldiers of the Fifty-second Pennsylvania, who had been recruited partially from Scranton, Pennsylvania, fought in the battles in and around Fort Wagner. When these men came home, they belonged to the integrated Ezra Griffin Post. Other Griffin Post members had enlisted in the Second Pennsylvania Heavy Artillery and may have fought at Chafin's Farm in the Petersburg campaign. During that battle, Robert Pinn won the Medal of Honor and the members of the Fifth USCT, including John Smith, found their own glory. Segregated units did not fight segregated battles, and this is critical to understanding why white posts accepted black members.[14]

Integrated posts were not always formed simply because an all-white organization chose to accept African Americans; some were formed because

African American soldiers capturing guns at Petersburg beside Ohio soldiers. From *Frank Leslie's Illustrated Newspaper*, 1896, in author's collection.

the founding members set out to create them. When Henry Harrison, a former first sergeant of the First USCHA, died, his death notice described him as a charter member of the Lamar McConnell Post, an integrated post in Maryville, Tennessee. Harrison's founding role in his post was not unique; black veterans chartered five of the twelve mixed-race posts in this state. North of the Mason-Dixon line, black and white veterans organized posts together. The *Cleveland* [Ohio] *Gazette* reported that "some of the charter members of the Austin Post G.A.R., of this city, were colored men." In Milford Centre, Ohio, a former first lieutenant of the 114th USCT and veterans of Ohio's volunteer (white) regiments, joined A. A. Logan, a former private of the Fourth USCT, to establish a local post. Three of the founding members of Palestine, Ohio's, post served as enlisted men in black regiments, including Samuel Paxton, former private of the Forty-second USCT. Three black Iowans, together with white veterans, chartered the post in Boonesboro, Iowa. In Covert, Michigan, one-third of the post's founders were African American. The presence of black veterans as charter members of integrated posts fundamentally challenges the notion that white veterans only grudgingly accepted African Americans into their posts.[15]

Membership in an integrated post, even as a founding member, would not have mattered if, as has been suggested, black veterans were second-class citizens in these groups. An examination of day-to-day life in integrated posts reveals that African Americans, like their white counterparts, attended meetings, participated in post activities, and accomplished the essential, but often mundane, work of their posts. Welch Post members Comrade Cox, formerly of the Fifth USCHA, whose application created such a stir, and Comrade Duffin, a former artilleryman, served on various committees. Both men supervised refreshments at the post's installation of officers. The post thanked them for furnishing "rations to all present which were thankfully and cheerfully received and disposed of." Cox belonged to a committee on music, and Duffin volunteered on the Memorial Day finances committee. African Americans in the Taylor Post served on the ad hoc committee that examined the applications of black recruits from Hartford. Gustavus Booth, veteran of the Fifth Massachusetts Cavalry (Colored), was often at the center of Taylor Post activities. One Memorial Day, Booth thanked Mr. William Smith "for supplying comrades with water upon their march last Memorials Day." Another Memorial Day commemoration prompted Booth to mention "the fine Memorial sermon . . . delivered by the Rev. E. L. Thorpe in the 1st M. E." When Booth suggested that this minister's services be secured for the next year, the post agreed. The GAR was no different than any other voluntary association; active members like Booth and Cox shaped post life.[16]

Examining the elected offices held by black veterans may be another way to gauge their status in predominantly white organizations. We have already met Robert Pinn and William Dupree, both commanders of integrated units, indicating that their posts fully recognized them as valued members of their organizations. Massachusetts posts honored other black soldiers with high rank. Former sailor William Benjamin Gould commanded his integrated unit in Dedham, and former sailor John Bond was the junior vice-commander of his racially mixed post in Hyde Park. Black members also represented their mixed-race posts at state encampments. William Singleton, former slave and veteran of the Thirty-fifth USCT, represented the Foote Post of New Haven. In Kentucky, integrated post member Levant Dodge told Kentucky officials that "one of our delegates today here is a negro, and we have no member for whose integrity and Christian character I have more respect."[17]

Since only one veteran at a time commanded a post, most veterans served in lesser offices, and African Americans often filled these secondary roles. Black members tended to occupy the guard positions—for example, officer of the guard. The Crocker Post elected Charles Willet of the Eighteenth USCT as a guard in 1889. Comrade Duffin acted as inside guard for the Welch Post in Ann Arbor. Gustavus Booth of the Fifth Massachusetts Cavalry (Colored) was perennially elected post sentinel in Hartford. The Veterans Post in Elgin included only two black soldiers among its ranks in 1893; one of these men, W. J. Harris, acted as officer of the guard. African American veterans may have been elected to hold these positions because a guard was not considered a leadership position. (This may be analogous to black veterans' failure to occupy the highest positions at the state level, discussed in Chapter 1.) It may have been difficult for some white veterans to elect black members to the top positions in a post because of racial prejudice. The failure of black members to hold higher office may also reflect class bias; poor white veterans rarely held high office either.[18]

African American veterans often occupied one of the most coveted positions in the post: color-bearer. A color-bearer carried the regimental or national flag in combat and was recognized as one of the most courageous individuals in the unit; a veteran assigned this duty likely was considered an honored member of this post. The *Washington Post*, reporting on the 1892 national encampment parade, described an integrated post from Haverhill, Massachusetts, as "noted for the several colored veterans in their ranks including Color Bearer Diggs and Walker." The African American newspaper the *Iowa Bystander* noted that "C. W. Henry [sergeant, Eighty-eighth USCT], of Post 7, Des Moines was appointed special aide and color bearer of the day," deeming this "quite an honor . . . [and] just recognition of a valuable soldier and a useful citizen." Frank Hamilton, who had been rejected by the Lyon Post in Hartford and then joined the Taylor Post, was appointed color guard, and his appointment was noted in this post's records; perhaps the adjutant noted this honor because of Hamilton's unusual history. Even more remarkable were the black standard-bearers in Tennessee. The state commander had expressed his displeasure with how little notice the department received at national encampments. To remedy this slight, he "determined to devise some plan by which [the state's] delegation would receive more attention than ha[d] been ordinarily bestowed upon it in the grand parade." The commander designed a large banner with the words "Loyal East Tennessee-'61-'65," to lead the state delegation in the annual review. Critical to this scheme was the standard-bearer, "Comrade John Talley, a colored comrade of [the integrated] Pat McGuire Post, No. 46, New Market," who represented the McGuire Post at the state encampment. According to the department commander, when Talley received the banner he pledged to "stick to it as long as a piece remains." Talley and other black veterans carried the Tennessee state colors in many subsequent years. A predominantly white group who appointed a black standard-bearer wanted observers to understand that African Americans were honored members of their organizations.[19]

Veterans joined the GAR to participate in parades and receive recognition for their service; unfortunately they could not always maintain their connection with this organization because of their poverty. Integrated posts, like all-black posts, had difficulty collecting dues from their members. The Welch Post suspended John Cox, former post sergeant major, because of his failure to pay his dues, just as it dropped white veterans for similar delinquencies. The Crocker Post of Des Moines suspended both an African American veteran and a white veteran because they failed to pay their dues. Posts struggled to maintain poorer members by remitting their overdue fees when possible. The Taylor Post of Hartford twice remitted the dues of C. H. Snyder, formerly of the First USCT, to avoid suspending his membership. The Long Post of Willimantic, Connecticut, carried John L. Harris, veteran of the Fifty-fourth Massachusetts, and Charles Buck, veteran of the Twenty-ninth Connecticut (Colored), on its books for years and never suspended them.[20]

Poor black veterans demonstrated the importance of their membership in the GAR, sustaining these organizations well into the twentieth century. A similar indicator of the importance of GAR membership is how long African American veterans maintained their membership in integrated posts. While it would be impossible to make a systematic assessment of the comparative longevity of black and white members, we have the experience of one black veteran who left behind a weather diary of his life in Worcester. Amos Webber, a former enlisted man in Massachusetts's only black cavalry regiment, joined his mixed-race post in Worcester in 1869 and remained a member until his death in 1903. A GAR membership in one post that spanned five decades was extremely rare and evinced Webber's tremendous loyalty to his comrades in the Ward Post.[21]

A post should be assessed as much by how it treated its dead members as by how it treated its living ones; honoring the dead was a fundamental function of a GAR post, regardless of a deceased comrade's race. As in any other post, when a member of an integrated post died, his comrades adhered to GAR mourning rituals. The death of Jerome Freeman, formerly of the 102nd USCT, prompted this resolution from the black and white members of Ann Arbor's Welch Post: "It has pleased our Heavenly Father to take unto him our late comrade in arms. . . . In him this community lost one of its best and most worthy citizens, and Welch Post, No. 137, G.A.R. a good member and beloved comrade." The post hung an "insignia of mourning" on its banner for thirty days to honor him. The Taylor Post of Hartford preserved an obituary for Comrade Gustavus Booth, longtime post sentinel, that described him as "a brave soldier in the War of the Rebellion." In the resolution marking his and other white comrades' passing, post members expressed their "high appreciation of the soldierly qualities that marked them as defenders of the Union, and of their manly characteristics shown in connection with our post during their membership."[22]

Integrated post members' concern for their African American comrades did not end with their death; they also cared for their deceased comrades' families. The Welch Post of Ann Arbor lamented the sudden death of Stephen Jacobs, a veteran of the Fifth Massachusetts Cavalry (Colored). His death was announced at a meeting and, as was customary, a committee was appointed to write a resolution of condolences published in local newspapers. The post attended his funeral together "in a body, to pay our last respects to our departed comrade." Initially, the post relief committee reported that Comrade Jacobs's widow needed no assistance. By the turn of the century, however, the post recorded that she "received our usual New Year present of provisions." In 1902, the post allocated "$6 a month from relief funds in favor of Mrs. Jacobs." The post later sponsored "a petition signed by a large number of citizens to Congress urging that Mrs. Jacobs be made special to the end that her name be placed on the Pension role at the proper rating." One year later, Comrade Childs "announced that the widow of our late Comrade Jacobs had been allowed a pension by a special act of Congress." The post formally thanked Senator Russell Algier and Congressman Henry M. Smith for their action on the post's behalf. Eleven years after their comrade's death, the post used its influence to secure his widow's future.[23]

But women other than widows of post members participated in the world of an integrated post. Lucy Nichols and Elizabeth Fairfax had been slaves in the South and joined white northern regiments—the Twenty-third Indiana and the Twenty-sixth Iowa, respectively—during the war and later associated with predominately white GAR posts. While neither woman ever formally enlisted, both were considered "members" of these units.

Pension bureau records provide extraordinary testimony to Lucy Nichols's wartime service and her membership in the GAR. According to one letter in her file, Mrs. Nichols had the "privilege of being an honorary member of a GAR post[;] she was voted this privilege for her good services during the war. . . . She came to the 23 Reg. Ind. Vols. at Bolivar, Tennessee in August 1862 and soon gained the respect of the regiment from Colonel to Private[.] In time of battle she was a great help to the surgeon and any of the men when sick." She stayed with these men for the rest of the war, all the way from Vicksburg, through the March to the Sea, and finally to the Grand Review

Elizabeth Fairfax, honorary member of the Baker Post, Clinton, Iowa. From author's collection.

at the end of the war. She went home to Indiana with her comrades and was considered "the best known [woman] in New Albany and respected by all who knew her." Lucy Nichols fully participated in the life of her post. She "turned out to funerals, attended church on Memorial Day and also marched with [the] post [on] Decoration Day to the National Cemetery." Despite her comrades' affidavits that described her service and a doctor's reports on her disabilities, the government denied her pension. Ultimately, over fifty members of the Twenty-third Indiana, one of whom could only sign his name with an X, petitioned Congress, and a special bill passed granting her a pension of twelve dollars a month, a small recompense for her service.[24]

Elizabeth Fairfax joined the Twenty-sixth Iowa at Vicksburg and performed a wide range of services as a nurse, a laundress, and even a scout. When the war ended she came home with the regiment to Clinton and made a living in a number of ways, including as a laundress and a peddler. A local newspaper described her as an "honorary veteran ... [who] became a member of the ... Baker Post." An extant photograph of her supports the newspaper's description of her status in the GAR. She wears a Baker Post ribbon on her chest, a privilege usually reserved to post members. Moreover, local businessmen paid her way to the national encampment in Boston. Had she not had a special status in the GAR, it is unlikely the community would have supported her efforts to attend this meeting. According to a Clinton County history written in 1946, "When Memorial Day came she always marched beside the boys, trudging along on bare feet, wearing a rusty black dress and an equally decrepit bonnet, her expression of mourning. She carried a bunch of flowers in one hand, and an American flag in the other and was never an object of derision,—rather [she] inspired reverence." Like the Sanderson Post, the Baker Post embraced a woman as a kind of comrade. Elizabeth Fairfax's status may have been circumscribed by her gender but not her race; the predominantly white Baker Post listed three black veterans on its official rolls.[25]

While black veterans were welcome to join integrated posts, given the choice, many may not have joined an integrated unit. Earlier GAR studies have asserted that black veterans formed their own posts because they were shut out of all-white posts, but that was not always the case. All-black posts were formed in almost any city or town where black veterans could sustain their own posts. Black veterans may have preferred their own organizations, if for no other reason than the importance of the black GAR circle to the African American community. Regardless of their preferences, black veterans believed that their membership in the GAR mattered. While much of the focus of this chapter has been on white veterans' willingness to accept black members, an integrated post existed because African Americans applied for membership and risked rejection. Without their courage, the integrated post would never have been possible.

African American veterans may have been willing to chance rejection from a majority-white post because, like their counterparts in all-black posts, they wanted a role in the battle for Civil War Memory. In cities and towns without all-black organizations, African Americans in interracial posts served as reminders of the black experience in the Civil War. The Ward Post of Worcester, Massachusetts, included a number of black veterans, and the history of this organization records that in 1896 "one of the largest audiences of the season gathered . . . to listen to the stories of the Colored Veterans, given by Comrades Hemenway-Phelps-Scott and Wiggins of the 54th Mass. Infantry, Webber, and Giles of the 5th Mass. Cavalry, [and] Watters of the US Col[ored]." The minutes recorded the presence of other members of the African American community: "A chorus from the A.M.E. Zion Church . . . was present and gave several selections—Rev. J. Sula of the church was present and his remarks were well received." Another member's story was recorded in the post's published history. Charles Clark belonged to the Twenty-sixth USCT, and shared with his comrades "a vivid recollection of the attack on Ft. Sumter." He witnessed the bombardment and had later joined the Twenty-sixth USCT. The post published a book highlighting its members' wartime experiences; an entire chapter is devoted to Clark's account of the opening salvo of the Civil War.[26]

Outside the post room, the larger community noted the presence of black veterans in the GAR, as the obituaries of members of Youngstown's Tod Post published in the local paper, the *Vindicator*, attest. It is unlikely that other African American citizens were accorded this honor. Virginia-born James Magruder was described as "as brave a soldier as ever fought for the flag of freedom." A picture of Oscar Boggess, a charter member of the Tod Post, accompanied his death notice, which described him as "a well-known colored-man" who "served faithfully, receiving a Medal for bravery [and] member of the Tod Post." The death notice of George Logan, titled "Gallant," described this "veteran of the Civil War [as] having served a First Sergeant in Company C 44th United States Colored Troops." Although Logan "served an apprenticeship as a bricklayer and laid down his trowel to fight for the freedom of his race," the paper noted, because he "received a good education and possessing a good memory. . . . Mr. Logan was an accomplished historian." Regardless of their education levels, black veterans acted as historians when they joined integrated posts. As individuals these men may have affected Civil War Memory in their cities; two of the three major Civil War monuments that feature black men stand in cities that hosted mixed-race posts. The Civil War memorial in Hartford, the place where Comrade Hamilton's application caused such a furor in one post and where he carried the colors for another, includes a slave as a soldier. Similarly, Cleveland, whose posts were integrated, honors a black sailor on a monument featuring both black and white veterans.[27]

The integrated post was not, however, as effective an instrument in the battle for Memory as its all-black counterpart. The existence of African American posts forced Americans to acknowledge that race, and therefore slavery, played a role in the Civil War. Individuals within integrated posts reminded Americans that black soldiers had served in the war; however, integrated posts could not and would not advance a race-conscious agenda. When William Dupree was asked to serve on a pension committee of the Massachusetts GAR, he declined, saying that "his name had been brought forward to represent the colored veterans. He was there as a delegate of Post 68 [an integrated post], not as a representative of any race or color." In his stead, the Massachusetts GAR chose a member of the all-black Bell Post of Boston. Integrated posts could not either literally or figuratively represent the race. Integrated posts were "forgotten" because they were what veterans hoped a regular GAR would be: a place where veterans of all races, religions, and social classes would come together as comrades.[28]

The remarks of a speaker at a Memorial Day service in Hartford, Connecticut, very likely an integrated group, explain how the GAR overcame the barriers of race, class, and ethnicity and how its members came together as comrades. "Noble veterans, survivors of this brave band of heroes," he observed, have a "strange power over other men[:] it is the consummate power of tragedy. . . . Its power over human hearts is universal and limitless." Understanding interracial comradeship requires a close examination of how the consummate power of tragedy allowed the black and white veterans of the GAR to create and sustain an interracial social organization.[29]

PART III

Brothers Ever We Shall Be: Black and White Comradeship in the GAR

9

Comrades Bound by Memories Many

An Irish private named Miles O'Reilly articulated an expansive definition of civil rights in his 1863 poem titled "Sambo's Right to be Kil't." O'Reilly proclaimed that "so liberal are we here, / I'll let Sambo be murthered in place o' meself." This plea for equality had practical benefits, particularly "if Sambo's body should stop a ball / That was comin' for me direct." Despite O'Reilly's frequent use of the racially derogative term "Sambo," he had faith in the fighting mettle of African American soldiers: "Though Sambo's black as the ace o' spades, / His fingers a thrigger can pull, / An' his eyes run sthraight on the barrel-sights, / From undher its thatch o' wool." O'Reilly challenged those who refused the black soldier's service and argued that "men who object to Sambo / Should take his place an' fight; / An' its betther to have a naygur's hue / than a liver that's wake an white." Some may consider this a racist call to include African American soldiers on the Civil War casualties list, but it was the author of this piece who drafted the order to arm South Carolina's slaves. Charles Graham Halpine, an Irish immigrant and journalist, wrote under the pseudonym of O'Reilly and served in the Sixty-ninth New York of the famed Irish Brigade before joining General David Hunter's staff. He penned this satirical piece to support Hunter's efforts to arm black Americans.[1]

While the poem advocating black enlistment is Halpine's best-known work, GAR men recited another of his efforts. This poem, titled "Song of the Soldier," described comrades as those who had marched "in marches many, comrades tried in dangers many, Comrades bound by memories many." Though rooted in soldiers' wartime experience, comradeship continued in the postwar era: "And, if spared, and growing older, Shoulder still in line with shoulder, And with hearts no thrill the colder, Brothers ever we shall be." GAR men recited the last stanza of this poem to explain their organization's multicultural fraternity: "Creed nor faction can divide us, Race nor language

★

can divide us, Still, whatever fate betide us, Brothers of the Heart are we!"
Sambo's right to be kil't evolved into black survivors' right to membership in
the GAR.[2]

If white veterans remembered the war as we do—either as the all-white
struggle portrayed in the movie *Gettysburg*, or the almost all-black battle de-
picted in the movie *Glory*—the GAR would never have accepted black members. African Americans' place in the historical Memory of the GAR, the Civil
War narrative articulated by members of this group, relied on the personal
memory of white veterans who fought in the same battles and campaigns as
their black counterparts. Because white soldiers remembered that they had
served near black soldiers, if not always directly at their side, this narrative
included African Americans. Moreover, GAR members defined comradeship
as encompassing broader ties than those binding veterans who had served in
the same campaign. Comradeship was about the shared experience of suffering; anyone who served and suffered to advance the Union cause—on the
march, in camps, in prisons, and in disease-ridden hospitals—was considered a comrade. Because most African Americans served in units that saw
little action—illness killed more black soldiers than rifles or bayonets—this
more expansive definition of comradeship ensured that black soldiers were
considered comrades. Comradeship may have been articulated as a function
of GAR's collective historical Memory, but its power came from the strength
of soldiers' personal memories. Civil War veterans' descriptions of the experiences that inspired comradeship included traumatic incidents that most
human beings find hard to forget. Quite literally, memories of the Civil War
allowed black and white veterans to overcome racial separation in an era defined by the color line.

Commander in Chief William Patterson understood the dual nature of
veterans' memories: "Each of the 2,000,000 men who wore the blue had
an experience that is all his own"—and thus had his own personal wartime
memories. Some soldiers served in hard-fighting regiments and saw a lot of
action, while others spent the war performing more mundane duties. Despite
their varied service records, veterans, Patterson argued, "share[d] in the great
achievements of the war; all have a mutual interest in the victories and defeats, in the joys and sorrows of the military service of the great Civil War."
Regardless of their individual wartime experiences, the GAR members had
a common history; they produced a historical narrative that encompassed
their combat experiences, their successes and their failures, and the more
mundane and sometimes more miserable day-to-day life of a soldier. It was
this combination of the personal memory and the collective historical Memory, Patterson maintained, that brought veterans "together in the fraternity

of the Grand Army of the Republic." Since Patterson sponsored the all-black Shaw Post in Pittsburgh and was regarded as its "father" by its members, he understood that this was an interracial brotherhood.[3]

This fraternity included white GAR members whose personal memories recalled black service; black men had literally served at their side. Louis Wagner, Pennsylvania state commander and later the commander in chief, had supervised Camp Penn, a training facility near Philadelphia. During a debate prompted by the reluctance of some southern departments to accept black veterans, Wagner, as "a man who organized 15,000 [black soldiers] and sent them to the front," argued that "the colored troops fought bravely, and we cannot, as an organization, refuse them admission." Robert Beath, the commander in chief in 1883, who had served with the Sixth USCT, also believed that African American soldiers were qualified for the GAR because of their service: "We are an association of survivors of the war, a confederation of men who preserved the name and fame of this great nation. We ask not in our council rooms what the religious creed, what the political prejudice, what the color or the nationality of a would be comrade; but we do ask is that he proved himself a true man in the hour of our nation's peril." Beath played an important role in forming the GAR's historical narrative; he wrote the first history of this organization.[4]

Other white veterans wrote about their experiences commanding black troops in the GAR's official newspaper, the *National Tribune*, and many of these articles were featured on the front page. The front-page story of a former officer of the Seventh USCT, titled "To Do or Die," described an attack made on Confederate forces around Petersburg as "a death struggle under the very muzzles of rebel guns" by four companies of his regiment. Can any "four companies of any regiment, white or colored, taken collectively . . . show such a record as these four of the 7th U.S.C.T.?" he asked. "I think not." "The Colored Troops, Unavailing Gallantry by Men and Officers" was the title of another front-page article by an officer in the Thirtieth USCT that detailed a failed attack on Petersburg. Western soldiers received their due in a five-part series describing "The Colored Troops, [their] organization and service in the Army of the Cumberland." The writer, Henry Romeyn, described routine matters such as "the process which made farmhands soldiers." Much of his account focused on their battlefield performance and the "Courage and Conspicuous Gallantry of the Negroes." Any white veteran who read this paper—and this journal would have been in many post rooms—might have agreed with Romeyn that African American soldiers stood beside their "white comrades [and] did [their] whole duty in the time that tried men's souls and on fields where the cravens had no place." The

GAR's historical Memory reflected the personal memory of its members who recalled the battlefield heroism of African American soldiers.[5]

Soldiers who had served in all-white units near black regiments also contributed to the Civil War narrative that included African Americans. No Civil War battle of any importance was fought by black troops alone. A black regiment may have been in an integrated brigade, a black brigade was likely part of a mixed-race division, an all-black division usually served in an integrated corps, and an all-black corps served in an army that included black and white units. Soldiers recounted their participation in struggles involving both black and white soldiers in their war sketches, memoirs of wartime service recorded by their local post. The memory of the final battles in the East, in particular, was etched on the minds of black and white soldiers. Rubin Lewis, formerly of the Fifth Massachusetts Cavalry (Colored), who later joined the all-black Shaw Post of Pittsburgh, remembered the "fierce battle in front of Petersburg on the 14th and 15th days of June 1864 when several of [his] comrades were killed and many wounded." Irish-born William McGee, veteran of the First Connecticut Heavy Artillery, described the intensity of this final year of campaigning: He "participated in the Siege of Petersburg Va. and Richmond Va. from May 1864 to April 1865[.] [S]pace will not allow the mention of the numerous engagements at those places as we were almost constantly under fire." The war sketch of James Ellesbury, veteran of the Sixth USCT and later a member of the Shaw Post, was more understated. "Some of the interesting events of my soldier life," he related, "[were] the battle of Petersburg and Springhill, New Market heights and Dutch Gap canal Virginia 1864." Garrison Cole, formerly of the Sixty-third Pennsylvania, summarized the final year of campaigning in the East in his war sketch: "The campaign from the Rappahanock [sic] to Petersburg Va. including the siege of that place—up to 1864 was among the most momentous and severe positions of service in which I was engaged. The earlier battles becoming by comparison little more than skirmishes."[6]

The explosion and assault on the Crater at Petersburg, involving an attack by a black division, appeared to have a distinct place in veterans' memories. John O'Reilly, Thirteenth Pennsylvania Cavalry, identified one of the most important events in his military service as the "engagement when our army blew up the rebel fort at Petersburg, VA." German-born Conrad Noll of the Twentieth Michigan, later of the Welch Post, reported that "at the Crater I received a minie ball in my left thigh the ball was lodged near my knee joint and was not extracted till April 13, 1870." Noll cited in his war sketch his experience at the Crater as one of the most important events; he was awarded the Medal of Honor for his heroism at the battle of Spotsylvania Courthouse.

William Fortin, a member of a prominent African American family, argued in a Memorial Day speech to an all-black Pennsylvania post, "It was once the pride of a Frenchman to say 'I fought on the field of Austerlitz,' I want you to hold up your head and say 'I was at Petersburg.'" Many black and white veterans could make that claim and would remember that both races had fought in this campaign.[7]

The experience of veterans in two posts, the all-black Shaw Post in Pittsburgh and the mixed-race Taylor Post in Hartford, demonstrated that segregated units did not mean segregated battles. When Taylor Post members Louis Falley and Frederick White, formerly of the Seventh Connecticut, listed their battles, they cited Olustee, as did Shaw Post members George Gross of the Eighth USCT and Oliver Steel of the Fifty-fifth Massachusetts. William Carroll served in the Fifty-fourth Massachusetts and remembered the "grand charge on Fort Wagner with my regiment," as did William Parker, another veteran of Shaw's regiment. Both men later honored Shaw's memory as members of the Shaw Post. Albert Fox and George Wetzel, both of the Sixth Connecticut, fought at Fort Wagner and later joined the integrated Taylor Post. Calvin Pike recorded his service at Fort Wagner and Olustee with a Connecticut regiment and his experience as an officer in the Seventy-fourth USCT. It is unlikely that Pike or any of the other Taylor Post veterans forgot the service of black troops.[8]

While Calvin Pike and other Connecticut veterans remembered Wagner and Olustee, the master narrative of the Civil War does not. The amnesia regarding certain engagements and campaigns led one historian to title the chapter in his book on the military service of Connecticut soldiers the "Forgotten War." While historians forgot Connecticut soldiers' service at Wagner, the Connecticut GAR did not forget. Clara Barton, Civil War nurse and founder of the American Red Cross, spoke to the 1883 encampment, twenty years after Wagner's fall. According to an observer, "The early part of her speech was devoted to a thrilling description of the gallant assault on Fort Wagner in Charleston Harbor in which the Sixth, Seventh and the Tenth Connecticut participated, and for fifteen minutes she held the audience in almost breathless silence." To the members of the Connecticut GAR, Fort Wagner was an important part of their collective Memory since it was so important in the personal memories of the state's veterans.[9]

Although Fort Wagner is well-known today, veterans appeared to be more familiar with the battle of Port Hudson—a failed attempt involving black troops to capture fortifications critical to control of the Mississippi River. Port Hudson may have been more memorable because more northern soldiers would have remembered their personal experience in this battle: at least thirty thousand Union troops participated in this battle, and over five thousand of these men were casualties. In contrast, five thousand Union soldiers attacked Fort Wagner in the charge that included the Fifty-fourth Massachusetts. The dead, missing, and wounded numbered just over fifteen hundred. At least nineteen members of the Taylor Post, including men from Maine, Massachusetts, and Connecticut regiments, cited Port Hudson as one of their battles. Some of these men were wounded in this engagement, making it even more memorable. Andrew Hall of the Twelfth Connecticut received a gunshot wound in the side of the face; William Silloway, formerly of the Twenty-fifth Connecticut, was injured when a piece of shell hit his left thumb. Harrison Soule, who served in the Sixth Michigan, cited Port Hudson in his war sketch as the most important event in his military career. Soule's description of the battle lacked literary flair and was recorded in a minimalist staccato, as were the memories in many other sketches: "the siege at Port Hudson, outer batteries stormed and taken. May 26 with storming party on the mainworks. June 14 with storming party Slaughterfield." Charles Puffer, formerly of the Twenty-fifth Connecticut, characterized his "duty in the rifle pits" at Port Hudson as "the most important event of my military history." Given the size of this engagement, a number of white veterans likely agreed.[10]

The personal memory of the thousands of white veterans who survived this battle may explain why the story of African American heroism at Port Hudson was told and retold by various members of the GAR and their circle. When Ivan N. Walker, the new commander in chief, received the GAR's standard at the national encampment in 1895 he asserted, "In accepting this flag I wish to use the language of the black sergeant in charge at Port Hudson. The colonel presented to him, and instructed him to die for them, if need be, but never to surrender them. He replied that he would return with the colors in honor or report to God the reason why." The color sergeant, Walker continued, "went down in that charge and when found was clasping the colors to his breast, and looking up to heaven." At an Ohio encampment, governor and future president William McKinley told the same story. The audience applauded when McKinley shared the sergeant's promise to defend the colors to the death and applauded again when McKinley told them that "he didn't bring them back, but God Almighty knew the reason why."[11]

Veterans may have known this story because popular works familiar to these men chronicled black heroism at Port Hudson. The *Grand Army Record* published the poem "I'll Report to God the Reason Why," which chronicles the sergeant's sacrifice, telling of how "bravely fought the dusky Black Brigade" who in "strife and battle won their right to liberty." Katherine Sherwood, president of the WRC, penned "The Black Regiment" as homage to the heroes of Port Hudson: "What did they wrest from the breach / Under the guns at Port Hudson? / The right to be men to stand forth / Clean-limbed in the light of freedom." In a poem with the same name, George Boker, a white playwright, tells the story of Port Hudson and the men who were "Glad to strike one free blow, / Whether for weal or woe; / Glad to breathe a free breath, / Though on the lips of death." In the final stanza he makes a plea for the regiment's black survivors: "Soldiers, be just and true! / Hail them as comrades tried; / Fight with them side by side[.]" When a Virginia official protested the exclusion of African Americans from other southern departments in 1887, he invoked the language of this poem, describing how "hundreds and hundreds fell, and now they are resting well" and demanded that his comrades be "just and true, hail them as comrades tried" and welcome the heroes of Port Hudson and other battles into the GAR.[12]

Serving together in the same campaign made soldiers comrades, but so did their other shared wartime miseries. Ohio's state commander used a chronological narrative of a soldier's life from enlistment to victory to describe comradeship: "A comrade is a brother. We have stood together and experienced to the full the heroic joy of placing our names side by side upon the roll of enlistment, . . . the sad but hopeful farewells to friends and dear ones as we marched away, . . . the unpleasant vicissitudes of camp-life[,] the hardships and torments of the march[,] the exhausting labor of entrenchment[,] the terrific carnage of battle[,] the untold agony of wounds[,] and the sad loss of comrades dear." The Illinois department commander also described comradeship in terms of the mundane but no less brutal aspects of a soldier's life when he described a comrade: "We have relieved him on the march, when footsore and hungry, and that under our own blanket we sheltered him from the storm and the sleet and the cold of the winter's day, and we are happier in the thought that through it all he was our pard and our companion. It means that we have drunk from the same canteen and shared the contents of the same old haversack." Nineteenth-century soldiers suffered as much from the everyday misery of military life as they did from the consequences of occasional battles. The state commander in Indiana spoke for his fellow Hoosiers when he defined comradeship: "It is the experience of camps and association of the camps, the march, and upon the battlefield, that unites us as comrades; and there has been sealed in privation and blood that fraternity which kept us 'elbow to elbow' as we have marched to the music of a saved Union." That veterans defined comradeship in terms of their wartime experiences both on and off the battlefields, with neither being privileged over the other, is one of the most surprising findings of this study. Since many African American soldiers served in units that had not seen much combat, interracial comrade-ship relied on this more expansive definition of a comrade.[13]

Veterans remembered that black soldiers had suffered regardless of their service record. The commander in Delaware explained his interest in the state's black post by reminding his comrades that "in the active stages of the war [black soldiers] performed the same duty, endured the same hardships, suffered the same agony, and gave their lives so that this glorious Union shall be one and inseparable." African Americans also believed that suffering pro-duced such a bond. Solomon Hood, commander of an all-black post in West Chester, Pennsylvania, who was identified by his white comrades in 1872 as a soldier who had "been in all the battles before Richmond and had fought valiantly for his country," explained comradeship in a Memorial Day speech in 1900: "Few things give stronger ties than common suffering. They who have tramped on long, weary marches together, lay down with the ground for a couch and the sky for a covering, felt the keen pangs of hunger and the burning thirst, faced death together, are bound by a tie others know not." Comrade Hood, and others like him, demonstrated the power of shared his-torical Memory to transcend racial barriers.[14]

Historical Memory may have defined comradeship, but the strength of this shared identity derived from the clarity of soldiers' personal memories. Only the enduring nature of these recollections allowed the GAR to over-come racial divisions. When the Indiana department commander reminisced about the war with his fellow Hoosiers, he "recall[ed] to mind a scene—it seems so real." He described the scene as if it were unfolding in front of him: "In my rear the sluggish waters of the Tennessee River run their serpentine course. Thousands of army tents dot its southern banks. . . . Peacefully rest-ing in open tents near rivers brink lay 60,000 brave men and true." Unto this rather idyllic scene, war came: "Hark! I hear the signal gun. . . . The air is filled with smoke and missiles of death, the cries of the wounded, heart piercing shrieks, ranks thinning rapidly. . . . The scene so grand two hours ago turns my face to ashen gray, the dead and dying everywhere, the groans of the wounded, the blood stained face of [the] hobbling trooper to the rear." This contrast between the peaceful scene and the later trauma was clearly etched in his memory. The power of this memory comes from its clarity, so many years after the battle.[15]

Veterans recalled more intimate but equally tragic scenes with uncanny clarity. Speaking to a group of Kansas teenagers, James Tanner, commander in chief of the GAR, recalled a hospital stay and "an Irishman who had been the joy of that section of the long ward, desperately wounded, yet making light of his wounds." Tanner explained that "he was more desperately wounded than he thought." A priest came to visit the soldier, "for he was Catholic, to break the news to him that God was calling him [home in] the immediate future." "I shall never forget the look that came over his face," Tanner said. "The mental struggle that was on him no one could describe." The unknown Irish soldier asked the priest to tell his wife and to "break it to her gently as you can that Pat comes back no more." The soldier died that night. Pat and his dying made an indelible impression on Tanner, who told the tale four decades after the war's end.[16]

Like Tanner, we all possess an almost uncanny ability to remember the circumstances surrounding a traumatic incident. Ask almost anyone where they were when President Kennedy was shot, or when the shuttle *Challenger* exploded, or the moment the Twin Towers fell, and they will be able to answer. In *The Seven Sins of Memory: How the Mind Forgets and Remembers*, Daniel Schacter maintains that the "sin" of traumatic memory is persistence: "In contrast to transience, absent-mindedness, and blocking, persistence involves remembering things that you wish you could forget." Schacter contends that "persisting memories are a major consequence of just about any type of traumatic experience: war, violent assaults or rapes, [and] sexual abuse." Schacter explains that these "intrusive memories . . . take the form of vivid perceptual images, sometimes preserving in minute detail the very features of a trauma that survivors would most likely forget." Moreover, scientists have recently identified the biochemical basis of this phenomenon. Strong emotions, such as fear, cause a person to release hormones that make memory more indelible, which likely explains the clarity of veterans' memories. The historical Memory of the GAR may be constructed, but it is built on the personal memory of its members. Enduring memories created enduring comradeship.[17]

Veterans' personal war sketches illustrate the indelible nature of traumatic memories. Even when veterans were asked to describe the most important event in their military service or, in the case of the all-black Shaw Post, the most interesting event of their military life, they frequently described instead the most memorable event. They often recounted the circumstances surrounding the death of a comrade, their own brushes with mortality, or their painful wounds. They also recounted their less glamorous but no less onerous experiences, such as hard marching on little food and sleeping on the cold ground, exposed to the elements. While comradeship was a notion that was defined in the historical Memory of the GAR, its strength came from the personal memory of its members and the fundamental nature of traumatic memories. The bonds of comradeship overcame the divisions of race because these men truly remembered.

Veterans' memories of wartime casualties were often the most enduring. Matthew Hamilton's war sketch is one of the longest memoirs left by
members of the all-black Shaw Post. Hamilton, a Pennsylvania native who
enlisted with the Fifth Massachusetts Cavalry (Colored), "was in front of
Petersburg, Va June 15th 1864 under the command of General Benjamin F.
Butler who commanded the 18th Corps." During this engagement, Hamilton
recalled, his "regt. . . . helped to capture a line of rebel works and about 200
prisoners and Seven pieces of artillery." Despite his pleasure in this triumph,
he recalled that "there was a goodly number of my comrades fell that day
killed and wounded." Hamilton maintained that he would "not soon forget
that day." George Washington of the Shaw Post, another Fifth Massachusetts
Cavalry veteran, recalled the same battle and that "there was several of the
comrades of my regiment killed and wounded." When soldiers remembered
the mass casualties, they also recalled their individual losses. George Washington remembered that "among the killed was Comrade Joseph Jackson
of my company." J. Edward Goodge of the 139th Pennsylvania survived to
record for posterity his memory of what was for him the single most important event of the war. A member of his unit was struck "in the back of the
head killed him—instantly—went back to Co. F and told his brother John."
In this case it was not only his comrade's death he remembers, but its aftermath, when he was duty bound to tell a man his brother was dead. George
Hawley joined the Fourteenth Rhode Island Heavy Artillery (Colored) when
he was seventeen. He cited as his most significant memory avoiding capture
by the enemy and the consequences for his comrades who were not as fortunate: "I was shot at three times on picket . . . but I made good my escape but
2 of my comrades were captured and . . . hung to a tree." A teenaged soldier,
traumatized by the loss of his friends in such a brutal manner, never forgot
this experience.[18]

Survival itself was frequently cited as the most important event in a soldier's service. Owen Harvey of the Fourteenth New York, who fought at Fredericksburg and in other battles, stated, "The most important event during
my military service was my getting home alive." George Gross of the Eighth
USCT was wounded at Olustee but also saw action at many engagements
around Petersburg and Richmond. The most "interesting event of my military life," he reported, "[was] that I was not killed in some of the battles that
I was engaged in." Postwar comradeship was, by definition, a bond among
the war's survivors.[19]

The memory of the circumstances surrounding severe wounds haunted
many veterans. William James, a Connecticut native who served in an Ohio
regiment, asserted, "I was the only native-born New Haven boy at Vicksburg

and am sure I was the only one who was shot through the head and lived to read his own obituary." Another Connecticut native reported that his brother died in the war and he nearly joined him. A. C. Bayne was severely wounded "and lay for three days and nights on the ground before receiving medical attendance." Veterans' descriptions of their wounds were frequently terse. Moses Ditcher of the Shaw Post who served with the Thirteenth USCT "was wounded in the nose at Nashville," and Perry Cox, Fifth Massachusetts Cavalry, reported his wounded groin. Both men belonged to the Shaw Post in Pittsburgh. George Washburn of the integrated Taylor Post and veteran of the First Connecticut Heavy Artillery said that he received a "gunshot wound in the seat and privates" at Antietam.[20]

Military medicine in this era made wounds even worse than they likely would be today. German-born Theodore Gelbert's service with the Twentieth New York ended at Antietam when he was shot in the arm. According to his sketch, the bullet struck "three inches above elbow, cut in two the main artery, arm was amputated the next day but it was poorly done, did not heal up and had to be amputated the second time in New York, June 4, 1863." Gelbert's terse commentary left unstated the agony he would have experienced between September 1862 and June 1863. When David Owen, a native of Wales, recalled his service with the 178th Pennsylvania he cited as "the most important event of his military service the loss of his arm at Murphreesboro, Tennessee in 1864." Members of Ann Arbor's mixed-race Welch Post left body parts scattered all over Civil War battlefields: Charles Mauly was shot three times, once each at Gaines Mill, Fredericksburg, and Gettysburg. His arm had to be amputated in Pennsylvania, which ended his service. Joseph Vallan lost an arm at Gaines Mill in 1863, Randall T. Van Valkenburgh lost two fingers in the Wilderness in the final year of the war, and Eli Mauly left his arm at Blue Springs in faraway East Tennessee.[21]

Amputation may have been preferable to capture, however; some Civil War prison experiences were so horrific that even death in battle would have been more merciful. Edward Logan recorded his experience as a POW when he almost shared the fate of George Hawley's companions. Logan, a native of Winchester, Virginia, enlisted in the Fifty-fifth Massachusetts (Colored) and was sent to South Carolina. "[I] was not there more than two weeks," Logan recounted, "before I with two others of my comrades was taken as prisoners. . . . We thought we was done for as Jefferson [Davis] the confederate President had issued orders to hang all Nigger soldiers that was captured fighting with the yankees. The rebels told us that they was going to hang us." Logan explained that "for some cause or other they did not hang me but they made up for it in the way of starving." Logan and his companions were treated so harshly that he "was the only one of the three that came out alive after being in their clutches for fifteen months." Logan likely spoke for many former prisoners, both black and white, when he stated, "I was in a much worse place than the battlefield." Daniel Donohue surrendered as a member of the Eighteenth Connecticut at Winchester—ironically, Logan's hometown. Donohue fared little better than his black comrade in prison. "I suffered in Belle Island [prison] and got to death's door on account of it," he recalled. Elijah Adams served in West Virginia Infantry and Artillery units. He was captured twice, once in 1862 and again in 1864. Not surprisingly, he deemed "the most important event in his services . . . the misery he underwent as a prisoner of war from June 19th 1864 and February 15th 1865."[22]

His second experience was so much worse than his first because the U.S. and Confederate governments stopped prisoner exchanges in 1864. In the early years of the war, the northern and southern governments traded prisoners; ten Union soldiers were released for ten Confederate soldiers of equal rank. These exchanges were suspended in 1864 because the Confederate government refused to treat black soldiers as combatants. More prisoners translated into overcrowded living conditions and poor treatment. The Confederate government established Andersonville prison to handle the overflow in the western theater. This "prison" consisted of a large field surrounded by a fence in which prisoners struggled to find shelter in holes covered by rags. Not surprisingly, 30 percent of all prisoners sent to Andersonville died, twice the death rate for all Union soldiers held in Confederate prisons.[23]

Members of the integrated Taylor Post remembered the Confederates' refusal to recognize black soldiers as combatants and their comrades' refusal to leave African American soldiers to the mercy of their captors. A Taylor Post member's obituary made a point of recounting how imprisoned soldiers from his unit refused to support Confederate efforts to abandon black soldiers in exchange for a chance for freedom. Many members of his regiment, the Hartford-based Sixteenth Connecticut, were confined to Andersonville because their unit surrendered at Plymouth, North Carolina. Similarly, a Connecticut official credited members of the Sixteenth Connecticut with rejecting a Confederate request to endorse their efforts to abandon "the niggers that [they] refuse to consider as prisoners of war," though it meant their continued imprisonment. Others members of integrated posts remembered Andersonville. A Tod Post veteran spent ten months in Andersonville and explained that he "could barely walk" when released. Welch post members had similar experiences. Oliver H. Perry, Seventh Michigan Cavalry, was captured and spent time at Belle Island before he was transferred to Andersonville. He described his liberation day in 1865 as "my last day in Hades." James

Saunders, a veteran of a Michigan infantry unit, recorded in his sketch that he weighed 162 pounds in May 1864. By March 1865, after four months in Andersonville, he weighed 90 pounds. The GAR and its members included the treatment of black POWs in their shared historical Memory because it was part of the personal memory of its members.[24]

Most soldiers were never captured; however, all shared the routine misery of military life. Veterans frequently cited suffering outside of battle as their strongest wartime memory. Charles Basset, a hospital steward who served with the Fifty-fourth Ohio Volunteers, fought in the battles at Shiloh and Vicksburg. "The most important event in my service," he maintained, "[was] the endurement of such extreme hardship, exposure, and affliction." Whereas Basset spoke generally about the misery of his wartime service, Isaac McWilliams, a veteran of many battles with the two different Pennsylvania regiments, had more specific grievances. When asked to cite the most important event of his service, he chose "the carrying of eight days rations (hardtack) on my back and sixty rounds of cartridges," which would have weighed at least fifty pounds. Cavalrymen appeared to suffer like infantrymen. John Sessions, formerly of the Seventh Michigan Cavalry, said his "hat was shot from his head in a charge at Gettysburg." While he remembered this close call, he gave equal time to his experience in Kilpatrick's raid on Richmond: "In the last engagement . . . my horses and equipment, tent and blankets were captured and my health was injured by exposure without shelter or blankets during the remainder of the raid, so that I was unsuited for duty for several months." A soldier's memory of exposure to the elements may have been as powerful as his recollections of battles, which, while harrowing, occupied a handful of days at discrete intervals over the months and, in many cases, years of military service.[25]

A soldier sleeping outside was probably even more miserable when he was hungry. Veterans often cited hunger as the most important, or at least memorable, "event" in their military career. Welch Post member William Acton, born in England and a veteran of the U.S. Regulars, said the most important event for him occurred at Lookout Mountain in the Chattanooga campaign, but not his service in battle. Rather, it was "being cut off from communication with the north and on 1/4 rations for a long time." Amos Simmonds, a Connecticut infantryman, contended that "the most important event of [his] military service was the seven day retreat from the Chicahomony to Harrison's Landing [1862], 3 days without food of any kind." Evan Jones, who served in the Second Maryland, asserted that the most important event for him was "the fighting two days and nights at Lynchburg—sick without a solitary morsel of food and sharpshooters kept up a steady fire at the well when we attempted to get a mouthful of water." The memory of marching or fighting on an empty stomach made an indelible impression on northern soldiers.[26]

Even well-fed soldiers suffered from that great scourge of nineteenth-century armies: disease. Sickness claimed the lives of 250,000 of the roughly 400,000 Union soldiers who died in the war; more Union soldiers died of disease than Confederates died of any cause. A Memorial Day speaker in Des Moines, Iowa, made sure his audience remembered the men who died "not alone in battle sternly fighting the foe but . . . [who] by the wayside sickened and died. In the hospital ward where fell disease raged its mad career, where fever, cruel and hungry, wasted and blighted once strong men, many 'passing over the river.'" The personal war sketches of GAR men included memories of wartime illness. Chester Elmer, a musician with the Thirty-fifth New York, ended his service before Antietam yet still managed to catch typhoid fever and had to spend time in army hospitals. Matthew Nesbitt served as a private in the Forty-fourth USCT and was captured by Confederate troops after receiving a blow to the shoulder from a musket. "On the march from Chattanooga Tenn July 1864," he recalled, "I was sick from the measles but I marched the whole way without medicine or attention to Rome Georgia the measles went in on me during my imprisonment [and] I suffered with the affect." He also tried to escape from prison twice, but to no avail. Although Perry Wehr served for only one hundred days in an Ohio regiment and saw no action, he "suffered more by sickness owing to the rapid changes of climate and way of living" because of his unit's "considerable traveling and in some cases hard duty." Disease was democratic, affecting soldiers regardless of their proximity to the battlefield.[27]

As is the case in every war, soldiers' suffering continued after the guns fell silent. If Civil War suffering had ended at Appomattox, then the GAR would not have been the most powerful social organization in the nineteenth century, and it likely would not have been an interracial group.

10

And If Spared and Growing Older

Eighteen-year-old James Tanner, a farmer's son, lay in a military hospital after the Second Battle of Bull Run with no legs. Two decades later, a former nurse remembered his condition: "Corporal James Tanner, a smooth-faced child, [was] a sight for a mother with an only son in the army. His stumps were not his only trouble. Having lost both legs, someone in kindness had laid him on a board on his back, and lying so long without attention, bedsores made inroads upon his frame. They also were full of worms, and when fully cleansed the naked bone was plainly seen." Tanner suffered from his wounds for the rest of his life. More than thirty years after the battle, a friend expressed his hope that surgery, in which more of both legs were amputated, would "result in complete relief to him from the exhaustion and excruciating pain from which he has suffered." As was the case for most amputees during this period, Tanner found little relief. Some veterans ached from pains in their amputated limbs. Nineteenth-century medical practices left some of the wounded still bleeding decades after Appomattox. For years after the war, former soldiers continued to suffer from wartime diseases of the body and maladies of the mind. These men had not sacrificed their lives during the war but gave the best years of their lives in its aftermath. Failure to chronicle the postwar suffering of Civil War soldiers has consequences: Many Americans seem oblivious to the final cost of this war. To paraphrase Robert E. Lee, it is good to know how terrible the suffering of veterans, because then we will not be so fond of war.[1]

Ironically, one of the activities directly related to the cost of veterans' service—the GAR's struggle to secure veterans' pensions—has affected how scholars view this organization. Early studies of this group, including Mary Dearing's, focused on the GAR as a political interest group lobbying for these pensions. According to Dearing, "at the height of their influence[, the GAR and its members] . . . were able to command benefits which cost the federal

★

government more than one-fifth of its total revenue." Dearing's distaste for both the GAR's political activities and the pensions veterans received is evident throughout her study. The author of another study of the Civil War pension system presented a similarly jaundiced view, describing these payments as a "system of exploitation by which the more mercenary element among the old soldiers was engaged in exploiting the grateful esteem of the northern public." The author viciously attacked James Tanner for his performance as commissioner of pensions. He described Tanner as having a "mania for pensions" and charged that his primary interest was to spend the government surplus and avoid lowering the tariff on imported goods—one of the primary pillars of the Republican Party in the late nineteenth century. While Tanner may or may not have acknowledged the virtue of tariffs to protect American industry, he understood the postwar suffering of his comrades and was more interested in their welfare than economy and efficiency in government.[2]

Focusing on pensions might have been the most profitable way for scholars to analyze the GAR. These payments proved that wartime suffering was not merely a memory. Disease still killed, wounds still bled, and hearts and minds remained broken for decades after the war's end. In 1913, the Illinois state commander assessed the war's toll on his generation: "How can we estimate the cost! The dead who fell in battle may be numbered but the anguish of the maimed who carry their pain on a daily basis until death releases them, the broken hearted fathers, mothers, whose sons sleep deep beneath the sod and whose cowed heads hasten to an early grave, the blighted home where the widow sits in darkness, the orphan children who were left to life struggle alone—the sum of the sorrow, and all the bitterness must be gathered and counted before the cost can be told." A speaker at an African American Memorial Day observance in Beaufort, South Carolina, commented on the aftermath of this struggle: "Many of the Nation's heroes are disabled for life, as a result of their bravery in the hottest thick of the fight, limbs shot off or amputated, sight, taste, hearing lost or defective, no eye to see, no nose to smell, no feet to walk." The GAR's struggle for expanded veterans' pensions, the source of so much scorn from scholars, represented only the most obvious way that its members dealt with the war's enduring legacy of pain and sorrow.[3]

Comradeship was not merely about the need for organized political action; instead, it was a complex synergy between the memory of wartime misery and the reality of postwar anguish. The Pennsylvania state commander, John Taylor, called upon his comrades to "be true as in the past to that fraternity, bound of all the toils, the privations, dangers in battle, pains of the hospital, horrors of the prison pen and death scenes; [to have] sympathy for the widows and the mothers and a parental care for the orphans of our fallen comrades; [to lend] a helping hand to our needy and disabled survivors, loyal to these as you were to your country and flag." Taylor linked veterans' memory of the wartime suffering of their comrades with the need to assist survivors. In his mind, there existed a direct connection between the past and the present, and that link was the bond of comradeship. A judge advocate in Ohio also spoke of this connection: "Remember those who fell, think of the sacrifices made by them, and my Comrades go into the houses all over this land; look at the empty sleeves; look at the maimed soldiers; look at the cripples, the widows still without comfort; look at the orphans, and think of the fathers as heroes and patriots that saved this nation." A Massachusetts official explicitly tied interracial comradeship to contemporary suffering when he described how "details of war-worn men from the posts are watching by some dying comrades bed[.] The men who bore the flag of the Commonwealth . . . may be found every night tenderly holding the hands of dying men, watching and nursing without any distinction of nationality or color, but because of the holy bond of combatant loyalty to the motherland." The powerful relationship between former soldiers may not have been as strong if suffering was a memory.[4]

Scholars may not have acknowledged the suffering of the Civil War generation because GAR members spoke of suffering in such sentimental terms, like "tenderly holding the hands of dying men." The horrors of World War I led many to reject sentimental language, particularly when describing war. Moreover, nineteenth-century American writers refused to describe the more gruesome details of veterans' suffering, particularly when, unlike James Tanner, many veterans suffered from diseases and not from more "honorable" agonies. Finally, American Civil War Memory often forgets not only that some of the hands of the Civil War dying were black but also the postwar agony of Civil War veterans; the "romance of reunion" had no room for the surviving human detritus of the battlefield.[5]

Language limits our understanding of the postwar suffering of veterans, and so does their poor record keeping. It is difficult to determine how many Civil War veterans suffered in the postwar era; no one ever counted the maimed survivors. The four hundred thousand wounded did not translate into four hundred thousand maimed survivors; a soldier wounded in one battle may have been killed in another, and a single soldier may have been wounded twice. Oliver Wendell Holmes Jr., the famous jurist, was wounded three times. Complicating any assessment of the Civil War's legacy is the unknown number of soldiers who fell ill during their military service. Since diseases killed more soldiers than battles did, we may assume that more veterans suffered from wartime diseases than battlefield wounds. Moreover, while diseases of the body were recognized, nineteenth-century doctors had little understanding of mental illnesses, particularly those that affected veterans. Today we have made great strides in understanding these kinds of psychological casualties, even if we do not always provide the resources needed to treat these injuries.[6]

Bureaucrats charged with administering the nineteenth-century pension system provided some hard evidence of the price paid by surviving veterans. In 1888, the commissioner of pensions reported to Congress the reasons that veterans obtained pensions. Since Appomattox, 117,947 pensions had been awarded for gunshot or shell shot wounds. Surprisingly, only 9,000 pensions had been awarded to amputees; perhaps these men received their pensions during wartime or their injuries were classified under the shot-and-shell category. The next largest pension category included those made chronically ill by the war; for example, the government awarded pensions to 55,125 veterans afflicted with one of the greatest killers of all, chronic diarrhea. In addition, 40,790 pensions were awarded for rheumatism. Few nineteenth-century Americans would have included the 22,517 individuals who suffered from diseases of the rectum, or the 2,119 men diagnosed with diseases of the scrotum and testes, in their tableau of Civil War suffering. A footnote to the commissioner's report explained that each reason cited did not translate to a single individual. Instead, "two or more disabilities exist in the same individual, as for example, a gunshot wound, hernia, and rheumatism"—which might be reassuring to the politician receiving this report, but not to the person burdened by these painful conditions.[7]

Behind these numbers were individuals. Members of the GAR described how their comrades suffered from these injuries decades after the guns fell silent. Joshua Palmer of the Eighteenth Connecticut Volunteers died in 1911, though he had "lived almost half century with a bullet near his heart," according to his obituary preserved by the mixed-race Taylor Post of Hartford. The obituary did not say whether he suffered pain from this wound or whether he worried that the bullet might move and kill him. A GAR medical official in 1894 reported the death of John Wade, who had "received a wound in the corner of his left eye, from the end of the limb of a tree." In an era without specialized eye care, the injury, which today would have been a relatively mild, "resulted in a discharging sore which ultimately consumed one eye, his nose and part of his face. Hence he was a great sufferer for years." That same year in Massachusetts, an official announced that Comrade Edward Hinks was dying. He had initially been "carried from the field of Antietam mortally wounded." Hinks, however, "partially recovered and took the field, to be again desperately wounded. And in consequence of said wounds and their resulting affects now lies on the point of death at his home in Cambridge." The second mortal wound claimed his life decades after the war's end.[8]

GAR members' postwar sketches chronicled the lingering effect of some wounds. Hugh Park served in the 155th Pennsylvania, and his sketch records his service in one of the last battles of the war: "He was disabled by a gunshot wound in both hips at the battle of Five Forks Va, First Day of April 1865. This wound has affected him through the balance of his life." W. H. L. Hamilton, veteran of the Sixty-third Pennsylvania Volunteers, managed to survive a wound in his right elbow at Gettysburg only to be wounded "in the right ankle joint by a minie ball at the battle of Mine Run" later in 1863. The wound "has afflicted his ankle at all times since." Surprisingly, in some cases, wounds still bled for decades. James Tanner explained that when he and another official were away at a GAR gathering, he was asked to dress this comrade's war wound. Tanner reported that he found out that night "that every day since Malvern Hill [in 1862] he had bled for his country." Tanner's experience was replicated in many cities and towns. At annual encampments and regular post meetings, veterans, literally and figuratively, re-dressed each others' still-bleeding wounds, which reinforced the bonds of comradeship among them.[9]

Since disease caused more deaths than combat during the war, it is likely that many soldiers continued to suffer from wartime illnesses after the war. At the 1888 encampment of the Iowa GAR, the state's mustering officer said the "muster of today" was much smaller than the "muster of 1861" because "thousands and thousands of our comrades have since that time received the final discharge, upon the battlefield, in prison pens, from diseases contracted by hardships, exposures and privation, and in the prime and meridian of their lives . . . met an untimely death." At the local posts of the GAR, veterans understood that the persistence of wartime illnesses was the most debilitating effect of their service. Comrade Solomon Hood, a black post commander from West Chester, Pennsylvania, described the phenomenon among his comrades: "Some [veterans'] . . . constitutions were shattered and broken by the Southern suns and fevers, though they escaped the bullet or the shell, and came home, have fallen victims to diseases contracted while in service and are gone on to the Great Beyond." The *Cleveland Gazette* reported that John Smith, veteran of the Fifth USCT and member of a mixed-race post, suffered "for some time from disease . . . contracted in the service

[from] which so many brave soldiers are passing away." Earlier, the newspaper described how he had been living in the street, which is the fate of many veterans today, and that it was only the aid of the members of his integrated GAR post that allowed him access to medical care. According to the *New York Age*, John G. Briscoe, former commander of the all-black Andrews Post in New York, gradually weakened and died "from a disease contracted in the line of duty as a sailor in the service of his country during the dark days of the Rebellion." Neither newspaper account mentioned their specific illnesses. Dying of disease may have seemed to nineteenth-century Americans, be they black or white, as an ignominious end for a soldier, particularly if a veteran died of a disease like chronic diarrhea.[10]

John Smith relied on his GAR post for succor, as did so many other ailing veterans. The meeting minutes of GAR posts demonstrate the centrality of charity or relief to these organizations. The committee charged with delivering relief to ailing veterans and their dependents reported to the post before any other committee at their regular meetings. The minutes do not identify the nature of the illnesses afflicting the men who received aid. Nor do they delineate whether these illnesses were the result of wartime wounds or of diseases contracted during the war or whether the veteran needed help because he had become sick or injured after the war. This may reflect a Victorian reticence to discuss certain kinds of illnesses. It is likely that the members of the all-black Shaw Post knew what was wrong with Comrade Peek, to whom they allocated two dollars a week. It is also likely that black and white members of the Welch Post in Michigan knew under what circumstances Comrade Jacobs died or they would not have worked so hard to get his wife a pension.[11]

The existence of such widespread suffering suggests that relief or charity work may have been more important to the GAR than scholars have realized. We know that women had always been at the forefront of efforts to take care of wounded veterans; for example, women's benevolence groups established the first soldiers' homes for disabled veterans. The women of the Civil War generation—the former nurse who spoke of Tanner's worm-ridden bones, for example—would have viewed providing assistance to suffering veterans as their primary duty. WRC records emphasize the organization's efforts to aid widows and orphans, but given the gendered conventions of this era, women may have been more comfortable recording their work with women and children than documenting their assistance to male veterans. Would they have recorded in their public records how they cleaned a veteran who lay dying in his own feces, or how, when an aged soldier became incontinent, they washed his bedclothes? Had they recorded these efforts, we might be tempted to deprecate such activities because they reflected conventional notions of a woman's role in that era, forgetting that these sacred ablutions were the final payment owed these men for their service and sacrifice.[12]

Nineteenth-century Americans may have been unwilling to discuss soldiers' more embarrassing physical illnesses, but they were unable to treat soldiers' psychological issues. Actually, it is surprising that, given the limited understanding of mental illness, the commissioner of pensions recorded 5,320 pensions for nervous prostration and another 1,098 for insanity or other psychological illnesses. Some of these men may have suffered from post-traumatic stress disorder (PTSD), one of the most significant postwar ailments affecting American veterans today. No Civil War soldier was diagnosed with PTSD, of course, since the disorder was not identified until the twentieth century. But nineteenth-century doctors understood that veterans experienced mental anguish related to their wartime service even if they did not fully understand it. Grand Army men with some medical training tried to explain the effect of the war on their comrades' psyches. Horace Porter presented a paper to the Northern Kansas Medical Society on the debilitating effects of military service on veterans' minds. He argued that "the common nervous troubles of old soldiers are the legitimate *sequelae* [sequels] of the degradation of nerve structure that had its origin in the neurokinesis of battle, in the tiresome watches of sleepless nights, in exposures to thermal extremes in the ever-varying vicissitudes of climate," and the other manifold hardships of military life. Dr. Porter understood that military service had an effect on the mental stability of soldiers, and he and others struggled to root this debilitation in physiological causes. In New Jersey, the GAR medical director asked post surgeons to document cases of "'Nervous Asthenia' a debilitated condition of the nervous system." Veterans suffering from this disease, he explained, "complain of languor and lassitude, aching of the limbs, mental depression." Medical professionals today believe that nineteenth-century physicians used the term "Nervous Asthenia" to describe PTSD.[13]

Nineteenth-century doctors' conclusions have been supported by modern psychiatrists who studied the records of 17,700 veterans to identify the effect of wartime service on their postwar health. They agreed with their nineteenth-century counterparts that cardiac issues were manifestations of veterans' wartime experiences. Doctors diagnosed Civil War veterans with "Soldier's Heart" for the postwar anxiety and associated heart palpitations many soldiers experienced. In addition, modern scientists identified gastrointestinal or stomach illnesses and nervous disorders as by-products of wartime ordeals. Some of the 7,745 soldiers who received pensions for stomach aliments and the 25,994 for cardiac issues may have been suffering from PTSD. Undocumented psychological illnesses that left veterans unable to work and take care of themselves might have prompted the GAR to fight for need-based service pensions that did not require medical evidence of wartime illness or injury.[14]

Lucy Nichols's membership in the GAR and the struggle for her pension may have been due as much to her comrades' recognition of her postwar suffering as the memory of her wartime service. To justify her disability pension, the GAR acquired an affidavit from her physician describing her illnesses that left her unable to perform manual labor. Like so many veterans, she suffered from chronic diarrhea and rheumatism, consequences of veterans' service in unsanitary conditions and exposure to the cold and rain. Although Nichols's doctor did not use the term "Soldier's Heart" in his diagnosis, he noted that she suffered from "palpitations of [the] heart with fainting spells due to some valvular trouble in the heart." Her doctor may have assumed that the pension board had seen this description enough to understand that, like diarrhea and rheumatism, her cardiac problems had their origins in wartime service. In all American wars, nurses like Nichols may have suffered from Soldier's Heart, an accurate description of the mental agony inherent in giving your heart to sick and wounded soldiers.[15]

Some may doubt that these men and women suffered the same ills as modern soldiers. Dr. Jonathan Shay, a noted psychologist and PTSD expert who works with Vietnam veterans, has documented the universal nature of this disorder in two studies, *Achilles in Vietnam* and *Odysseus in America*. He identified PTSD in the demigods and mortals in the *Iliad* and the *Odyssey*— for example, in Achilles's response to the death of Patroclus—which echoed the experiences of the Vietnam veterans who had lost beloved comrades. If it is true that so long ago ancient poets understood the psychological toll of war, then we should listen more carefully to the somewhat inchoate musings of Civil War veterans and their efforts to describe the mental anguish of their generation.[16]

While Civil War veterans had little understanding of mental illness, they knew that some of their comrades had neurological problems associated with the war. James Tanner described this type of suffering: "In the years that have been since the war closed, the wounded soldier suffers not only by shot and shell, but, as the years roll on its effect upon the nervous system are felt more and more, and he is made to pass the night with groans and finds that the hours of the night do not bring him rest." John Mitler served in the Fourth Pennsylvania Cavalry and "considered the most important event in the line of his military service was being wounded and taken prisoner at Petersburg and that has caused him the most anxiety and trouble." Few veterans recorded the psychological effects of their experiences, though it can be assumed that Mitler was not alone in his postwar anguish. Members of the Welch Post of Ann Arbor encountered mental illness in one of their longtime members, Comrade Fred Markley. According to the post's meeting minutes, members "were somewhat reluctant [to speak] of his illness."This is likely because Markley's suffering was not related to more "honorable" battlefield wounds. Comrade Dean spoke to them and "kindly relieved this situation by giving the post the true version of Comrade Markley's indisposition." He described Comrade Markley as a "true blue soldier. The hardship he endured during his active soldier's life might have something to do with his mental balance." Comrade Markley, who had served for three years with the Fifth Michigan Cavalry, noted in his personal war sketch that he had never been wounded or sick during his service. Ironically, he decided that "the most important event in [his] military history" was "being discharged with a whole skin." While physically unharmed, he was scarred mentally by his service.[17]

It is no coincidence that Americans discovered postwar suffering in the aftermath of the Vietnam War and have been blind to the physical and mental anguish of northern Civil War veterans. If American wars were placed on a continuum, the Civil War—a war for a worthy cause that ended in victory—would be placed at one end of the spectrum and Vietnam—a war not seen by many as worthwhile that ended in defeat—would anchor the other. If a war is won or the cause is just, we seem to turn a blind eye to the price paid by its survivors. The only war comparable to the Civil War would be the "Good War," World War II. As was the case for Civil War veterans, veterans of this later war came home in silence to little public awareness of their physical or mental anguish. The nation lived secure in the belief that the GI bill alleviated postwar suffering—except, of course, for those with broken minds and bodies who did not go to college or buy homes.[18]

Comradeship binds former soldiers in any war, but we may never see a bond that was as wide or as deep as that between Civil War soldiers for several reasons. Civil War battles were particularly deadly: the combination of lethal rifled muskets and primitive military medicine made wounds and disease more likely to kill and more painful for survivors. Moreover, never again would such a large part of the U.S. population be mobilized and serve in combat units. Today, more soldiers supply the front lines than serve there. At the end of this supply line stands a well-fed, well-dressed soldier who did not march to war but instead rode there in a truck, tank, or plane. When wars end, a safety net of veterans' hospitals and pensions assists the soldiers and their survivors. We have become better, as one usually does with practice, at addressing soldiers' agony. Despite these advances, a hard word to use in regard to war, soldiers still suffer; in Iraq, improvised explosive devices have left thousands of troops suffering from amputations and traumatic brain injury. Veterans still sleep in the streets of American cities, and it is likely new generations of soldiers will fight and lose their final battle.

NOT SURPRISINGLY, members of the Civil War generation, who still suffered so much physical and mental anguish, were angry at their former enemies. The sheer level of vitriol against the Confederacy and its cause would surprise scholars who argue that Union soldiers embraced their former enemies at the expense of their former allies—slaves and slave soldiers. The following is just a small sample of Union soldiers' antireunionist sentiment. When members of the integrated Tod Post in Ohio objected to a Memorial Day unveiling of a monument for Confederate prisoners of war in Chicago, they explained that they entertained "no sentiment of bitterness" toward their former enemies; however, their description of Confederates as "those whose treason cost the lives of more than four hundred thousand of our gallant comrades; and caused more than a million of mothers, widows, and orphans to mourn their loved ones" suggests that they had not yet forgiven Confederates. A GAR official cited the popularity of Jeff Davis and how his "path was strewn with roses in Alabama." In contrast, he believed his path should "be strewn with the ghosts of skeletons of comrades pointing their bony fingers of infamy—of comrades who fell in battle a death of honor and a death of glory, who starved in prison pens, for which the damnable creature was the responsible party. Let these ghastly skeletons be even present in his sight, so that he may consider it a release to be taken from the land of roses, to a land where fire burns and is never quenched." An article in the *Grand Army Record* titled "A Romance of the Rebellion" bitterly satirized the sentimental romance novels that popularized sectional reunion. The story reminded its readers of how unromantic the war had been by describing the current condition of a veteran: "He has seventeen wounds in his body, four of which are in his left thigh and are now open and discharging. The left forearm and hand are numb and almost entirely useless; hearing of the left ear is gone and sight of the left eye [is] badly impaired." Those who saw little romance in rebellion rejected the romance of reunion.[19]

Some veterans embraced their former enemies and overcame their bitterness; however, they were not willing to do so if it meant forgetting the cause for which they suffered. A woman who spoke to the Illinois encampment rejected reconciliation because it demanded historical amnesia: "In these days when there is so much talk of peace, when there is this almost a maudlin sentiment for the defeated soldiers of the South, there is [a] . . . danger of the issues of the great conflict being blurred, almost obliterating the line between treason and loyalty. . . . There must be no peace, except that which comes through surrender and contrition for the great wrong attempted to this country." A West Virginian who embraced reunion wanted it clearly understood that he and his comrades "rejoice at the return of fraternal feelings, and . . . clasp hands with our ex-Rebel brethren even at our campfire and reunions . . . yet without debate we shall always demand recognition of the fact . . . that the war for the Union was eternally right and that the war for Secession was wrong, everlastingly wrong." Commander in Chief Russell Alger explained that socializing with former enemies did not constitute an endorsement of their cause: "You may go from one end of this country to another and . . . you will not find one disrespectful word uttered against the men who faced us on the field. While we meet with them socially, and compliment their gallantry, we never forget nor fail to teach our children's children that we were right and they were wrong." If these men knew that accepting Confederate soldiers as American heroes would cement the victory of the Lost Cause in Memory, they might have been less enthusiastic witnesses to southern courage. Regardless of their willingness to reconcile with their enemy, most GAR members had no tolerance for the notion that their cause was the moral equivalent of the Lost Cause.[20]

What did these men and women remember as their cause? When the GAR members and their associates dressed still-bleeding wounds, felt the phantom aches in their amputated legs, struggled with the pain and the indignity of chronic diarrhea, what would they have said made the agony worthwhile? We have already seen the comfort that these men took from their comradeship, but they also found solace in their cause. The Texas state commander understood that while "veterans were united by ties of comradeship of defeat, victory, death—by the sacred remembrances of toils, danger, battles, hungers, [and] thirst," these melancholy memories were balanced "by the more glorious remembrances of the great fact that the cause for which we sacrificed our youth was so completely triumphant." A chaplain in New Jersey made the same connection between the bonds of comradeship and the northern cause: "No ties are so strong as those that were 'welded in the fires of battle,' no earthly fellowship so sweet, as that which grows out of the memory of mutual suffering endured for a holy cause." Ironically, scholars are correct; Memory mattered. What white and black veterans' remembered as their cause was as important as their memory of their comradeship and explains interracial comradeship in the GAR.[21]

PART IV

The Won Cause: A Meaning for Their Suffering

11

Liberty and Union, Now and Forever,
One and Inseparable

What They Remembered They Won

Human beings need to find some type of meaning for their suffering. A careful reading of the musings of James Tanner, the "legless corporal," and his comrades demonstrates that they, more than most, needed to know that their sacrifices were made for a worthy cause. James Tanner's contemporaries considered him the most eloquent orator in the GAR; in this role, he advocated the Won Cause of the Civil War. Tanner argued that his cohort had fought not merely to preserve the Union and the old order but to create a new nation with freedom for all. Initially, Tanner admitted, "the cry, I remember in '61 was 'the Union restored with all the rights of the States conserved.'" Upon reflection, Tanner believed that since "it was legally right . . . to tear the wife from the arms of her husband and the babe from the breasts of the mother, and sell them, as you sell your hogs and your calves, and cattle at the auction mart," preserving the antebellum Union may not have been a worthy cause. Tanner explained to a group of Kansas teenagers that slavery made the prewar flag "a living lie," and it was only during "the course of the war we tore that lie out of its folds and . . . made it for the first time in its history, the flag of the free." Surprisingly, Tanner maintained that he was grateful for the initial failure of Federal forces. It was only when he and the army "got licked on that line . . . [that] pressed in upon the brain of our leaders among the people and we humbler persons" that they realized this contest would not end until they "ceased to defy the Divine power, . . . ceased to deny rights to a man, because God had seen fit to create some black and some white." Tanner reminisced with comrades in Ohio about the effect of emancipation on his morale: "Oh, then it was that our bosoms swelled with manly pride, when around our camp-fires at night and on our march by day,

★

we were thrilled by the grand *Battle Hymn of the Republic*—'Christ Died to Make Men Holy, while we died to make men free!'" James Tanner's status in the GAR—eventually commander in chief—suggests that his was not merely a voice in the wilderness.[1]

While northern veterans dealt with the physical and psychological aftermath of the war, they also dealt with a more spiritual crisis—finding something to redeem the sacrifice of their generation. Although northerners failed to articulate a Won Cause, at least not in so many words, they shared many common understandings of what they had fought for, what cause had been worthy of their generation's agony. Black and white veterans and their female associates had very similar understandings of what they had won with their shared sacrifice, though they diverged on what it meant in the decades after the war's end. The northern Civil War generation, or at least the segment represented by the GAR and its associates, believed that the dual cause of preserving the Union and ending slavery redeemed the sacrifice of their generation. Reinterpreting Daniel Webster's plea, "Liberty and Union, now and forever, one and inseparable," members of the GAR rejected the notion that the Union could or even should have been preserved with slavery intact. They believed that slavery undermined national unity and that only black freedom and the achievement of true liberty ensured a more perfect Union. While the rhetoric of American political culture shaped their political understanding of their cause, it was the Christian faith that most of these men and women shared that explained why they came up with a remarkably cohesive interpretation of the meaning of the Civil War. When they reflected on what they achieved, they echoed the Old Testament, asserting that, like the prophet Moses, they helped deliver four million human beings from slavery. When they contemplated the New Testament and its lessons, advocates of the Won Cause interpreted their blood sacrifice as redeeming a nation from the sin of slavery. Only such a divinely inspired cause was worthy of the suffering and sacrifice of their generation.[2]

Northerners born after the Civil War seem to have been less clear as to exactly what cause northern soldiers fought for and appeared more impressed by southerners' better-known, and more successful, Lost Cause. Having a name for the southern cause probably helped. While there never has been a formal appellation for its northern counterpart, Union soldiers, at least those who joined the GAR, appeared to have a definite idea of what they had fought for and won.

I coined the phrase "Won Cause," just as Edward A. Pollard coined the term "Lost Cause" in 1867 when he wrote *The Lost Cause: A New History of the War of the Confederates*. A brief review of the fundamental tenets of the southern Lost Cause may be needed to understand its northern counterpart. First, its supporters justified secession as a constitutional assertion of states' rights and rejected the notion that it constituted rebellion or treason. Second, the advocates of the Lost Cause denied that the breakaway occurred because of slavery. Finally, southern partisans argued that Confederate soldiers, led by preeminent leaders such as Robert E. Lee, prevailed in every battle until they were overwhelmed by sheer numbers. Implicit in their argument was the notion that such heroic deeds could only have been inspired by a noble cause, which did not include destroying a nation to establish a slave republic. Not surprisingly, Won Cause advocates disagreed and remembered the war and its causes and courses differently.

GAR members fought attempts by Lost Cause advocates to advance their version of Civil War history, particularly in school textbooks. The historian of the Kentucky GAR objected to the "systematic effort . . . being made by the United Confederate Veterans through their historical society, which is quite an important adjunct of their organization, to get written a new and fictitious history of the war and its causes, incidents and results." The aim of this society was to "glorify the cause of secession and to throw about the War of the Rebellion, on its southern side, a glamour of romance that they fondly hope will obscure in the minds of the generation now coming on stage of action the fact that the war fought forty years ago was at the time uncalled for, unnecessary, and useless and that the vast destruction of life and property and human misery entailed thereby, could and doubtless would have been avoided but for the firing on Sumter in April, 1861." Lost Cause advocates' efforts to define Civil War Memory incensed veterans because of the importance of this battle. A Missouri official explained that "all educators agree that impressions received in the school room on the youthful mind are the most lasting and the most difficult to efface." New Jersey officials monitored school texts to ensure that such "histories are used as properly reflect the spirit of truth and loyalty and justly record the deeds of the men who followed Grant, Sherman, and Sheridan in the great struggle for Unity and Liberty." Pleas against "False School History" as a "Lost Cause of Historical Truth" headlined an article protesting school texts in a Massachusetts GAR newspaper and, ironically, prophesied the Lost Cause's victory when advocates of the Won Cause lost a battle, though not the war, for Civil War Memory.[3]

Northern veterans directed much of their wrath at school texts that adopted a neutral stance, refusing to comment on the morality of the Confederate cause. The Indiana GAR complained that in one text there was "an entire absence of any statement therein, indicating which side was right and which wrong in the greatest conflict." These Hoosiers wanted the text revised "to indicate clearly that our comrades, living and dead . . . were in the performance of their highest patriotic duty, and that those who fought against them were in the wrong." Missourians also demanded a moral judgment: "The Grand Army is not willing that their children be taught in public schools, or elsewhere, *even by inference*, that the cause of the Union, for which we fought, and which cause we believed then and believe now, with an intensity that cannot be uttered, *was not right*." Union army veterans rejected neutrality in school texts since they assessed the struggle that had consumed many in their generation as both victorious and morally right. If these men objected to what these books said, what would they want them to say? What did they believe was the southern cause?[4]

Grand Army men repeatedly invoked the idea that the rebels seceded from the Union to protect slavery. Kansans wanted school histories to teach that "the rebellion inaugurated by Davis and his companions was wholly without cause and was a crime in every possessive sense. The election of Abraham Lincoln served as the pretext. . . . Separation had long been held in contemplation. Slavery was the direct and inviting cause." At a New York encampment, veterans cited a textbook that, in their view, accurately explained the cause of the war: "Why did the Southern States secede? To be fair to them we must seek the answers in the speeches of their leaders. Your voter, said Jefferson Davis, refused to recognize our domestic institution [slavery] which preexisted the formation of our Union—our property [in slaves] which was guaranteed by the Constitution." Massachusetts officials wanted textbooks to characterize "the attempt of the Southern Slave holders and their sympathizers to destroy the Union" as "treason and rebellion, and moreover that it was a crime against humanity." Why did the war rise to the level of a crime against all mankind? Bay State veterans maintained that the war was "between the advancing civilization of the nineteenth century and the barbarism of the middle ages, as represented by Negro slavery." Union veterans wanted schoolchildren to understand that the Civil War was caused by slavery.[5]

Veterans argued that slavery caused the war and that their victory saved the Union and freed the slaves. In the District of Columbia, veterans explained the "Truth of History" and their role in the war: "The Boys in Blue saved the Union established by our fathers, and in doing this freed a race." Massachusetts veterans described exactly what school texts should say about the Civil War: "The war between 1861 and 1865 was a rebellion; that it settled for all time that secession was treason and would not be permitted; that it destroyed slavery; that it showed the strength of the Republic; that it proved that there was not air enough on the continent to float two different flags."

Northerners had been accused of forgetting emancipation as critical to the causes and consequences of the Civil War. Did GAR members only remember a war against slavery in public battles against their old enemies? What did they say to one another, outside of these public debates over textbooks, about what they remembered they fought for? What was the Won Cause of the Civil War?[6]

Some GAR members believed they had fought a war for preserving the Union rather than one that freed the slaves, but it was the rarity of this belief that made it noteworthy. A GAR official addressing a reunion of the Army of West Virginia in Ohio maintained, "[We] can go back twenty years and look into the cause that created the grand army of Union, and you will remember that it was called into being alone for the preservation of our nation." African Americans agreed that U.S. forces wanted to preserve the Union with slavery intact. Black veteran and historian George Washington Williams argued: "The South was determined to retain the Negro in bondage, while the North was willing she should do so. The North did not care to soil its spotless hands in the slave traffic; did not care to be partaker in the sins of the South; but from the heart she endorsed the terrible crime, and by her laws and armed forces drove the fugitive back to the hell of slavery. . . . The North declared her intention of maintaining the 'Union' at any cost. On her escutcheon was written in burning letters '*The Union as it is.*'" The New York state commander agreed, explicitly rejecting the idea that northern soldiers fought for liberty: "While our fathers have fought to create a government which should be forever dedicated to liberty, we fought to preserve and continue the same government as handed down to us as a rich heritage by these forefathers." A New Jersey official made no mention of liberty at all, maintaining that he and his comrades fought because they loved the "flag and the Union . . . [and] resolved that it [the flag] and the Union should and must be preserved."[7]

When GAR members discussed their desire to preserve the Union and the status quo, most of them were usually explaining why they enlisted at the beginning of the war. Even James Tanner understood that northern soldiers were initially motivated by preserving the Union. "Who of us at first supposed we were going out to free the slaves?" he asked. "We went out to fight for the reestablishment of the old order of things." William McKinley, future president and popular GAR speaker, explained to Ohio veterans, "There was not a comrade who went from Ohio that didn't believe that the purpose was to save the Union as it was, with the Constitution as it was, with slavery . . . undisturbed. . . . That was the horizon of human vision; that was the chalk line of human purpose and yet the result overleaped the resolution; for you never can stop the results of revolutions in advance." This generation recognized that the initial impulse to preserve the status quo transformed into a revolutionary effort that redefined the meaning of freedom.[8]

African Americans understood this evolution and argued that military necessity was the cradle of revolution; the federal government needed to replace dead white soldiers with living black soldiers. Initially, northerners refused to consider arming African Americans. Rev. Solomon Hood, a black GAR member, recalled the congressional debate over recruiting black soldiers. Hood argued that Congress understood that if African Americans served in the army that slaves "must be freed, and this was one of the great objections [to black enlistment], for most of the men in Congress at the time wanted it clearly understood that the war was not waged for the freeing of the slave, but for the restoration of the Union." Another minister explained in a Memorial Day speech why northern officials changed their minds: "In 1862 [black recruits] were not wanted, but when the struggle became more desperate there came a time when the government was ready to taking anybody who would fight." In an address to the Bell Post, George Washington Williams cited the bloody failure of Federal forces in the early years of the war as the reason for northerners' changed attitude: "From Bull Run to Gettysburg our Army met with signal defeat. Her ranks were thinned by the enemy's bullets, and wasted under a Southern sun, while victory perched upon the enemy's banner. A hundred thousand Northern sons perished, . . . Columbia was weak from loss of blood, and her war-eagles wearily flapped their wings in the blood-damped dust of the nation." Williams contended that it was only military necessity produced by these military failures that led to emancipation. "It was not that the country had come to see the wrong of slavery," he argued. "It was not that the country was willing to loose the yoke of bondage which had galled the Negroes neck, but, it was that emancipation was *an absolute necessity*. It was the advent of the Negro soldier that brought victory to our national arms."[9]

Some white GAR members agreed that military failure led to emancipation. The GAR chaplain in New York gave thanks for "the early defeats of Bull Run, Ball Bluff and Little Bethel." It was only because of these defeats that the war became a war of emancipation and the tide of battle turned, "and then Mobile and Charleston fell, and Savannah, and then Sherman went like a winged eagle to the sea, and Grant thundered on to Richmond, and Sheridan swept the Shenandoah like the beacon of destruction, and Appomattox and Five Forks brought a close to our strife." A former chaplain in a Maine regiment told an Ohio GAR post that in the beginning of the war his comrades went out for the flag and the government but "in both logic and fact the Government [meant] bondage, and the flag [meant] slavery." With a level of cynicism that many would not tolerate today, he explained, "Our armies were beaten back. Panic shouted the word, disaster followed. . . . Brave men died gallantly but without any positive and significant purpose to seal their blood." However, after the Emancipation Proclamation, "The sword was grasped by the idea with a heart in it. It was the 'Sword of the Lord and Gideon,' . . . and the victory was won." In Delaware, a loyal slave state, a GAR official admitted that at the outbreak of the war "an effort was made to overthrow the rebellion without any attempt to wipe out slavery. . . . As long as the government of the United States attempted to do this it met with reverses and defeat on the battlefield." As soon as "Lincoln issued his Emancipation Proclamation," however, "victory perched upon the banners of Federal troops and victory after victory was achieved." The initial failure of the U.S. armies in the eastern theater were not, therefore, attributable to either southern heroism and military proficiency or northern cowardice and incompetence. Rather, these setbacks represented the will of God—an interpretation that was likely embraced by more than a few members of the Army of the Potomac.[10]

Perhaps it is not surprising that veterans from the Midwest and South, where Union armies experienced initial military successes, cited another reason for the transformation of the Federal cause: slavery divided the Union, and only slavery's end could ensure its survival. Mrs. Clark, president of the Ohio WRC, maintained that "with the evil of servitude there was discontent. It was not peace. The question of its existence hung in the balance, and finally we were launched into a great conflict, and the great Ohio River, upon whose banks we are now encamped, was the dividing line of this great struggle of the North and the South." Tennessee state commander Newton Hacker recognized the same fundamental schism in the prewar Union: "Two antagonistic ideas found a foothold on the American continent. The Mayflower landed at Plymouth Rock, and a Dutch vessel landed near the mouth of the James River. The first carried a cargo of men and women who were seeking a refuge from religious persecutions of the old world, the other carried a cargo of African slaves." A chaplain in Illinois also described the arrival of these ships in America. These two ships, he explained, carried two ideas, "slavery and freedom." From this small beginning, the chaplain asserted, came "two nearly equally balanced systems, between which grew up an irrepressible conflict, settled only by the march of the millions of men, the light of burning cities, and the tears of brothers, mothers, wives and orphans." Men and women associated with the GAR argued that since slavery represented the root of this struggle, only its end settled this conflict.[11]

While recognizing that defeating slavery was key to saving the Union, members of the GAR and their associates went even further, and arguing that slavery "blotted" the prewar Union. The Massachusetts commander in 1915, John M. Wood, looked back fifty years to what had been accomplished at Appomattox. "The Union was restored," he explained, but not as it was. "Human slavery, the foulest blot and greatest curse in our national life, has been forever removed." An LGAR official in Indiana maintained, "The conditions that existed which caused our Civil War will remain a black blot upon our nation forever, but what comfort, gratification and relief to know that you men rose in one mighty body, a solid phalanx as it were, to set aright and make recompense for that terrible evil." A nonveteran welcoming the GAR men to their encampment, the Honorable R. F. Downs, reminded them, "You fought for a principle; you fought for freedom; you fought to remove the one black spot that remained on American institutions; for the abolition of human slavery; for the freedom of all mankind in this our country." The notion that the prewar Union needed to be cleansed of slavery in order to survive was not a view held by merely a handful of aged veterans.[12]

Advocates for the northern cause invoked the image of a national flag stained by slavery. In 1901, Commander in Chief Leo Rassieur asserted that the Federal victory "made it possible to keep the flag stainless . . . as it is today as it was not in '61 in the South where human beings were held in bondage." Rassieur's belief that slavery stained the flag flying in the South was unusual; most GAR commentators indicted the flag, wherever it waved. Ohio's WRC president described how slavery debased this banner. The flag that had "fostered, protected, and defended human slavery from the foundation of the government came out of that struggle . . . cleansed and baptized in the blood of 300,000 patriots . . . not a slave to gaze upon its folds and mock the flag that says 'you are free.'" The Massachusetts chaplain argued that on Memorial Day comrades plant "above their sleeping dust . . . the loved colors under which we marched together, and the ensign of a country they died to save. . . . The last foul stain upon [the flag] has been removed by the combined valor of the volunteer armies of which they were a part. Through their sacrifice it is the flag of the free." A prominent nonveteran repeated this argument. Mayor John Fitzgerald of Boston greeted the GAR in Boston twenty-nine years later and contended that these men "went out to fight for the black man, in order that there might no longer be the stain of slavery upon the flag." Both men, from two different generations, agreed that only emancipation cleansed the American flag.[13]

According to some GAR men and women, the blame for this stain rested upon the shoulders of the founding fathers. A GAR official explained to the

1904 Massachusetts encampment that they fought "to bring completeness to the great temple of freedom, whose foundations were somewhat imperfectly laid by our fathers." Thirty years earlier, a veteran, identified only as Captain Brumm, maintained that Union soldiers sacrificed their lives to ensure that "the theories inculcated by our forefathers put into practice by immortal Lincoln" would succeed. Brumm defined the result of these men's sacrifice: "three millions of slaves were liberated and clothed in the panoply of freedom." At a New York 1882 Memorial Day commemoration, the speaker denounced the founding fathers: "Let us be truthful; all of our fathers were not true to themselves. . . . They were not great enough to appreciate the grandeur of the principles for which they fought. They ceased to regard the great truths as having universal application. 'Liberty for all' included only themselves. They qualified the Declaration. They interpolated the word 'white,' they obliterated the word all." The chaplain who described the postemancipation army as the "Sword of the Lord" commented similarly: "The Declaration of Independence, by the concession of the fathers, ignored the fact of human slavery." The mistake, he maintained, was "remedied at last, and now, but at what cost." Had the founding fathers addressed slavery, "their children would not have had to correct the mistake with their blood and their lives."[14]

Other GAR members and their associates argued that their victory in the war fulfilled the founding fathers' vision. The war not only "saved, though at great cost, our national unity," according to one Pennsylvania veteran; it also "fulfilled the promise of the Declaration of Independence making the land in fact as well as name, the land of the free." Rhode Island's state commander also linked the end of slavery to the realization of this document's promises: "I rejoice with you . . . that the privilege was ours to make freedom a fact, the Declaration of Independence a truth, slavery a thing of the past." Black Americans agreed. Mrs. William Scott, an African American orator, spoke for many advocates of the northern cause when she declared to the New York GAR that the "Boys in Blue, who marched to battle determined that only one flag should float over this land, and that the land should be free, and that the part of the Declaration of Independence which says that all men are free and equal shall have its full meaning."[15]

The black and white members of the GAR and their female associates did not believe that the war was either for Union or for freedom but felt the two causes were inextricably linked. Mary Tapley of the Illinois LGAR advised the GAR state meeting, "Hold in grateful remembrance all the glories of that terrible conflict which made all men free and retained every star on the flag." A WRC official told another GAR meeting in Illinois, "We all know the glorious work you did in the early sixties, of the trials and hardships you endured to accomplish the work of blotting the curse of slavery from our land and preserving the Union and this glorious flag." An Illinois state commander argued that the Grand Army "was grand in its results. It saved the Union, it freed the slave." Mrs. Wall of the LGAR told the Kansas men that they represented "the grand invincible army who preserved the unity of this republic and freed a race from the chains of slavery." The Arkansas state commander attacked the Lost Cause and articulated the dual nature of its counterpart: "If the orators of the Lost Cause are to be believed, the time may come when the living may have to beg pardon for the part our dead comrades took in that terrible war for national existence and human freedom." Comrade O'Neall asked his comrades in Ohio, "Dare we not look history in the face, aye, challenge the generations yet unborn to gaze upon the record we writ of the pages of that country's history, in the morning of our lives?" What did he believe future generations would see? "We look at the close of our efforts, and then we see a rebellion conquered, a country welded together, a race freed, a flag purified."[16]

Across decades, into the next century, and through new wars, members of the GAR and their associates demonstrated a remarkable consistency in their belief in the Won Cause. Less than twenty years after Appomattox, a Decoration Day speaker in New York declared, "For the preservation of this Nation, for the destruction of slavery, these soldiers, these sailors, on land and sea, disheartened by no defeat, discouraged by no obstacle, appalled by no danger, neither paused nor swerved, until a stainless flag, without a rival, floated over all our wide domain, and until every human being beneath its folds was absolutely free." His remarks were met with "thunders of applause." Orlando Summers, a commander in chief of the GAR, voiced similar sentiments thirty-six years later at the 1918 national encampment, held in the shadow of the war to end all wars: "In the book of the Grand Army of the Republic will be the eloquent story of 'A REPUBLIC SAVED AND A RACE REDEEMED FROM BONDAGE.'"[17]

African Americans, naturally, remembered the war that freed their race, but they also valued their role as defenders of the national Union. The Reverend Charles Dickerson spoke at the all-black Tucker Post in Newark's annual celebration of the Fifteenth Amendment. He maintained that African Americans "fought for a chance to save the Union. We urged our way to the field of battle amid showers of stones flung by the hands of prejudice." George Washington Williams's Memorial Day address to the Bell Post connected the maintenance of the Union to African American freedom: "And it will ever be the glory of the colored people of this country that they unlocked their own prison-house; that they saved the '*Union*' and that they purchased their citizenship, with all its immunities; that they tore down the walls of the slave institution; that they built a new government upon the broken shackles of four and one-half million of slaves. This is the Negroe's place in history;—his own deliverer; the defender of the Union." The commander of an all-black New York post explained in the *Age*'s GAR column why graves must be decorated on Memorial Day: The dead must be honored as a "token of our love and patriotism for our country, and again to pledge allegiance to the old flag and the preservation of our Union." Like so many of his generation, this black veteran tied the preservation of the Union to emancipation when he expressed his hope that "future generations [would] be inspired by these acts and ever remain true to the loyal teachings of the land, where treason is dead and where no traitor dare show his head, where the liberty of one is the liberty of all." Advocates of the northern cause, black and white, shared an understanding that slavery made the national Union untenable; therefore, emancipation and national preservation were inextricably linked.[18]

GAR members frequently invoked the terms "Liberty and Union" as a way of summarizing their cause. The Massachusetts state chaplain contended that he and others "served faithfully in the cause of Liberty and Union." A loyal Tennessee veteran concurred: "The Grand Army stood for Liberty and Union during the dark days of the Rebellion." A Pennsylvanian declared, "The proudest boast of our prosperity will be that their fathers' lives stood in the vortex of war and fought for Liberty and Union." Mrs. Sanders, a WRC member, agreed. She thanked Illinois veterans for their "fidelity that gives us 'Liberty and Union,' one and indivisible." One of the most eloquent orators in the GAR, Commander in Chief John Black, spoke to veterans in Lincoln's home state and described northern volunteers as "the citizen soldiery," and "the purpose for which they fought, 'Liberty and Union,' then and now, and forever, one and inseparable."[19]

Rutherford B. Hayes revealed the origin of this expression, a speech made by Daniel Webster invoking "Liberty and Union, One and Inseparable" thirty-one years before the attack on Sumter. Hayes, former president and a member of an integrated post, asserted that "every schoolboy almost knows the closing words by heart" of this "the grandest speech ever made on the American continent." In this speech, Webster argued against nullification advocates who believed that South Carolina's right to void tariffs was more important than national unity. Webster's passionate denunciation of this view included a plea to the heavens: "When my eyes shall be turned to behold, for the last time, the sun in heaven, may I not see him shining on the broken and dishonored fragments of a once glorious Union; on States dissevered, discordant, belligerent; on a land rent with civil feuds, or drenched, it may be, in fraternal blood!" Or would his "last feeble and lingering glance rather behold the gorgeous ensign of the republic, now known and honored throughout the earth, still full high advanced, its arms and trophies streaming in their original lustre, not a stripe erased or polluted, nor a single Star obscured . . . everywhere, spread all over in characters of living light, blazing on all its ample folds, as they float over the sea and over the land, and in every wind under the whole heavens, that other sentiment, dear to every true American heart—Liberty and Union, now and forever, one and inseparable!" Webster died in 1852 and thus never lived to see this apocalyptic vision become a reality. The Civil War generation, however, lived to see a shattered Union caused by the incompatibility of Liberty and Union in a slave republic.[20]

Hayes did not reject Webster's sentiment but rather reinterpreted Webster's remarks given the experience of his generation. Hayes asked his fellow GAR members, "[Has it] ever occurred to you when Webster said 'When my eyes shall turn and behold for the last time, the sun in heaven, may I not see him shining on the broken and dishonored fragments of a glorious union; on states dissevered, discordant, belligerent; on a land rent with civil feuds or drenched in fraternal blood,'" that this was "a prayer, an aspiration that he might not suffer shame and disgrace?" Hayes answered his own question: Webster's prayers had been answered "by your victory in the war." According to the transcript of this speech, this comment was greeted with applause. Hayes continued, "We can all say, each one for himself: 'When my eyes shall be turned to behold for the last time, the sun shining in heaven, I shall not see him shining on the broken and dismembered fragments of a once glorious nation. I shall not see upon the flag any such miserable sentiment as this: Liberty first and Union afterwards; but I shall see written all over in letters of living light, on its ample folds, as they float over the sea and over the land, and in wind under the whole heavens, those other words dear to every American heart, Liberty and Union now and forever one and inseparable!'" Prolonged and enthusiastic applause greeted these remarks. The cheering veterans believed that Webster's plea for a permanent Union was achieved only with the end of slavery.[21]

GAR members and their female associates often appeared to have derived the most satisfaction, and even joy, from their part in the liberation of enslaved African Americans. A WRC official in Illinois believed that reminding Americans that the Civil War had been about slavery represented an important task for this group. "It would remain so," she argued, "as long as time shall last, . . . so long as the W.R.C. be in existence [it will] tell the old story of our redemption from slavery and how it was our glorious country remained the 'Land of the free and the home of the brave.'" The Massachusetts GAR issued a general order for 1894 Memorial Day declaring that veterans commemorate this day to honor "our comrades [who] made the air 'too pure for a slave to breathe' and broke the shackles from the limbs of more than three millions of human beings." Another veteran explained to Ohioans that American emancipation was "the greatest act of modern civilization in freeing over four millions of people who for nearly 100 years had been slaves." The New York state commander remembered the end of the war, "when peace was declared, when with torn and shattered flags, weary limbs, yet happy hearts, these old soldiers came back to you, covered with the glory of a victory won in a holy cause. Four hundred thousand [*sic*] slaves set free, the Union restored[,] the flag saved." The latter speaker may have erred when he tabulated the number of slaves set free, and the former may have gotten wrong the number of years slavery had prospered in the New World, but they, like other members of the GAR, derived enormous satisfaction from their role in freeing the slaves.[22]

Much of the GAR circles' pleasure in emancipation derived from their view that their service in a war to end slavery not only saved the Union but was also part of God's plan to destroy the peculiar institution. As Mrs. Florence Baker, president of the national WRC, put it, "The war of the rebellion, which has no parallel, was undoubtedly part of God's fixed plan from the beginning, and America the ordained tablet on which our Maker, just and wisely, ciphers out the problems of history and humanity!" Rev. Solomon Hood, a black GAR post commander, agreed: "We have said that the Negro was neither wanted nor trusted, and it was only from almost absolute necessity and then with great doubt that the Negro was armed. God, the eternal, forced it upon this nation, as he did emancipation." William McKinley, comrade, governor, and soon to be president, maintained that initially veterans had enlisted "to save the old Union as it was. But God would not have it so." The speech transcript notes the applause prompted by this remark. "From Him who is sovereign of soul and limb came our ordeal of battle," McKinley asserted, "that he might be God, and that man might be free." Again, his comments were met with "great applause." The intense religiosity of these men and women prompted them to interpret their experience in light of their faith.[23]

Given their religious beliefs, it is not surprising that some members of the northern Civil War generation construed the war as God's punishment for the sin of slavery. According to a Kansas chaplain, "God had directed our forefathers to this godly land," but America did not stay in God's good graces when "we began to oppress our fellow beings." As a consequence, God "didst lay the rod of correction upon us until we proclaimed liberty throughout the land to all the people." Similarly, the chief mustering officer of this state recited a poem that described the graves of veterans "as silent witness, as the years passed by . . . of a nation's wrong, And How, when sore depressed by wrath divine, That Nation made its bondsmen free." Not surprisingly, African Americans agreed that God punished the nation for enslaving their race. George Washington Williams explained that Memorial Day reminded "the nation how great its sin was, and how large a price it had to pay in precious life and golden treasure to cancel that sin." African Americans recused themselves from much of the discussion of the war as a punishment since their race was the sinned against and not the sinner.[24]

Many GAR men and their women affiliates spoke of American slavery and Americans' experiences during the war in biblical terms. They often invoked the story of Moses and his chosen people because it was a familiar one and seemed an apt analogy. Just as Egyptians lost their firstborn male children, many white Americans lost sons as soldiers in the Civil War. Commander in Chief Washington Gardiner compared the plagues on the pharaoh to wartime suffering: "Not until . . . the one [child] lay dead in thousands of households, not until the wail of sorrow went up from the northland and the southland, not until the habiliment of woe darkened the homes and shadowed the streets of the North and South alike did the people rise up to the great Lincoln, 'Let them Go.'" In Pennsylvania, a comrade who was also a minister maintained, "Throughout all our Southland we had humanity in the bonds of slavery and under cruel taskmasters, but like the children of Israel bound under old Pharaoh they multiplied until their numbers became legion, and God in his own due time raised up for these people in the Southland a leader, just as he had in the olden time, a leader for the Children of Israel, and . . . they attained their freedom."

Some veterans and their associates compared wartime losses to sacrificial offerings placed upon an altar, just as Abraham had offered to sacrifice his son Isaac. A comrade addressing the Ohio GAR described the group as "that grand organization who in the dark days of the country's need, laid all upon its altar, in order that 'government of the people, by the people and for the people should not perish from the earth.'" The Tennessee state commander argued that GAR veterans should not weep for the dead because "their blood was a libation upon the altar of human liberty and national unity." An LGAR official in Illinois likewise maintained that her cohorts should "drop a tear on the grave of those who cemented, by blood that poured out like rain on the Altar of Freedom and forever annulled the fatal fallacy that this land could remain part slave and part free, disunited and dismembered."[25]

A comrade in Ohio recalled that in his "youth, though not the son of a prophet, but claiming to be a prophet, I said that the stupendous crime of slavery could only be atoned by blood." Pennsylvanians heard a former state official describe their wartime exertions: "Every manly heart was laid upon the altar of country, and . . . they were ready to shed the last drop of blood in their veins to win the victory." As a result of this offering, he concluded, "this nation of ours shall be forever free, for God hath ordained it so out of the sacrifice that was poured out on this sacred soil." Attendees at a Massachusetts campfire heard Commander in Chief Torrance describe their organization as "a small remnant of the once glorious and triumphant host . . . whose bayonets and swords blazed a path of freedom around the globe, whose blood washed out the last stain upon the flag." Twenty-four years earlier, another GAR official, the Massachusetts state commander, was "grateful to God that in the agonizing hour of the great motherland, I was permitted to humbly share your baptism of fire and shed my blood on the same triumphant side of human rights with you." The commander lost an arm during the war.[26]

In the same way that the men and women of the GAR circle used the phrase "Liberty and Union" to describe what their cause achieved for human beings, they used lyrics from the "Battle Hymn of the Republic" to explain what they accomplished in the name of God. A former national president of the WRC contended that "from the time the Union forces were driven back at Bull Run until beneath the apple blossoms at Appomattox, you could hear the glory hallelujah of the Union soldiers who cried, 'As he died to make men holy, let us die to make men free.'" In 1903, Thomas Stewart, the commander in chief of the GAR, asserted, "We stand at the portals of a new century, and [look] over that just closed, the most important probably of all time." He believed the nineteenth century was so critical because during this period, "the problem of human liberty" was solved. How was it solved? "[By] the great union army and navy, thousands of whom have died to make men free, as Christ died to make them holy." Forty-seven years after the war ended, another commander in chief used similar language: "Now that peace is secured, and men are free and the Republic survives, you and I and all the great citizenship of the Republic can change the last verse of that magnificent hymn and read it: . . . As He lived to make men holy, let us live to keep men free! While God is marching on." The resonance of this hymn demonstrated that the Memory of a war for freedom gave members of this generation tremendous solace as they remembered their losses.[27]

The religious imagery the GAR and its associates often used to describe their cause reflected the Christian faith of black and white Americans of this era and evinced their need to find solace for a generation's anguish. These men and women described the full range of wartime suffering that occurred in battle, on the march, in hospital and prison, or on the home front, but they always then spoke of the cause that they deemed worthy of their sacrifice. At the national encampment, Henry Castle, the Minnesota state commander, detailed the suffering of northern soldiers and their accomplishments: "They died amid the battle clangor of five hundred crimson fields; they died in the hospitals where nerves were highways for steps of fever scorching feet; they died in dismal prison pens unshorn, unsheltered, hungering, thirsty, desolate, despairing; they died four hundred thousand of them died, in the dewy efflorescence of a beauteous youth, that the slave might be unshackled, freedom apotheosized, the nation saved." In his Memorial Day address to a black post in West Chester, Pennsylvania, W. H. Banks argued that "it was to save the stars and stripes from dishonor and the Union from destruction that caused thousands of our comrades to fill unknown graves in the ever-glades of the South." However, Banks added, these men were also "martyrs to principles as comprehensive as the universe. It was the idea of American nationality, universal freedom and equality before the law that impelled and inspired them in that bloody conflict." Reminiscent of Oliver Wendell Holmes's famous description of the Civil War generation as one that was "touched by fire," the GAR's chaplain in chief explained to a Connecticut encampment that GAR members had suffered in "a hell so hot that it melted and welded our hearts together." But their time in hell did more than make them comrades; it also "wiped out the curse of slavery from our land, and set all men free, so that our flag was no more a lie, but it was really the flag of freedom." This juxtaposition of suffering and its justification was so ubiquitous among black and white members of the GAR circle that it became the most consistent characteristic of the Won Cause.[28]

More directly, these men and women queried, in one form or another, "Why did we suffer?" and their responses leave little doubt about the association they made between their sacrifice and their cause. Comrade Winship of Cleveland asked his fellow veterans, "For what did these men fight; for what did these men die?" He specifically rejected the notion that preserving the Union was a sufficient cause for these men's suffering. "Was it simply that they might maintain the geographical integrity of this country for the few years they might live? Could you have not lived here in the Western Reserve [Cleveland area] the years you had to stay, even if the country had been dismembered?" Rather, he concluded, it was for "the cause of human liberty throughout the world that these comrades died." Speaking to Missourians, the senior vice-commander in chief reflected on the "sufferings of the great army that saved this Union." He asked his comrades, "Did it pay us to sacrifice the immense number of lives? Did it pay us to suffer in every conceivable manner?" When he answered, he did so "in the name of four million colored men from whom the shackles of bondage were struck." In their name and in the name of the war dead and the grief-stricken survivors, he exclaimed, "Yes, yes, we did right."[29]

Comrade Gibson of Ohio embraced the cause of black freedom as a salve that helped alleviate the pain of wartime losses. Gibson, like so many others, left his wife and children at home when he went to war. He recalled how he mounted his horse to leave for his unit: "[My] little boy three years old came running across the yard, and when I leaped to my saddle, in his coaxing way, he said 'Papa, I want to kiss you again.'" "When I was in camp in Kentucky," Gibson continued, "and the telegraph news came that little boy was cold in death—died in the arms of his mother, and I was in the army, my country's army." Soon, another son was gone, "racked and transformed by disease—[I] just got to him in time to hear him say with his dying breath, 'Meet me on that beautiful river.'" After relating these tragedies, he asked, "Why is it we sacrificed?" He answered: "Great God, when Sumter's guns were heard one-eighth of the people under the flag were bought and sold— flesh, blood, wives, children—sacred souls, that were brought by the same blood on Calvary that bought your pardon and mine." Gibson cited the fifth verse of the "Battle Hymn of the Republic": "In the beauty of the lilies Christ was born across the sea . . . and as he died to make men holy let us die to make men free." Gibson concluded, "And we made them free, and today we are all free."[30]

While Howe's famous hymn resonated among Union supporters, perhaps the words of Abraham Lincoln, this generation's most eloquent spokesman, best articulated the connection between suffering and slavery. Lincoln's second inaugural, best known for its expression of hope for a future with "malice toward none and charity toward all," included a concise and eloquent meditation on the causes and consequences of the war. Lincoln pondered the irony of such a religious nation embroiled in Civil War, both sides praying for victory: "It may seem strange that any should ask a just God's assistance in wringing the bread from the sweat of other men's faces." The soon-to-be-martyred president did not, however, argue that the war was a punishment to the South. Rather, Lincoln maintained that the war represented divine retribution directed toward the entire nation for the "offence" of slavery: "If we suppose that American slavery is one of those offences which . . . He now wills to remove, and that He gives to both the North and the South, this terrible war, as the woe due to those by whom the offence came, shall we discern therein any departure from those divine attributes which the believers in a living God always ascribe to Him?" Lincoln accepted God's judgment.

"If God wills that it [the war] continue, until all the wealth piled by the bond-mans two hundred and fifty years of unrequited toil shall be sunk, and until every drop of blood drawn with the lash, shall be paid by another drawn with the sword, as was said three thousand years ago, so it must still be said 'the judgments of the Lord are true and righteous altogether.'" The GAR and its associates carried the message of Lincoln's second inaugural address, his last political testament, into the next century.[31]

African American veterans and their associates differed from their white counterparts in one significant way: they wanted freedom to mean more than just the end of slavery. The African American men and women of the GAR shared what David Blight described as "the emancipationist vision, embodied in African Americans' complex remembrance of their own freedom, in the politics of radical Reconstruction, and in conceptions of the war as the re-invention of the republic and the liberation of blacks to citizenship and Constitutional equality." James Wolff used his bully pulpit as head of the Massachusetts GAR to advise his comrades against extending "the hand of friendship and fraternity to those on the other side" because of "the hundreds of thousands of men of darker hue [who in the South] have no rights, loyal men who wore the blue." He demanded that southerners "respect American citizenship regardless of religion, race or color." When the national president of the WRC presented the American flag to the all-black Sumner High School in Kansas, the African American principal, J. E. Patterson, recalled the "over 180,000 [that] bled upon the battle-fields of the late war in order that this banner might float to-day, not over this institution only, but over the entire race—the entire race of Negroes of this country—guaranteeing to them [the] right of liberty, the rights of every citizen in this country." Professor William H. Day, who exhorted the all-black George F. Smith Post to fight the battle for Civil War Memory alongside black women, would have agreed with Patterson, but he went one step further, reminding his audience that "theory, is all very well, but it is for the members of the Grand Army of the Republic to make it practical before the world." But what did making this practical mean to black veterans like Gibson and white veterans like Tanner? If white veterans and their associates believed that the northern Civil War generation redeemed the nation from the sin of slavery with their own blood, how could they abandon black Americans to the southern solution to the race problem: Jim Crow and disenfranchisement?[32]

12

The Won Cause at Century's End

Malvina Shanklin Harlan observed the frustration her husband, Supreme Court justice John Harlan, experienced as he attempted to write his dissent to the majority opinion that struck down the Civil Rights Act of 1873. "His dissent," according to his wife, "cost him several months of absorbing labour, his interest and anxiety often disturbing his sleep." Mrs. Harlan reported that he had "reached a stage when his thoughts refused to flow easily. He seemed to be in a quagmire of logic, precedent, and law." In a desperate attempt to alleviate her husband's frustration, and demonstrating a modern understanding of the importance of Memory, Malvina replaced Harlan's inkwell with one that had been used by his predecessor Chief Justice Roger B. Taney. "The memory of the historic part that Taney's inkstand had played in the *Dred Scott* decision, in temporarily tightening the shackles of slavery upon the Negro race in the ante-bellum days," Malvina wrote in her memoir, "seemed that morning to act like magic in clarifying my husband's thoughts . . . and his pen flew on that day and, with the running start he then got, he soon finished his dissent." The memory of slavery prompted Justice Harlan to defend black civil rights nearly two decades after Appomattox.[1]

This would not be the first or last time the "Great Dissenter" was at odds with the majority of his colleagues. However, Harlan is better known today for his lone opposition to the *Plessy v. Ferguson* decision, which stood for decades as the legal basis for Jim Crow and de jure segregation. In this dissent, Harlan demonstrated racial attitudes typical of his time and his origins; before the war he had been a slave owner. He argued that "the white race deems itself to be the dominant race in this country. And so it is, in prestige, in achievements, in education, in wealth and in power. So, I doubt not that it will continue to be for all time." Despite these views, Harlan rejected the majority opinion that enshrined the separate-but-equal doctrine. Just as his memory of the *Dred Scott* case informed his earlier dissent, his memory of

★

the Civil War shaped his response to this case. If segregation statutes were to be upheld, he contended, "citizens of the black race in Louisiana, many of whom, perhaps, risked their lives for the preservation of the Union . . . who are not excluded, by law or reason of their race, from public stations of any kind, and who have all the legal rights that belong to white citizens, [will] be declared criminals, liable to imprisonment, if they ride in a public coach occupied by citizens of the white race." Since Justice Harlan, the sole northern veteran on the court, was the only dissenter, his actions failed to stop this pivotal ruling, which would define race relations in the United States for almost sixty years.[2]

Harlan's generation has been indicted for forgetting their cause and their comrades because at the turn of the century the United States rolled back the civil rights gains made by African Americans since emancipation. David Blight identifies distinct, but interrelated, phenomena connecting Civil War Memory with the status of black Americans. First, he links reunionism, the reconciliation of northerners and southerners, with the triumph of white supremacy in the South. Second, Blight contends that northerners, including former soldiers, forgot that the war had ended race-based slavery; he sees this surrender in the battle for Memory as a condition of national reunion. Finally, he argues that this amnesia was critical to northern acquiescence to Jim Crow, disenfranchisement, and lynching. Blight implies a relationship between Memory and action: remembering emancipation and rejecting reunionism would have prompted Americans to fight southerners' attacks on black civil rights. However, most GAR members and their associates were reluctant reunionists who rejected the notion that forgiving their enemies meant forgetting their cause. Moreover, it is clear that they understood the central role of slavery and emancipation in the causes and consequences of the Civil War. How, then, did the GAR, a politically powerful interracial organization, figure into the calamity that befell African Americans at the end of the nineteenth century and the beginning of the twentieth? The answer to this question explains one of the great quandaries at the heart of the American experience in the twentieth century: how could a nation so dedicated to advancing freedom overseas be so blind to the need for freedom at home?[3]

The Grand Army of the Republic rejected reunionism and remembered slavery, but neither their personal memories nor their collective Memory prompted these men to protect African American rights at the turn of the century. African Americans' efforts to use northern Civil War Memory often succeeded within the GAR; however, blacks often failed in their attempt to use the Won Cause to advance their own civil rights outside the GAR. As has been the case for so many generations of white Americans, racism shaped the GAR's response to contemporary issues involving black Americans, particularly those who were not veterans. Racism, however, did not cause veterans to forget emancipation. Rather, these men and their associates believed that the victory of Liberty and Union represented another necessary milestone on the road to fulfilling American national destiny—becoming a "city on the hill" for the whole world to emulate. Only a united nation of free men could be a model of freedom to the rest of the world, in a way that a nation that had slavery could not. Further, only a united nation could, when necessary, spread freedom by force of arms, as northerners and southerners had done during the Spanish-American War. The men and women of the GAR circle demonstrated a prescient understanding that they had lived to see the dawn of the American Century, in which the United States became the most powerful nation in the world committed to the defense and expansion of freedom. Most would have seen this development as the ultimate affirmation of the northern cause and an outcome worthy of their suffering and their sacrifice. The status of African Americans would have been as irrelevant to these men and women as it would be to generations of Americans who lived through wars fought to make the world safe for democracy, or for the four freedoms, while denying basic democracy and freedom to African Americans at home.

Benedict Anderson's theory on nationalism and the nation as an "imagined community" may help explain this ideological disconnect. He argues that the community "is *imagined* because the members of even the smallest nation will never know most of their fellow-members, meet them, or even hear of them, yet in the minds of each lives the images of their communion." I may not know anyone in North Dakota, for example, but North Dakotans and I share a bond of national identity. Anderson contends that shared nationality does not make individuals equals. The nation is "imagined as a *community*, because, regardless of the actual inequality and exploitation that may prevail in each, [it] is always conceived as a deep horizontal comradeship." White veterans embraced black veterans as comrades but were not concerned with their equality because members of an imagined community need not be equals. In addition, African American veterans were referred to as "Colored Comrades," indicating that race mattered even among men who shared the bonds of comradeship. Finally, Anderson ties the imagined community of the nation to its wartime experiences: "It is this fraternity that makes it possible, over the past two centuries, for so many millions of people, not so much to kill, as willingly to die for such limited imaginings." Irrespective of their limited nature, these imaginings are powerful. Civil War veterans found solace in their Won Cause of comradeship and nation—composed of free but not necessarily equal Americans—an imagined community worthy of their suffering and sacrifice.[4]

White veterans made a direct connection between their Won Cause and the status of African Americans within the imagined community of comradeship. Clay Hall, a senior New York official, declared that the GAR "excludes no man from comradeship by reason of rank, of color, or of sect." He then told his black colleagues to "look around upon this gathering and see here and there the face of one of that race which for so many years was held in bondage under our boasted government of freedom. They are our comrades and our brothers." The brotherhood of the GAR was based both on veterans' personal memory and on their collective Memory of black service and slavery.[5]

Black veterans hoped that they could use the Won Cause and the Memory of slavery to inspire white veterans to defend African American rights outside the GAR. When Comrade Little, the commander of the all-black Garrison Post in New York City, was nominated for state office in the GAR, the speaker described him as "a little dark horse. He is a first class soldier, through him this department can recognize the race to which by your act you gave liberty." But Little wanted more than just recognition for his race; he wanted the GAR to act to protect black citizenship. He submitted a resolution to the New York GAR in 1890 demanding that it condemn a Senate bill, proposed by Senator Butler of South Carolina, to sponsor African American emigration from the United States. Little asked these men to remember "that in the army which conquered American independence, as well as the Army that saved the Union were soldiers of the colored as well as the white race, fighting side by side to make this nation a living fact; and that [the nation's] blessings and privileges, should, therefore be enjoyed by both races, and all schemes to expatriate the colored people should be heartily condemned as unjust, ungenerous, and un-American." The committee on resolutions recommended that no action be taken on the matter.[6]

Usually, the disapproval of the committee signaled the failure of a resolution, but Comrade Little and several white veterans would not let this measure die. Addressing the state meeting, Little exhorted, "Remember, comrades, that it is you that have made it possible for me to be here upon this platform as your political equal, and I thank you for that blessed privilege." Little made his "appeal for 186,000 colored troops who bore arms in some 281 battles for the Union and who lost 37,000 men in the field." Little invoked a familiar refrain to these men when he asked, "Must their bones molder in vain?" The transcript recorded the audience's reply: "no, no." He then reminded the men of their cause and of the "4,000,000 of our people you helped to liberate." He asked these men to "adopt this resolution . . . and show these people down South that they can not banish us from the country we have fought for." The crowd responded to the concept of banishing these men with the cries of "no, no." At the end of his appeal, the encampment applauded Little.[7]

Other comrades joined the debate. Another member invoked veterans' duty to their comrades: "The bill . . . implies the expatriation of members of the Grand Army of the Republic, and it is incumbent on us to notice it." Another comrade tied his opposition to this measure to his memory of what he fought for: "I, as an Irishman, protest against any such action. . . . For three long years I fought to free these men, and if necessary I will fight again to free them." Comrade Tanner, the legless corporal, asked, "To whom have the colored people a better right to look for protection than to the Grand Army of the Republic?" According to the black-owned *New York Age*, the resolution was "unanimously adopted as the expression of the encampment, and is a magnificent tribute to the justice, equality and manhood existing in the G.A.R."[8]

As Comrade Little and his comrades hoped, some state organizations seemed willing to protest particularly egregious attacks on black Americans. Minnesotans, for example, were willing to make a stand against racially motivated violence. In a resolution offered by an integrated post in that state, members expressed their "inexpressible horror [at] the recent cowardly attack upon, and the brutal murder of, the postmaster of Lake City, South Carolina, the fiendishness of which acts were made still even more inhuman by the shootings of the other members of the family and the killing of his helpless babe in his mother's arms." The family was slain "for no other cause than that these victims had black skins and the father had been commissioned by the nation as its postmaster at that place." Post members also noted, however, that the leading South Carolina newspaper offered a substantial reward for information about the killings. They cited this as "encouraging evidence of a better sentiment for the rights of human beings without regard to race" and expressed their "faith that such newspapers voice the demands of the brave men of the South who opposed the veterans of Grand Army of the Republic on the field of battle." These men may have placed too much faith in the goodwill of their former adversaries. Another Minnesotan, J. Adam Bede, denounced the brutal murder of a black American in a northern state. He described an incident in which "eight thousand people stood upon the streets of Leavenworth in Kansas, with a Federal Army but a few miles away in a fort, and the police force of the city in their hands and witnessed the burning at the stake of a Negro, unconvicted of a crime." "When you [are] doing that in the Northern states," Bede concluded, "the race problem is not yet solved even in this great Republic."[9]

Most of the time, however, protests against extralegal violence appeared to require that the person relating the attacks describe them as interracial. Illinoisans, who in 1904 denounced lynching and "the frequent accounts of the hanging, shooting, burning of offenders, and supposed offenders of the law, white and black, by mobs throughout our beloved land . . . [r]esolved, that we most earnestly protest against the continuance of these inhumane practices and found them as the acts of enemies of our governments and against the laws of God and humanity and alien to all that stands for the highest type of American citizenship." Veterans approved the resolution. Kansas protested the Ku Klux Klan because "in many of the states of this Union, loyal citizens, thousands in number, many of them ex-union soldiers had been scourged and our comrades assassinated by that traitorous and cowardly organization." A comrade protesting this violence demanded that the GAR proclaim that the Ku Klux Klan "cannot murder our comrades, no matter whether they be white, or black, Democrat, Republican, Prohibitionist, or Union Labor without our denunciation of [its] foul deeds." If the GAR failed to act, he added, "all of the four years of suffering and death were a sham and a delusion." Veterans emphasized that these were attacks on black and white Americans, but their strategy worked: Kansans passed this resolution by an almost unanimous vote. While this debate demonstrates the GAR's willingness to protest the Klan's actions, it also delineates some limits to their outrage. They acted when comrades were attacked regardless of their color, but they did not state their policy on victims who were not veterans. By implication, it is likely the Klan could victimize Americans who were not comrades without fear of the GAR's condemnation.[10]

State organizations sometimes refused to pass resolutions to protest violence. The Kentucky GAR, for example, refused to go on record against lynching. A brief summary of what was likely a very lengthy debate appears in the records of Kentucky's 1899 meeting. Comrade G. W. Ward of Post 189 offered a resolution "condemning the recent lynching of citizens of Georgia." After the committee on resolutions rejected this proposal, a debate occurred on the floor. Unfortunately, the encampment transcript contains only terse summaries of the speakers' main points. A number of comrades agreed with A. J. Thorp, who opposed the resolution because, in his mind, "the question was political." A Kansan made the same point when opposing a resolution against Klan violence in this free state. "Political" in these instances might refer to the Republican Party's historical, but often ineffective, commitment to black civil rights. Another comrade in the Kentucky debate rejected charges of partisanship, arguing that "it was the duty of this body to condemn lynch law, whether the victim was white or black." Once more, a veteran portrayed criminal acts as affecting both races, likely understanding that this might help his case. Ultimately, however, the resolution failed, and Kentucky did not go on record opposing lynching.[11]

Kentucky was not alone in its failure to support African American rights; other GAR departments refused to challenge discrimination against black Americans. Comrade McKie, commander of an all-black post in New York City, appealed to the state encampment to help African Americans obtain civil service jobs under the state's veterans' preference policy. According to McKie, "In the two departments of the city of New York, known as the police and fire department, there has been seemingly a barrier thrown in the way of colored veterans, deterring them from presenting themselves for examination on account of color." He asked the New York GAR to ensure that "any man who is a citizen, who served in the army or navy and was honorably discharged, shall not be prohibited from being examined for the position of policemen or firemen if he be colored." There was no debate on this issue; it was merely recorded that the committee on resolutions made no report on this proposal. It may have been easier to take a stand against colonization overseas, as the GAR did a year later at Comrade Little's prompting, than employment discrimination at home.[12]

Interracial comradeship was not always a useful weapon to fight the kind of racial prejudice that kept black New Yorkers out of the police and fire departments since most African Americans were not veterans. Most white veterans did not believe that military service by some African Americans translated into a higher status for all African Americans. A black veteran had proven his manhood and, according to nineteenth-century gendered norms, deserved a measure of equality among other men. As a Memorial Day speaker in New York explained, "In ancient time the monarch of the realm smote with his sword his supplicant subject, and he rose a knight. Americans, following her ancient custom on a mighty scale, reached out her hand and with a blood-stained sword smote thrice her kneeling blacks, and they rose up knighted with everlasting manhood." In white veterans' minds, African Americans who had not served did not deserve the same recognition. When a city in southwest Missouri wanted to host the state meeting, GAR members demonstrated how accepting those who had served did not mean they had changed their racial attitudes toward those who had not. Local veterans assured the state encampment that they had "as much love for the old colored soldiers as they have in any other section of the State. We have a good many colored people among us and they are treated properly, and I can assure the colored comrades that they will be treated just as well as though they were white comrades." When the Massachusetts GAR considered holding its next encampment in Boston, the group decided to do so "provided the hotels would take in colored comrades." The GAR was aware that Boston hotels maintained a color line; however, segregation was only an issue if it affected black veterans and not when it applied to nonveterans.[13]

The GAR debates discussed so far were exceptional; most GAR departments took little note of racial issues. In previous chapters, much of the focus is on what the GAR said and did; in this case, what the GAR failed to say and do is the most salient point. Instances in which white veterans objected to racial discrimination were rare. Virtually all the discussions of racial issues that I found in my research have been explored in this chapter or in previous sections. The Memory of a war fought to free black Americans only rarely prompted these men to action, and generally they were only willing to challenge egregious attacks on black rights such as banishment or lynching. And even then, a resolution denouncing the violence required assurances that the violence was interracial. Even when veterans protested attacks on civil rights, their objections usually took the form of internal resolutions with about as much weight outside the GAR as the paper on which they were written. Finally, white veterans never challenged the more routine but onerous manifestations of racial discrimination. For most northern veterans, segregation and other civil rights violations were not pressing issues. African Americans hoped the Civil War would help them with their struggles; clearly, it did not, since Memory did not translate into action from the one group that so clearly remembered the price paid for African American freedom. To paraphrase Corporal Tanner: "Whom could the colored people ask for protection if not the GAR?" The answer was no one, not even the GAR.[14]

Ultimately, most white veterans and their nonveteran contemporaries shared the same racial views. They were ordinary Americans who had lived in extraordinary times and were called to uncommon sacrifice; they had no special education, no unusual experience outside that moment—aside from the occasional GAR meeting—that might allow them to transcend contemporary racial mores. Even on the encampment floor, in the same venues where they so passionately extolled the sacrifices they made for black Americans, white veterans demonstrated that they were, indeed, men of their times. In his annual address to the Arkansas GAR, the department commander reported that he had "visited colored as well as white posts and succeeded in establishing in many instances a better feeling between the races," indicating that racial problems existed in posts in this state. But his comment also demonstrates that the state's senior leadership believed that racial discrimination required their attention. What we do not know is whether the commander's concern about the racial attitude of veterans extended beyond the boundaries of the GAR post room. A New York official, on the other hand, had a more laissez-faire attitude toward racial discrimination within the GAR. When Comrade Little, who had successfully appealed for the condemnation of black emigration, complained "of the treatment that two comrades of his color had received at the hands of some Post of the Grand Army who had denied them admission merely on account of their color," the newly elected state commander replied that he "hoped no such act would occur during his administration" and "hoped the matter would be reported to the Commander of the Post, and he knew the Commander would see that it was corrected." If the GAR felt uncomfortable acting against race-based exclusion within its own ranks, it is unlikely it would be willing to fight racial discrimination outside its ranks.[15]

Since some GAR members refused to welcome blacks into their posts, it is not surprising that some white veterans resented African Americans when they asserted their political rights on the encampment floor. A former New Jersey department commander, commenting on the fact that an African American nominated a white comrade for office, explained, "We are tainted to a greater or lesser extent with a prejudice that has not been removed in this generation." He seemed somewhat embarrassed by this admission since he "had the honor of marching at the head of a colored regiment." In his annual address, Levant Dodge, Kentucky department commander, appealed to his "white comrades, who have chafed at the presence of the colored soldiers in our department." He exclaimed that "no nobler specimens of the manhood which is dear in the sight of God can be found than are present in large numbers among the dark-skinned comrades of Kentucky." At the same time, however, Dodge, president of integrated Berea College, member of an integrated post, and self-described "champion of the colored people," warned black veterans against too vigorous an assertion of their political rights. According to Dodge, since former commanders would always be able to vote, African American posts elected new commanders more frequently than white posts in order to increase their political power in the encampment. Doing so may have increased their voting power, Dodge argued, but this "course is a leading factor in creating whatever prejudice or hostility exists." Despite Dodge's assertion, it is unlikely that this was the principal cause of racial prejudice in this former slave state.[16]

Given that white veterans in this state chafed at the presence of their dark-skinned comrades, it is not surprising that a General Order for the annual state meeting explicitly endorsed segregation in 1913. Black veterans were assured that at the encampment in Barboursville, "the colored visitors will be amply cared for by the colored people of the place. We are thoroughly assured of that." A list of the quarters to which various black and white posts were assigned for the national encampment in Louisville describes groups of posts as colored, something that GAR records almost never did. Accompanying the list was the mandate that "if by mistake any white posts are in these number they should report the fact immediately to these headquarters, that a change can be made." The GAR in Kentucky enforced its own brand of Jim Crow in a state with de jure and de facto segregation.[17]

White veterans in northern states understood that there were racial issues in American political life. In 1890, a committee of Allegheny County, Pennsylvania, veterans, which may have included representatives from the Shaw Post, asked the state GAR to protest "the ex-Confederates who since the war have regained their citizenship in the United States, and at this late date [are] raising the question of the race problem." The resolution did not ask the Pennsylvania GAR to do anything except object to "any such question being raised [in] America [since] . . . the race question was once and forever settled at Appomattox, in Virginia, in 1865." In their minds, the end of slavery had solved the race problem. When James Wolff, the African American Massachusetts department commander, completed his term of office in 1906, James Tanner was commander in chief of the GAR. In a speech to Massachusetts veterans celebrating Wolff's tenure, Tanner acknowledged black progress since emancipation, noting "that the colored race has occasion to congratulate itself since Abraham Lincoln struck the shackles from their feet that they have climbed so high as they have and it is my amazement that they have risen to their present height." "If there were more James H. Wolf[f]s and Booker Washingtons in this nation," Tanner continued, "the great race problem would be solved by the character and the integrity of such men." Tanner, who had so clearly articulated the GAR's Won Cause, clearly placed the blame for the "race problem" squarely on the shoulders of African Americans.[18]

Even if Tanner and his cohort assessed contemporary racial issues through the prism of Civil War Memory, it may not have changed their views because GAR members did not always see slavery as a racial issue. Speaking to an Ohio meeting, the newly elected state commander argued that "slavery was only an incident; the flag was only an emblem. The Union itself and the Constitution were of no importance as compared with the necessity of at once and forever putting down the doctrine that, in this country, an oligarchy should rule; that one man should be the master and the great mass of men should be slaves." He contended that racial slavery was only about race in so far as it was based on the inferiority of African Americans. "The negro was a serf simply because they took advantage of his ignorance and of his super-stition and the prejudice against his color, and made him a slave. But they proposed to make a slave of every man who was compelled to work for a living. It was the plantation order; it was not the farmer. It was the oligarchy which the South proposed to build up on this continent." Slavery was not a racial issue; it was a class issue. Rutherford B. Hayes, the former president and a member of a mixed-race post, asked his fellow Ohioans at the annual meeting, "What did we gain by the war?" He answered: "The war taught us that when the public conscience of the people of the United States is aroused on any great question it will settle it. Laboring men need have no fear. The war has proved that the United States will permit them to suffer no injustice because they are poor." A Kentuckian described the Lost Cause strictly in terms of social class: "The cause that was lost in the War of the Rebellion was the cause of Aristocracy against the Common People—the cause of Human Slavery and Barbarism." Emancipation was a blow not against racial injustice but against economic injustice.[19]

To northerners who came of age in the Civil War, the triumph of free labor over slavery did not require social and political equality for black Americans. Eric Foner has demonstrated the compatibility of racism and free-labor ide-ology. Antebellum white northerners believed in the superiority of free labor over slave labor and the inferiority of the men and women who labored as slaves. Abraham Lincoln articulated this view in his first debate with Senator Douglas when he argued that while he had no desire "to introduce political and social equality between the white and black races," he maintained that African Americans deserved the right "to eat the bread, without the leave of anyone else, which his own hand earns, [and in this] he is my equal and the equal of Judge Douglas, and the equal of every living man."[20]

Three decades after this famous debate, veterans described posteman-cipation equality in similar terms. "Today," a Kansan argued, "there are no masters and there are no slaves under the sheltering fold of the flag, but all men in this great government are free to eat the bread of honest toil with an equal chance in the race of life, unvexed by the lash of the master or the brutality of the overseer." Commander in Chief Ivan Walker made a similar allusion in a speech to the 1896 Massachusetts encampment. He defined lib-erty as "the right of a man to compete for his livelihood wherever he may. It means the freedom of the individual to control and use the products of his hand and brain. It means free speech, or a free press and a free and unfet-tered conscience." A year later, Commander in Chief T. S. Clarkson argued that because of Bay State men's efforts, they had a "united country where all are free and equal, where all have equal opportunities, where a field of honest effort is open to all and the very humblest may obtain high position." Given that these latter two speeches were made after the Supreme Court decided *Plessy v. Ferguson*, white veterans did not see the failure to guard black civil rights as a critical indicator of the status of American freedom in the aftermath of emancipation. The triumph of free labor and an African American's right to eat the bread earned by his or her own efforts was sufficient, even if he or she could not eat that bread in the same train car as a white person or vote for a politician who promised him or her more bread to eat.[21]

The remarks of the ubiquitous James Tanner, who spoke to an Ohio encampment the same year the Supreme Court decided *Plessy*, summarize the viewpoint of white veterans, and indeed his generation, who did not see the relationship between the end of racial slavery and the existence of racial equality: "And out of it all there was brought back from that awful sacrifice a flag triumphant, a nation redeemed, a race freed, a stain wiped out." However, he also argued that race and racism were unrelated to the importance of American emancipation. "All of you may pronounce the word 'nigger'; you may spell it with two 'gs' and you may put all the scorn in the expression you can, but whether at home or abroad, the form of an American citizen stands straighter and holds his head higher as we walk on earth, because we have relieved ourselves of the reproach foreigners were so wont to give us that our flag was a living lie; that it was not the flag of freemen, but only the flag of free white men." Finally, the fundamental compatibility of accepting racial inequality and remembering emancipation suggests that amnesia about slavery does not explain the dismal state of African American rights at the turn of the century. In a society that embraced race-based slavery for centuries, race and racism were independent variables with no necessary dependence on the triumph of any particular Civil War Memory. The true "Lost Cause" may have been racial justice.[22]

Like Tanner, white northern veterans assessed the enduring significance of emancipation not by considering the status of African Americans within the United States but rather by looking outside national boundaries. The American war against the fading Spanish empire became the first major overseas event that GAR members viewed through the prism of Civil War Memory. Veterans invoked their Won Cause, Liberty and Union, freedom and national unity, when interpreting the meaning of the Spanish-American War. A comrade welcoming the Indiana encampment to the small Hoosier town of Warsaw directly associated the national unity exhibited during the Spanish-American War to emancipation: "Through your heroism and valor this nation is to-day a united nation, as proved by the unanimity of action in the Spanish-American War. Because you swept from this fair land slavery and made it not only free in name but in fact." The Illinois department commander contended that the 1898 war was a "blessing, for it has obliterated any sectional feeling between the North and the South." He argued that the Spanish-American War indicated that southerners accepted both Union and Liberty. "The Blue and the Gray are ready to go together singing '. . . as He died to make men holy let me die to make men free.'" The Spanish-American War—the first war of a new century—began an era in which an emancipationist vision writ large would triumph in foreign affairs, even if it had no effect on domestic policy.[23]

While GAR members proclaimed their pride in the U.S. victory in the Spanish-American War, they also believed that this was part of a much larger development: the emergence of the United States as a world power that, either by example or by the power of its new status as an imperial republic, would spread freedom throughout the world. In 1888, an Ohioan saw a "glorious future" for the United States that he and his comrades would not live to see. He described the current thirty-eight-star flag of the United States and how "in the lifetime of a child who now lives . . . these stars shall be swollen to fifty, when 100 senators gathered from the golden sand of Sacramento shall sit down with senators coming from Plymouth Rock." He had lofty ambitions for these fifty states. "The islands of the sea shall be called from darkness by the brightness of our example and the dark continents of earth shall hear the glad tidings of Christian Civilization and . . . freedom . . . [will] spread to the uttermost parts of the earth by the potency of the example of my country." While being a model was sufficient for some, other veterans went further, arguing that, when necessary, the United States should spread freedom by force of arms. A Kansan declared that his generation fought to ensure "that the constitution of these states might be saved from the stain of human slavery—a perpetual shield for human rights and orderly liberty everywhere under the sun; and that this republic should be an immortal asylum for the oppressed of all lands and an enduring example to all subsequent generations." This veteran saw the United States as both a model and a global shield for freedom, implying that military force may be needed, as it had been when his generation ended slavery. It is noteworthy that he saw no conflict between the United States as an asylum for the oppressed of other lands and but not for those oppressed in his: black Americans.[24]

Overseas expansion and the emergence of the United States as an imperial power also shaped the evolution of the Won Cause rhetoric and the views of its advocates. In 1899, an Iowan maintained that "since Appomattox, we have gone on and expanded. We have been lifted up from the valley of isolation and placed upon the very highest plane upon the nations of the world. And we stand today, second to no nation that ever existed. Our flag and our freedom that follows it, the right of suffrage, of home, of liberty, of equal rights before the law has been planted upon the fertile soil of the islands of the sea and there it will remain." The islands of the sea can only mean Cuba and the Philippine Islands. The Kansas department commander foreshadowed future American conflicts when he argued that the soldiers of 1898 have an even "greater mission, . . . to say that no government on earth is strong enough to starve and murder its citizens in the Western Hemisphere, while old Glory waves over Uncle Sam's domains to say in thunderous tones that over whatever land our flag waves, at the cost of American blood, there shall ever remain and the people of the land shall be free." Echoing these sentiments, the Massachusetts department commander described with great satisfaction how the Spanish-American War had "shed new luster on our arms, vastly enlarged the boundaries of human liberty, and although it has brought us face to face with new and untried problems, has gained for our country a new title to respect as the friend of all weaker peoples and the proudest and most powerful nation on earth." This official looked forward to that "glorious day when our flag shall wave—the symbol of law and order, of justice and love—above the free hearts and homes of an imperial republic on whose dominions no sun shall set." [25]

Veterans and their associates took great solace from the United States' status as a world power because this development, a direct outcome of the victory of the Won Cause, redeemed the tragedy that shattered their generation. As the Tennessee state commander argued, "It was the blood of our comrades that paid the price and cemented our states into one indivisible Union, breaking the shackles of slavery and giving universal liberty. The Union formed in the blood of our fathers, cemented and solidified in our blood, we hand down to our descendants." The United States these men bequeathed to their posterity was, according to this Tennessean, "one of the first powers in the world. It stands as one of the foremost in the advance of civilization, the part we took in our struggle has had much to do with this." Charles Partridge, an Illinois official, argued that his comrades "with undaunted heroism . . . performed the arduous duties of military life, and their sacrifice not only made citizens of slaves but maintained the unity of a Republic that to-day is a world power." Florence Newlin of the LGAR agreed: "The world knows and it should never forget that by the valor of those who perished where heroism saluted death, in the name of liberty and humanity, and by virtue of you who survived the storms, this benign republic was redeemed to become the brightest day star in the firmament of nations." While she detailed the economic and social progress of the United States, she emphasized freedom and "the greatest of all, freedom and equality of the human soul, made possible by your sacrifices and heroism."[26]

It would be difficult to imagine these men and women forgetting slavery since they viewed emancipation as central to their understanding of what made their generation's sacrifices worthwhile. It is equally unlikely that members of the northern Civil War generation would have embraced the idea that the status of black Americans somehow degraded their achievement. Had they done so, they would have been saying that all their sacrifice and suffering was meaningless. So, instead, these men and women embraced the status of the United States as an imperial republic as their ultimate triumph, one that was only made possible by their sacrifices in the war. Only northern victory, the creation of a united nation of freemen, allowed the United States to stand as a symbol of liberty and, when necessary, to spread liberty using the military power of a united nation. In the decades after the Civil War, the United States would spread liberty to a number of nations and act as a shield for human rights while denying freedom and these same rights to black Americans at home. The failure to see the fundamental contradiction between these two seemingly antithetical actions mirrors the compatibility of racism and emancipation in northern Civil War Memory.

Every generation must answer for its particular failures; however, the GAR should not be blamed because the Lost Cause has, for most of the twentieth century, defeated the Won Cause, at least in Memory. The men and the women in the GAR never believed that they would lose the battle for Memory. The Massachusetts department commander assured his comrades, "The trophies of the Union soldier are the Union saved, slavery abolished, the constitution purified, and constitutional liberty preserved for the world. Everything that you . . . contended for was completely and honorably obtained, and such will be the final verdict of impartial history." The mayor of St. Paul, Minnesota, a comrade, agreed: "Cynics or weaklings may doubt, sensational or foreign prejudice may deride, but history cannot forget you nor tarnish the luster of your deeds. They are engraved upon the imperishable tablets of memory of a country redeemed of a race of bondsmen enfranchised." Responsibility for the triumph of the Lost Cause in the battle for Civil War Memory should not be laid at the feet of the men who vigorously contested this interpretation of the war and clearly articulated that they had fought and died for black freedom. We have to explain to these veterans something that may be obvious in our more jaded and cynical times: that history is not impartial, nor is Memory imperishable.[27]

13

A Story of a Slaveholding Society that
Became a Servant of Freedom

The Won Cause in the Twentieth Century

One warm, sunny morning in Elgin, Illinois, the local veterans' posts commemorated Memorial Day by gathering near the soldiers' plot in the local cemetery. A young African American boy read the Gettysburg Address. The strength and power of his rendition impressed the audience. According to the local newspaper, he "captured the power imbued in the speech." A black veteran named Floyd Brown delivered the main speech of the day. Brown used this speech to claim American citizenship. "[I am] a father, husband, neighbor, and veteran," he declared, "[but] . . . most of all I'm an American, which is what makes Memorial Day so important." When "Taps" was played at the end of the service, an elderly white veteran struggled to his feet for a final salute to fallen comrades. An African American woman from a veterans' auxiliary organization rushed to his side and held him up by his elbow. Later, she gently eased him back into his seat. Beneath crumbling government-issued tombstones two men of the local GAR post, a veteran of the Thirteenth USCT and a member of the Fifth Pennsylvania Cavalry, bore silent witnesses to this ceremony.[1]

Had these men been alive on this day, they would have found this ceremony both similar and different from those they had attended in the past. The role of African Americans would not have been unusual; however, the main speaker did not belong to the Colored Troops. Rather, he had served in the first modern war fought by an integrated American military, the Korean War. Memorial Day services on May 30, 2000, were commanded by a woman veteran, representing the newest members of the honored dead in the wars of the twentieth and twenty-first centuries. While black Americans also fought in these wars, it was only a victory at home — the civil rights victories of the

★

second half of the twentieth century—that allowed Brown to claim his place in the imagined community of our nation and say, without irony or qualification, "I am an American."[2]

An American living at the beginning of the era of Jim Crow could not have imagined its end less than seven decades later. As the Civil War generation passed into Memory, most white Americans seemed satisfied with the southern solution to the race problem. Scholars have argued that accepting Jim Crow required amnesia about slavery and emancipation and that this Memory loss served the interest of national reunion and reconciliation. However, white Americans did not forget slavery; they remembered a romanticized version of it, and they seemed comfortable with this institution. Reunion and reconciliation required amnesia, but not about race and slavery. If any aspect of the war needed to be forgotten, it was secession and disunion. Had they not minimized the threat of the South's actions to the survival of the American nation, northerners could not have reframed the Confederate military experience as an example of American valor and patriotism. The mythology that defined our imagined community could include heroic slave owners in a hopeless cause, but not soldiers intent on destroying the very real community of the American Union. Ironically, the Won Cause lost to the Lost Cause in Memory because the southern version of Civil War Memory was more useful for the United States as an emerging world power with increasing military responsibilities, a development that was such a source of pride for GAR members and their associates. As the decades passed, and the United States fought so many wars for freedom, the Lost Cause version of the Civil War tightened its grip on American Memory. Wars require national unity, and the myth of the Lost Cause seems more inspirational than the forgotten Won Cause. Meanwhile, black Americans realized that Civil War Memory was of little use in their contemporary freedom struggles decades after Appomattox. Instead of focusing on shaping Civil War Memory, black Americans emphasized the service of contemporary African American soldiers. In the first seven decades of the twentieth century, African Americans used their participation in the same wars that reinforced white Americans' embrace of the Lost Cause to create a second front in order to achieve their long-cherished hope: equality for black Americans at home. Ultimately, after a war in which black men like Floyd Brown fought at white men's sides, the Supreme Court's *Brown v. Board of Education* decision overturned *Plessy*, signaling the beginning of the end of the Jim Crow era.

The dawn of the twentieth century was the twilight of the Civil War generation. Delaware veterans memorialized three of their junior vice-commanders, all former commanders of the all-black Sumner Post in Wilmington. Pennsylvanians recognized the passing of its two black members by giving them an unusual honor: the state records included eulogies for these men, a privilege almost always reserved for senior officials. Edward Harris was "at the time of his death . . . in his seventh consecutive year [Post 27] commander. As a comrade and a citizen, he was respected by all with whom he came in contact." Samuel Jones of another Philadelphia post was described as "the embodiment of the genial, affable comrade; as a soldier and a citizen his record was unimpeachable. His example was one that will be ever cherished." When James Wolff of Massachusetts died in 1913, the fiftieth anniversary of both Gettysburg and Fort Wagner, he was memorialized as "a loyal comrade . . . held in high esteem by all his comrades." Two years later, Lucy Nichols's guardian wrote a long letter to the commissioner of pensions reporting her death and describing her honored place in his GAR post. The letter was more than a bureaucratic formality; this GAR member wanted someone outside the community of New Albany to know about Lucy and her membership in the GAR. I like to think that he knew someone, some day, would be going through her pension files and would tell the world her story.[3]

As these men and women passed from the scene, the number of Americans with personal memories of the Civil War dwindled; veterans and their associates understood this. As early as 1896, Comrade Searle commented to the New York encampment that "to more than half the people in the community the war is beyond the limits of experience and of memory." Similarly, the commander in chief remarked: "Today we find ourselves surrounded by a generation who has come upon the stage of life since the close of the great civil conflict. Of those times they know nothing save the beneficent results which are enjoyed in the peaceful pursuits of the present." Commander in Chief Rhea spoke to the District of Columbia's GAR about his generation's personal memory of slavery. "I can remember as you can also, many times that along the streets of this city chained gangs of human beings were drawn, men driven in shackles along the streets to be sold as slaves," he remarked, understanding that most Americans did not. A WRC official understood the consequences of forgetting slavery and freedom. She recalled when "justice and humanity asserted themselves, and a race was born to freedom" but worried that "when these memories die out something far better must have taken their places, or something worse must follow." Scholars today would argue that something worse did follow.[4]

Newspapers frequently commented on the passing of the Civil War generation on Memorial Day. In 1913, the New York World understood that "there is a generation that was born after the smoke of battle had cleared away, it is a generation prone to forget how much blood and iron have gone into the winning and holding of human liberty." A Maryland newspaper editor remarked, "A full quarter of a century [has passed] since most of the men whose graves will be decorated fell upon the battle field. Time seems to be moving on so rapidly that the war of the rebellion is getting to be ancient history." He acknowledged that "those who lived through it retain . . . lively recollections of its stirring scenes as if they had occurred but yesterday." A Pittsburgh, Pennsylvania, editor in 1885 made a distinction between personal memory and historical Memory: "[The] stirring events which are recalled" on Memorial Day "become more of a memory and less of a recollection." A century before Memory became a popular notion in historical studies, the editor understood this critical distinction.[5]

When the mayor of Trenton, New Jersey, spoke to the GAR in 1905, he demonstrated his grasp of the distinction between recollection and Memory. "[I belong] to a generation to whom the great Civil War is but history," he remarked. "I have no stirring recollection of those stirring times." His knowledge of the war came "from the pen of the historian of the causes which led to that awful conflict and the sacrifices of blood and treasure made to preserve the unity of our nation." Though he did not remember the war, the mayor maintained that he understood its lessons: "We have learned, with the flight of years, to respect the honor, the valor of those who fought and shed their blood for a cause for which they believed right. Time has healed all wounds. No bitter memories are revived by recalling these events of the past. The reconciliation has been complete." Had the mayor had any real recollection of the war, bitter or sweet, or had wounds that had not healed, he might, like GAR members, have been less sanguine about sectional reconciliation.[6]

In 1900, in Lancaster, Pennsylvania, an editorial on Memorial Day defined a true American in terms of his or her Civil War Memory. He imagined what different generations recollected as they watched the Memorial Day parade. He speculated that the older generation remembered the "power . . . of *Uncle Tom's Cabin*, the uncompromising fierceness of Horace Greeley's *Tribune*, . . . Thaddeus Stevens, the great debate of Lincoln and Douglas, 'squatter sovereignty,' the Christiana Riots, the Harper's Ferry Raid, and all the fearful storm of the anti-slavery movement." The editor obviously understood that the war had been caused by slavery. The "true American," however, understood that "the [Civil] War made each section respect the bravery of the other; that the tombs and the cemeteries of both armies are perpetual monuments to American Bravery, and finally that the day came when the Sons of Confederates and Federals . . . Stormed the hill of San Juan and thundered their guns at Santiago and Manila Bay." "True Americans" forgot about slavery and freedom as the cause and the consequence of the war because their personal memories included the Spanish-American War and the shared service and sacrifice of northern and southern soldiers. In contrast, Americans who had no personal memory of the Civil War may be able to view the Confederate military experience as an honored part of the American military experience. They did not share the GAR members' understanding that Confederate courage served a cause intent on destroying the American Union.[7]

Veterans of the Civil War may have lost the battle for Memory when the younger generation created a new mythology about the war to inspire the young people of all sections to serve and die in the wars of the twentieth century. A Memorial Day address by Thomas Stewart, deputy superintendent of the Harrisburg, Pennsylvania, public schools, explained how Memory could inspire ardor for the military among the nation's youth: "It is necessary that the rising generation have instilled in their minds the memory of the sacrifices made by their fathers that in a similar crisis their patriotism would call them forth to die bravely fighting for the honor of our reunited nation." While he may have meant Pennsylvania's sons, it is not hard to see how this could be seen as a broader mandate for all American children. The Spanish-American War marked the debut of the United States on the world stage, and the conflicts inherent in its role would require the service of a number of new generations of American soldiers.[8]

Before Americans fought in these battles, they found time to commemorate another. Fifteen years after the USS *Maine* sank, starting one war, and two years before the sinking of the RMS *Lusitania*, which set the United States on the road to another, Americans commemorated the fiftieth anniversary of the battle of Gettysburg. Approximately fifty-three thousand veterans of the Blue and Gray attended this event, about the same number killed, wounded, or missing in the three-day battle. Woodrow Wilson, the chief orator of the day was not a northern Civil War veteran but a civilian born in Virginia, a Confederate state. Woodrow Wilson spoke at this commemoration. He proclaimed, "We have found one another again as brothers and comrades in arms, enemies no longer, generous friends rather, our battle long past, the quarrel forgotten." According to David Blight, Wilson's speech "struck the mystic chord of memory that most white Americans were prepared to hear." Many scholars, in fact, view Union veterans attendance at this reunion with their former foes as acquiescence to Wilson's inclusive definition of comradeship. The reunion at Gettysburg has been cited as illustrative of how Civil War Memory had changed in the years since Appomattox, that by attending the reunion northern veterans approved of this change, which included amnesia about slavery and emancipation as the cause and the consequence of the war.[9]

It is ironic that Wilson's address has been portrayed as such an important milestone in the evolution of Civil War Memory because he said so little about the Civil War. In his opening remarks, in fact, Wilson explained that he had no intention of discussing the war since it would be "an impertinence to discourse about how the battle went, how it ended, what it signified." Most of his speech advocated peacetime service as opposed to wartime sacrifice. He explicitly asked the crowd to eschew militarism, to "not put uniforms [near] by," and, instead, to turn away from the Memory of the war and "put the harness of the present on. Lift your eyes to the great tracts of life yet to be conquered in the interest of righteous peace, of that prosperity which lies in a people's heart and outlasts all wars and errors of men." He concluded his speech with an appeal for all Americans to be comrades in peace, to "serve our fellow men in quiet counsel, where the blare of the trumpets is neither heard nor heeded and where the things are done which make blessed the nations of the world in peace and righteousness and love."[10] It is ironic that Wilson's address, which advocated turning away from swords in favor of plowshares, has been portrayed as such an important milestone in Civil War Memory.

Although the silence of the veterans attending this speech has been characterized as assent, evidence suggests that many of them rejected Wilson's message. A front-page article in the New York Times declared, "Gettysburg [was] Cold to Wilson's speech, 10,000 Veterans Cheer Perfunctorily, but Say he Failed to Catch the Spirit of the Hour. . . . [T]he comments on the speech afterward were not complimentary." The Times reported that although the veterans believed it "a good speech, [they thought it] ought to have been made at some other place, but not at Gettysburg." Veterans' silence was likely a respectful acknowledgment of Wilson's status as commander in chief. These men probably understood that the next generation used the Civil War and its commemorations for their own purposes. In Wilson's case, this use may have been more objectionable than most because northern veterans understood that had they heeded Wilson's advice and not donned uniforms thirty years earlier, he would not have been speaking as the president of United States.[11]

While Wilson's remarks seem to minimize all soldiers' efforts, it has been the treatment of African American veterans at this gathering that has been noted by scholars examining the event. Because historians have not found pictures of these men or accounts of their activities, they assumed that African Americans did not attend this reunion. However, newspapers noted their participation in this commemoration. According to the black-

African American veterans attending the 1913 Gettysburg reunion.
Property of the Edgecombe County Memorial Library, Tarboro, N.C.

owned *New York Age*, for example, when former southern soldiers reenacted their famous war cry at Gettysburg, "the Negro veterans there looked on in silence and listened to the Rebel Yell without responding to it." The *Cleveland Gazette*, an African American newspaper, similarly reported that "the Negro veterans and many white G.A.R. veterans there looked on in silence and listened to the Rebel Yell without responding to it." In addition, a white newspaper, the *Harrisburg Patriot* of Pennsylvania, reported the departure of local GAR posts for this gathering, including the local black post. Out of the 184 veterans who went to the event, the paper reported, "144 were from post No. 58, 28 from post No. 116 and the remainder from post No. 520." "Post No. 520," the *Patriot* noted, "is a colored post and as it only contained 25 members, practically the same [percentage] went from this post as the rest." A southerner attending this gathering thought black veterans' presence noteworthy; he included a picture of them in a photo album.[12]

A Philadelphia paper commented on black veterans at the Gettysburg commemoration, and its description of these men revealed how the next generation "remembered" the Civil War. "More than 300 [black veterans] are here," the journalist reported, "gathered from a score of states." He speculated that the men recalled "how they traveled 'the underground railroad' and returned South in blue uniforms to fight the men who wanted to keep them in slavery," but he added, "They still love their masters; nothing better pleases them more than to recount plantation days." When these men sing, he continued, they sing not of freedom but "jubilee songs that echo with the crooning of a southern mammy and the frolics of picaninnies." The journalist and his generation viewed slavery and former slaves through the prism of the romantic portrayals of plantation life in popular culture. While the article illustrates an educated white American's view of slavery at the turn of the century, it also demonstrates that black veterans still fought the battle for Civil War Memory by their presence at these kinds of commemorations. The caretakers of Memory, however, were men like Woodrow Wilson and this newspaper reporter, not GAR members, black or white, who had a less sanguine view of the peculiar institution.[13]

Editorialists would have approved of this story because they, too, downplayed slavery; however, they also dismissed the importance of secession. Commenting on the reunion at Gettysburg, a *Washington Post* editor declared that the war "settled for the country the two great questions of secession and slavery." But then he minimized the importance of these great questions. Secession, the editorialist argued, was a "political and not [a] moral issue," which makes the dissolution of the Union sound like nineteenth-century tariffs or twentieth-century taxes. On the other hand, the editor allowed that slavery "involved a moral principle," adding, "But admitting as such, no particular part of the people was responsible, unless, indeed, the burden should be shouldered by the North for its introduction." If southerners were not responsible for slavery, then northerners could not receive credit for ending it. Similarly, the *New York World* commented: "It is not merely that slavery was destroyed, it is not merely that the doctrine of secession was crushed." Rather, "a new nation came into being, with new ideals, new aspiration, and new principles. The baptism of blood was indeed a consecration." Northern veterans would have agreed with that latter sentiment but rejected the former. Under no circumstance would a northern veteran accept the association of the word "merely" with saving the Union and freeing the slaves. Racism explains the editorialists' casual attitude toward slavery; providing an explanation for their indifference toward secession represents more of a challenge.[14]

While historians have emphasized the country's need to forget slavery to achieve national unity, reuniting a nation also required amnesia about secession and disunion. Speeches by politicians and newspaper accounts reveal the true agenda of the Gettysburg reunion: reimagining the American community to include southerners by embracing Confederate veterans as American patriots. "There are no more patriotic people at the present time than Confederate veterans," the governor of Kentucky declared during his reunion speech. "They are today as patriotic and loyal as the men who carried the stars and stripes during the war." Newspapers went to great lengths to describe southerners as patriotic. One newspaper, commenting on the arrival of the Blue and Gray in Gettysburg, waxed poetic: "Whether feeble or faltering with their advanced years or crippled and maimed from old-time wounds, not one is less stern of eye or mien or weaker in patriotic purpose than when he marched into Pennsylvania that long ago June day to the strains of 'Dixie' or the 'Star Spangled Banner.'" Newspaper reporters and editorialists were from a generation that had no memory of that march into Pennsylvania and could characterize the men who defended the state as equally patriotic as the men who attacked it.[15]

In contrast, members of the GAR consistently characterized the failed Confederate national experience as treason. Today, if the Confederacy and its supporters are condemned, it is usually because of their association with human slavery; however, northern veterans repeatedly cited treason as their greatest transgression. An Ohio official condemned the Confederate cause and its followers: "The Army and the Navy fought against treason. It was an understanding during the war of the rebellion the boys on the side of their country were loyal and those opposed to their country and flag were traitors. We believe that yet." The Ohio chaplain objected to decorating the graves of Confederate dead. He asked his comrades, "What are the lessons taught when the mounds of the Blue and Gray alike share the honors of the day? . . . Who was it who filled the land with graves, and tears and death? From every hill and valley came the answer, the 'Gray.' . . . We cannot honor the 'Gray' for treason and disloyalty to our country and flag." The Indiana department commander expressed his willingness to "meet a Confederate and acknowledge and honor his bravery," but he also wanted it clearly understood that these men had to answer for actions. "Treason is a crime, not a sentiment," he asserted. "Scores of people have tried to say it was a sentiment not a crime, but it [was] a crime." Members of the GAR and their associates refused to fully pardon their former adversaries for this transgression. Given an opportunity, successor generations may, or may not, have forgiven southerners for attempting to destroy the Union; however, newspaper reporters and editorialists removed from the national dialogue the notion that slave owners were considered traitors by their opponents. Reunion did not require that the nation forget race; it required amnesia about disunion and treason.[16]

Not satisfied with merely overlooking treason, newspaper editors decided that the true American heroes who marched into Pennsylvania in the summer of 1863 were the Confederate soldiers in Pickett's brigade. The headline of an article describing a reenactment of this famous charge read, "GRAY MEN TOTTER TO BLOODY ANGLE—Cheers, Not Shots, Greet Pickett's Heroes Fifty Years Later—150 of Immortal Brigade Traverse Route of Charge." The article reported the remarks of the Speaker of the House of Representatives, who proclaimed that "the valor displayed in the war was not Northern Valor, it was not Southern valor, but I thank the almighty God it was American valor." It may have been only a happy coincidence that this article appeared on the Fourth of July 1913. The pantheon of American heroes now included Pickett's men; Americans incorporated southern suffering and sacrifice into American national mythology. In his recent study of the Civil War in movies and popular art, Gary Gallagher argues that even when movies portrayed slavery and emancipation as critical to the cause and consequence of this struggle, they ignored the battle to preserve the Union. If we acknowledge that the fight was to save the Union, we would have to acknowledge that the Confederate army tried to destroy it. The Lost Cause and its emphasis on southern military heroism won the battle for Civil War Memory because it was more important to reincorporate southerners into the imagined community of the American nation than to pay homage to the men who had saved the Union, the real community of the United States.[17]

Contemporary Americans' urgent need to integrate the Confederate army into the American military experience is partly explained by the next group of visitors to this battlefield. Two days after the veterans left, the *Washington Post* reported that "young men, active, alert and ambitious to learn the war game" arrived at the battlefield. The newspaper's use of the term "war game" demonstrates that decades of romanticizing the Civil War had taken its toll; Americans had forgotten what veterans so clearly remembered—the horrors of war. A newspaper described these college students as "the posterity of the reunited North and South," making a direct connection between these students and a Civil War Memory that emphasized reunion over disunion. A *Washington Post* editorial argued that "nothing could possibly more be impressive or more inspiring to the younger generation than [the Gettysburg] gathering," and these young men's presence on this battlefield only days after the reunion was probably not a coincidence. These young men belonged to a new military training program for college students; we know it today as the Reserve Officer Training Corps (ROTC). Created just prior to World War I, ROTC supplied officers for the wars of the twentieth century and continues to do so in the twenty-first. Five years after their visit, some of these men might have been in the Meuse-Argonne; and in thirty years, their sons might have been on Normandy Beach or a few years later, storming Inchon, their chil-

Dethroned. This painting, which appeared in *Pictorial Review*,
a popular women's magazine, in 1919, illustrates that contemporary Americans
understood that World War I soldiers and their tales of valor were displacing
Civil War veterans. From author's collection.

dren's children in Danang, and their great-grandchildren in Baghdad. The
United States' involvement in these overseas wars for freedom reinforced
Americans' need for a useful Civil War Memory that advanced the cause of
national unity rather than one that encouraged a retreat from the cause of
racial equality. American racism required less inspiration than American
nationalism.[18]

Editors of black newspapers understood that the Gettysburg celebration
was part of a broader agenda to advance national reunion and reconciliation, but they did not cite black participation in this gathering to counter the
effort. While the *Cleveland Gazette* and the *New York Age* described veterans' responses to the rebel yell, no other details of the Gettysburg reunion,
including the activities of African American GAR members, were reported
by black newspapers examined for this study. The *New York Age* failed to
mention Post 520's visit to Gettysburg, though the local white paper had believed its attendance worthy of note. If fact, none of the *Age*'s correspondents
reported that black veterans in their cities participated in the commemoration. If at least three hundred black veterans attended this gathering, some of
the black posts in cities covered by the *Age* correspondents must have trav-

eled to Gettysburg. Ironically, the only specific mention of a black soldier at Gettysburg in the black press was of "the only bona fide colored Confederate veteran" in attendance, "Levi Miller of Relief, Virginia." His presence likely was mentioned to demonstrate that few black Americans served the Confederacy. The failure of the black press to report the presence of the bona fide Union veterans, however, aided those who wanted these men's loyal service erased from historical Memory.[19]

Hostility toward this gathering may have prompted the black press to ignore it. The editor of the Washington *Bee*, for example, denounced the event: "The occasion is to be called a Reunion! A Reunion of whom? Only of those who fought for the preservation of the Union and the extinction of human slavery?" No, he explained, it was for "those who fought to destroy the Union and perpetuate slavery. . . . The Spirit which prompted the threat of Toombs that he would call the roll of his slaves on Bunker Hill—a spirit which denied the Negro the right to emancipation, either physical, intellectual or moral—still dominates the southern whites as evidenced by Negro disenfranchisement, jim-crowism, peonage and the many unjust laws and customs to which the race is subjected." In 1913 the African American community focused its attention on the contemporary status of black citizens, an understandable priority given their desperate plight.[20]

The postreunion commentary of a *New York Age* editor displayed an impressive understanding of how newspapers and the next generation of white Americans orchestrated the Gettysburg reunion. The editor understood that while veterans were commemorating the "most memorable event in their lives" at this gathering, they did not control the celebration. Rather, he argued, "the Newspaper Syndicates and the newspapers had their way. They made the Gettysburg celebration what they wanted and not what it was. . . . The truth of history was smothered by the commercial fiends who bolster the falsehood that 'good trade relations must subsist between the sections!'" The *Age* understood the nationalist agenda behind the event: journals and syndicates "decided long in advance of the celebration that . . . now [has] come a time when there was no North and no South, but one country and no Union or Confederate soldiers, but one soldier; and no loyalty and no treason but just a 'misunderstanding' between brothers which time had made plain in which the Confederates have proven that the Union soldiers were in the wrong and the Confederate soldiers were in the right." Despite the reports of the mainstream press, the *Age* observed, "the mock lovefest at the Gettysburg celebration did not conceal the skeleton in the national closet. Negro Grand Army men who attended the celebration have told us that there were constant disputes and rows among the Union and Confederate veterans." The

Age understood that newspapers were biased observers of the Gettysburg gathering. Newspapers edited out the presence of black veterans and penciled in Confederate soldiers, creating a specific dramatic tableau in which southern and northern soldiers were courageous Americans simply wearing different uniforms. However, black newspapers may not have realized that they missed an opportunity to pass on the story of African American soldiers in the Civil War to their own younger generation and to challenge the notion that this was an all–white brothers' war.[21]

It is interesting to note that when the *Bee* attacked the Gettysburg reunion, it also observed that "the colored soldier was peculiarly inconspicuous" and wondered why there was a "studious avoidance of celebrating events in which the Negro soldier has prominently figured." But when the opportunity came for the *Bee* and other black newspapers to celebrate the anniversary of the battle at Fort Wagner, they failed to do so. A letter from a black veteran sent to the *Cleveland Gazette* and other newspapers inviting his comrades to attend the fiftieth anniversary of this battle was the only acknowledgment that a celebration was taking place. Eventually, the *Age*'s Boston correspondent reported on the "semi-centennial celebration of the Battle of Fort Wagner . . . [which included] a reunion of the veterans of the 54th and 55th Massachusetts regiments and other colored Army and Navy veterans at Faneuil Hall." The report was buried on page seven and followed other news from Boston's African American community. This was quite a contrast to the treatment of the Gettysburg reunion, a front-page story in white newspapers. The only other paper to acknowledge the anniversary was the *Indianapolis Freeman*, which reported that an AME church had held a memorial service for Robert Gould Shaw and recorded the remarks that honored his Memory.[22]

An examination of African American newspaper coverage of Memorial Day events at the beginning of the second decade of the new century demonstrates that Civil War commemorations in general, and Memorial Day in particular, were not as important as they once had been. While in 1913 the *Savannah Tribune* and the *Indianapolis Freeman* reported Memorial Day services on page one, coverage of these activities declined overall. The *New York Age*'s correspondents, who had always reported the activities of local African American GAR posts, made no mention of their activities. Although a number of black posts still prospered in Baltimore, the local correspondent failed to report their Memorial Day celebrations. Instead, the Baltimore correspondent's letter to the *Age* included a description of a prominent African American woman's funeral. Similarly, while the Philadelphia correspondent covered the 1912 Memorial Day activities of the all-black Jackson Post, in 1913, the only Decoration Day activity discussed involved a branch of the black fraternal organization, the Odd Fellows, which held its "eighth annual field day, review and parade" on this holiday. A decade earlier, no African American newspaper would have focused on the activities of a fraternal group at the expense of the GAR. One explanation for this lack of coverage may be that most African Americans reading these papers had not served in the war, so they could not be members of the GAR; naturally, they were more interested in groups they might actually be able to join. Moreover, Civil War Memory appears not to have been very useful in addressing contemporary racial issues, perhaps because even those who remembered that the war was about slavery, like the GAR, did not connect the struggle against slavery during the Civil War to racial issues. Black newspaper editors probably understood, better than modern scholars, the limits of Memory, and how it had not been an effective instrument to advance the cause of African Americans at the beginning of the twentieth century.[23]

The black press's apparent lack of interest in Memorial Day observances did not reflect an emerging antimilitarism since newspapers still chronicled the activities of African American soldiers. They appeared to be more interested in contemporary soldiers than in Civil War soldiers, however. On the fiftieth anniversary of the second day at Gettysburg, when the Twentieth Maine made its stand on Little Round Top, the Age reported the activities of a contemporary black regiment: the mostly black "10th Cavalry [was] en route to [its] Summer Camp . . . at Winchester, Va., and is carrying full-strength of twelve troops, machine gun platoon, hospital corps and a band of twenty-eight pieces." While the New York Age's Memorial Day 1912 edition included a cartoon of an elderly GAR member with the caption, "Remembering his Comrades," there was no article nearby explaining why his comrades should be remembered. Instead, next to the illustration was a letter from members of the predominantly black Ninth Cavalry, who "issued an appeal to the Negroes of the United States to get closer together along business lines. To show that they desire to play an important part in bringing about a closer racial feeling the cavalrymen have made it known that they have $110,000 available for investment." They proposed "to establish a department store to consist of a banking system, millinery and dry goods, shoe, drug and grocery, soda fountain, restaurant, and cigar departments, such a store to be opened in one of the cities where a large population of Negroes is found." Contemporary black soldiers could do more for the African American community than elderly veterans could.[24]

Much of the emphasis on the present at the expense of the past must be credited to black elites' faith in the power of race progress, that is, that African American economic, social, and cultural advances represented the best weapon against charges of racial inferiority. Ultimately, African Americans hoped that demonstrating sufficient race progress might make white Americans more likely to support black civil and political rights. The *Indianapolis Freeman* published in its July 5, 1913, edition a long letter from its soldier-correspondent in the Twenty-fifth Infantry, a predominantly black unit, in which he described the world of black soldiers at Schofield Barracks in Hawaii. "The soldiery of the Twenty-fifth Infantry and of the various regiments turned out en masse to hear [a musical] recital," he wrote. "The men were dressed in the regulation service uniform, but the ladies were beautifully gowned in dresses of the latest design." After describing the recital in detail, the correspondent described the activities of the regiment's literary society. The writer emphasized the social refinement of these men, an indicator of race progress, not their martial prowess.[25]

The African American press also focused on black regulars because they, like their civilian counterparts, experienced racial discrimination. The *New York Age* expressed its concern in 1913 that "leading army authorities at Washington have under serious consideration the expediency of recommending the disbandment of the four Negro regiments of the regular Army." The *Age* objected to this action because these units had "a record of service and efficiency second to no other four regiments of white soldiers. They have stood the fighters' test of bravery and deportment in times of war and peace." The *Cleveland Gazette* ran a cartoon and an editorial protesting the 1906 dishonorable discharge of 167 members of the Twenty-fifth Infantry, who "[Roosevelt] and his secretary of war, William Howard Taft 'Lynched' when they discharged them without honor as a result of the ALLEGED Brownsville, Tex., 'riot.'" Given the ongoing struggle of modern African American soldiers to obtain fair treatment in the U.S. military, it is not surprising that black papers focused more on their contemporary struggles and less on the Memory of Civil War soldiers.[26]

Closer to home, African American newspapers advocated for local all-black National Guard units. The federal government had organized the state militias into National Guard units, and some of them were all-black. On the fiftieth anniversary of Pickett's Charge, the front page of the *New York Age* reported the formation of the "first company for new [all-black regiments]." The paper also noted that black New Yorkers had "been fighting for a colored regiment for the past three years." In 1913, the Memorial Day edition of the black-owned *Chicago Broad Ax* featured a front-page article on a sermon delivered to the all-black Eighth Regiment, Illinois National Guard, accompanied by a picture of its commander. The John Brown Post of Chicago must have observed the most sacred day in the GAR's calendar with some type of public commemoration, yet the *Broad Ax* made no mention of it.[27]

Black newspapers actively supported the struggle to ensure that black officers would command African American soldiers in the Eighth and other regiments. The *Age* was outraged when it discovered "a movement [afoot] to assign white field officers to the colored regiment of infantry" of the New York National Guard. In its Memorial Day 1913 edition, the Washington-based *Bee* published a letter to the Secretary of War asking the army to include African Americans in its officer training courses. "The male students of Wilberforce, Howard, Fisk, and Lincoln Universities et al. have physical intellectual and moral competency," the paper asserted. "Would it not be to the interest of the public . . . to include the training of colored students as officers of colored regiments?"

Black newspapers also chronicled the activities of the handful of black officers in the regular army. The *Indianapolis Freeman* noted that "Lt. Benjamin O. Davis and wife have returned from Liberia. Lieut. Davis has now gone to Fort Huachuca to join his command in the United States Army." Davis became the first African American general in the U.S. Army. His son, a West Point graduate and commander of an all-black fighter squadron, rose to the rank of four-star Air Force general. Advancing the cause of black officers during the First and Second World Wars was an important part of the struggle for racial equality in the United States.[28]

Black Americans may have abandoned the use of Civil War Memory because they understood that it would not prompt action, at least on civil rights issues. Civil War service by some black Americans had not translated to broader civil rights gains in the late nineteenth century. Moreover, the GAR and its members understood, better than any group outside the black community, that the war had been about slavery. The GAR was not, however, inspired to take any serious measures to ensure black rights decades after emancipation. Given the GAR's indifference to racial issues, African Americans' emphasis on contemporary military service, at the expense of reminding Americans of their Civil War service, may have been a more effective tactic in their battles for political and civil rights.

Black Americans had faith in the notion that military service represented a claim to citizenship and equality. African Americans such as W. E. B. Du Bois and the leadership of the National Association for the Advancement of Colored People (NAACP) hoped that the wartime service of black Americans making the world safe for democracy would advance democracy at home. African American leaders fought for, and partly won, African Americans' right to fight in combat units and advanced the cause of African American officers in World War I. The Harlem Hellfighters, the 369th Infantry Regiment, a black National Guard unit from New York, distinguished itself fighting alongside French forces and vindicated the African American community's faith in its citizen-soldiers.[29]

White Americans' allegiance to Jim Crow and their understanding that wartime heroics might lead to postwar demands for greater equality prompted the government to segregate most black soldiers in support units that provided logistical services. They could do this partly because the United States came late to the fight. While the losses the United States experienced were certainly grievous enough—approximately 320,000 soldiers died or were wounded during this conflict—the other allied powers sustained many more casualties. Harlem's Hellfighters were greeted with open arms by French troops, who had seen more soldiers fall in a single battle—Verdun—than the United States lost in the entire war. Had the United States joined the allies earlier on the western front, military necessity might have forced the United States, just as it had under similar circumstances during the Civil War, to form more all-black combat units.[30]

Since the Great War was not, as many hoped, the war to end all wars, African Americans once again served in a crusade for freedom overseas while enjoying precious little freedom at home. During World War II, the African American community initiated the "Double V" campaign, victory over fascism in Europe and victory over discrimination at home. While black leaders struggled to ensure that black soldiers served in ground combat units, they wanted them to fight in the air as well. The Tuskegee airmen, commanded by Benjamin O. Davis Jr., represented an important victory in the Double V campaign. African American leaders also began to push for the integration of the military. Personnel shortfalls forced the integration of some units toward the end of the war, but once again the United States calculated its dead in the hundreds of thousands, while other nations mourned millions. The war ended when the atom bomb, dropped on two Japanese cities, killed tens of thousands in an instant.[31]

Ultimately, President Harry Truman—a World War I veteran—integrated the military at the dawn of the atomic age when it seemed to some that war itself had become obsolete. Surely, the first atomic war would be the last. The Korean War, fought by black and white Americans in the same units, demonstrated that nuclear weapons did not necessarily mean the end of war, just as the integration of the military was not the end of the black Americans' struggle for civil rights. It may have signaled, however, the end to wars that were fought by large armies that required the mobilization of the entire population. When the government needs more soldiers and the support of even its more marginalized citizens, such as African Americans, it broadens the notion of the imagined community to include these men and women. Because modern wars require only a small percentage of volunteers, the idea of the imagined community, at least one built on the notion of shared sacrifice, may itself become marginalized.[32]

Despite the changing nature and scope of American wars, the rhetoric of the Won Cause dominates the oratory justifying these conflicts. It resonated through the twentieth century when the United States fought in Europe to make the world safe for democracy and free an enslaved continent from fascism and defeat communism in Asia, and it continued to do so in the twenty-first in the Middle East in our efforts to establish democracies in Iraq and Afghanistan. If the United States has demonstrated anything in the last one hundred years, it is that the Won Cause has partly prevailed, since black and white, southerners and northerners, and now men and women in succeeding generations have adopted Liberty and Union, freedom and nation, as worthy of their sacrifice. Perhaps the resilience of this rhetoric is best demonstrated by its survival into the twenty-first century. In the first month of the first year of the third millennium, George W. Bush explained his version of American history as "a story we continue, but whose end we will not see. It is the story of a new world that became a friend and liberator of the old, a story of a slave-holding society that became a servant of freedom." While some scholars have been preoccupied with discrediting the Lost Cause, perhaps we should remember the Won Cause and the interracial blood sacrifice that redeemed, transformed, and made possible the modern United States — the living legacy of the black and white comrades of the Grand Army of the Republic.[33]

Epilogue

All One that Day If Never Again: The Final Days of the GAR

Surprisingly, the GAR, including the remaining black member, lived to see the atomic age. The GAR was made of tough men who had lived through a horrific war, and they took a long time to die. After the fiftieth anniversary of the battle at Gettysburg, the First and Second World Wars, and even through the Korean armistice, the GAR marched ever so slowly into the sunset. In the waning years of the GAR, African Americans still ran for office and won. Illinoisans nominated an African American from the John Brown Post of Chicago to run for junior vice-commander in 1928. A veteran supporting his nomination asserted, "You have plenty of salt on the ticket, let it be sprinkled with a little pepper the same as it was in the Army." The only white candidate withdrew in his favor, stating, "It is fitting at this time that we should be represented in the Grand Army and the Department by one of our colored veterans that stood up in the ranks and met the bullets that we did." In the thirties, a black New Yorker sat on the Council of Administration; in the forties, another "Colored Comrade," Isaiah Fosset, one of the last surviving members of the GAR, became the department commander in Delaware.[1]

Black GAR posts struggled to survive much longer than one would have imagined. The Shaw Post in Pittsburgh, whose members shared with us the hospitality of their post room, if only in our imagination, survived until the fourth decade of the century, as did a small post in Christiana, Pennsylvania. The Stevens and the Andrews posts of New York City, and the Delany Post of Indianapolis lasted long enough to welcome the second president named Roosevelt. The integrated Hartford-based Taylor Post, home of Gustavus Booth, Fifth Massachusetts Cavalry (Colored), held its last meeting in 1937, as did the integrated Welch Post in Ann Arbor, whose members may or may not have confused the colors black and white when voting for an Afri-

★

African American veterans from Louisiana and Mississippi attending
the national encampment parade in Denver, 1928. Courtesy of the Western
History and Genealogy Department, Denver Public Library.

can American member. When these posts died, interracial posts were almost
forgotten. Identifying the black and white members of these posts returns
black veterans to their proper place in the GAR—marching alongside their
white comrades.[2]

The women affiliates of the GAR circle continued to prosper in the early
decades of the twentieth century and beyond because membership was not
confined to the Civil War generation. Julia Mason Layton, the long-serving
African American secretary of the WRC in Washington, D.C., pronounced a
fitting epitaph for the GAR as modern soldiers escorted the dwindling ranks
of the GAR in a national encampment parade in the early 1920s: "The escorts were largely of World War boys. Sometimes it was a solid Guard of all
Colored boys in khaki—sometimes all white—sometimes they were mixed.
They were all veterans—all one that day if never again." The black and white
members of the GAR were all one in their day, if never again or anywhere else.

Julia West Hamilton, another black official of the Washington, D.C., WRC, carried the battle for Memory to a 1928 congressional hearing on a proposed African American memorial and museum. Arguing that black Americans deserved this tribute, Hamilton declared, "In every war of our Nation's history, on land as well as on sea, Negro blood has been freely shed and has sanctified the battle fields of American freedom, liberty, and independence." She specifically invoked their Civil War service and the example of the soldiers of the Fifty-fourth Massachusetts Infantry, who "with fearless, steady step and aim . . . were determined that not one star should be effaced from the beautiful diadem of Old Glory; they were determined that Americans should remain a free and united country." In the next decade, segregation formally separated African American women and their corps from the District's WRC. Outside the nation's capital, women's groups also persevered. The all-black Biddle Circle of the LGAR still held meetings in the years after the Korean War. The Sumner Circle in Chestertown, Maryland, the first LGAR unit in the state, survived into the 1930s. The post hall that the black men and women of Chestertown built still stands today, and the town works to preserve this crumbling edifice and the Sumner Circle's legacy.[3]

African American veterans also endured. In 1922, William Singleton, formerly of the Thirty-fifth USCT and a member of New Haven's Foote Post, wrote a narrative of his days as a slave. To counter the sentimentalized portraits of slavery so popular among successor generations, he described the reality of slavery: "I was born a slave. . . . I had no rights that anybody was bound to respect. For in the eyes of the law I was but a thing. I was bought and sold. I was whipped." He reminded his readers that while he was slavery's victim, he was not passive: "[I] wore the uniform of those men in Blue, who through four years of suffering wiped away with their blood the stain of slavery and purged the republic of its sin." Singleton highlighted the service of modern black soldiers, observing, "When a nation across the seas sought to enslave the world as once my race was enslaved, I saw the boys of my race take their place in the armies of the Republic and help save the freedom of the world."[4]

African Americans still paraded at national encampments, and in 1935 a journalist in Grand Rapids noted their presence and its meaning: "The cheering throng gave added applause to the three Negro marchers, men who ran away from slavery to join the Union forces and help preserve the Union. Their comrades in the reviewing stand gave them a special salute also for it was that cause that all should be free and no man bond servant to another that the war had been fought." Three years later, William Singleton joined his comrades at the seventy-fifth reunion at Gettysburg, serving as a living

A postcard of William Singleton, a veteran of the Thirty-fifth USCT, who attended the 1938 Gettysburg reunion and died at the national encampment later the same year. From author's collection.

reminder that the Civil War was not an all–white brothers' war. A few weeks later, Singleton attended the national encampment. Though it was ninety degrees and he was ninety-eight years old, he insisted on marching fifteen blocks in the grand parade, as so many African Americans had before him. It was his last stand in the battle for Civil War Memory; he died of a heart attack only a few hours after the parade. In 1949, eleven years after Singleton died, the last encampment of the GAR was held. Joseph Clovis of Michigan, the sole surviving black member of the GAR, was one of only six veterans in attendance. When Clovis died two years later, the GAR's existence as an interracial group ended. The organization itself did not last long after his passing; the last GAR member died in 1956, and thus the GAR passed quite literally into memory.[5]

Two years before the last GAR member died and in the immediate aftermath of the first war in which black and white soldiers served side by side, *Brown v. Board of Education* overturned the separate and never equal doctrine of *Plessy v. Ferguson*. Justice Harlan's lone stand for his comrades was, at last, vindicated. In the decades that followed, the Civil Rights and Voting Rights Acts implemented the Fourteenth and Fifteenth Amendments, almost a century after they were ratified. Exactly eight years after George W. Bush described the story of a slaveholding society that became a servant of freedom, after two more American wars added to the interracial roll of the honored dead and even more to the ranks of America's scarred and maimed veterans, Barack Hussein Obama was sworn in as the forty-fourth president of the United States. In the end, the Won Cause finally won. If Americans are to live together, perhaps they have to die together.

Appendix I

African American GAR *Posts*

The following is a list of the all-black posts I was able to identify for this study (others may have existed, but these are the ones I found). The list is incomplete for the very reason that made this organization unique: the GAR almost never officially labeled a post as "Colored." I found only one instance in which a small "c," similar to a footnote, was placed next to a post's name indicating its racial composition. Occasionally a GAR official described a post as "Colored." In a report of the failure of a black post in Pennsylvania, for example, a state official included the names of successful African American posts in the state. Newspapers also revealed a post's racial composition. White papers sometimes described a post as "Colored" when it reported on its Memorial Day activities. Similarly, if a black newspaper provided extensive coverage of a post's activities, one can infer that it was a black post. The muster rolls of some states listed the members of each post and their ranks and regiments and were the best means of identifying all-black posts. States sometimes included in their annual encampment records a list of the soldiers who died in a given year, including their ranks and regiments, and these lists also helped to identify black posts.

This list is neither comprehensive nor necessarily error free. It relies on the GAR having accurately recorded information, such as the unit a veteran had served in during the war. In addition, the spellings of post names and their locations are not always correct in GAR records. Unfortunately, the men recording this information were not as careful as we would like them to have been.

Identifying African American posts and their locations is an ongoing process. I intend to include this list and any necessary corrections to my website devoted to African Americans in the GAR (www.blackgar.com). If readers

★

know of any black posts that I have not listed here, please contact me at bagannon@mail.ucf.edu. I would be grateful for any information related to these groups.

STATE	POST NO.	NAME	LOCATION
Arkansas	7	Judson	Little Rock
	23	Sumner	Fort Smith
	30	Washington	Hot Springs
	103	Hutchinson	Brinkley
	121	Shaw	Marianna
District of Columbia	4	Morton	Washington, D.C.
	9	Sumner	Washington, D.C.
	21	Douglass	Washington, D.C.
Delaware	4	Sumner	Wilmington
Florida	6	Gabriel	Jacksonville
	14	Logan	St. Augustine
	18	Montgomery	Palatka
	22	Hunter	Tallahassee
	23	Stephenson	Pensacola
	30	Hamel	South Jacksonville
Georgia	8	Shaw	Savannah
	15	Delany	Brunswick
Illinois	50	Brown	Chicago
	233	Shaw	Quincy
	578	Bross	Springfield
	598	Foster	Cairo
	599	Cobb	Metropolis
	630	Mound City	Mound City
	663	Delany	Chicago
	687	Governor Yates	Jacksonville
	728	Murphysboro	Murphysboro
	749	Pennock East	St. Louis
Iowa	413	Pratt	Keokuk
Indiana	70	Delany	Indianapolis
	351	Penney	Jeffersonville
	541	Grills	Evansville
	556	King David	Mount Vernon
	581	Fort Wagner	Evansville
	585	Brown	Charlestown

STATE	POST NO.	NAME	LOCATION
Kansas	10	Sumner	Kansas City
	208	Shaw	Leavenworth
	321	Fort Pillow	Topeka
	365	Walker	Lawrence
	486	Steele	Fort Scott
Kentucky	10	Rouseau	Louisville
	15	Jackson	Carlisle
	18	Johnson	Round Hill
	32	Fremont	Midway
	43	Blackburn	Covington
	44	Monroe	Frankfort
	45	Bacon	Hopkinsville
	48	Smith	Somerset
	61	Sumner	Lexington
	68	Brown	Paris
	88	Hanway	Bowling Green
	107	Martin	Central City
	112	Shaw	Henderson
	125	Young	Danville
	130	Sedgewick	Richmond
	142	Miller	Nicholasville
	146	Terrell	Harrodsburg
	156	Delany	Louisville
	166	McKenevan	Maysville
	167	Connors	Bardstown
	181	Searcy	Lawrenceburg
	192	Douglass	New Castle
	197	Fry	Anchorage
	200	Bacon	Hopkinsville
Louisiana	3	Hamlin	Baton Rouge
	4	Lincoln	Thibodeaux
	9	Callioux	New Orleans
	10	Bassett	New Orleans
	11	Grant	New Orleans
	12	Crowder	New Orleans
	13	Sheridan	New Orleans
	14	Orillion	New Orleans
	15	Ellsworth	New Orleans
	18	Shaw	New Orleans
	19	Garfield	Shreveport
	20	Delany	St. Bernard
	23	Brownlow	Vidalia
	26	Morton	Cheatham

STATE	POST NO.	NAME	LOCATION
Louisiana (cont.)	27	Custer	Port Hudson
	31	Hayes	Jesuits' Bend
	33	Lynch	Port Gibson
	34	Lake Providence	Lake Providence
	35	Phelps	Lafayette
	37	Canby	Houma
	39	Fairchild Bayou	Goula
	40	McKinley	Port Allen
	41	Plaquemine	Plaquemine
	48	Wilson	Alexandria
	49	Thomas	Donaldson Ville
	51	Butler	Boutte
	52	Pearsall	St. Martinsville
	53	Sherman	Franklin
	56	Shaw	Iberia
Maryland	7	Lincoln	Baltimore
	12	Sheridan	Annapolis
	16	Guy	Baltimore
	19	Ellsworth	Baltimore
	23	Logan	Baltimore
	25	Sumner	Chestertown
	26	Brown	Cambridge
	31	Lyon	Hagerstown
	33	King	Baltimore
	34	Kilpatrick	Frederick
	40	Stevens	New Windsor
	51	Mead	Berlin
	54	New Shining Light	Tyaskin
	55	Choate	Ridge
	56	Goldsborough	Centerville
	60	Butler	Princess Anne
	61	Johnson	Tunis Mills
	62	Morris	Salisbury
	63	Graper	Fishing Point
	64	Ames	Millington
	68	Armstrong	Pocomoke City
	70	Horner	Rockville
	82	Birney	Baltimore
Massachusetts	134	Bell	Boston
	146	Shaw	New Bedford
Michigan	184	Brown	Detroit
	341	Artis	Calvin

STATE	POST NO.	NAME	LOCATION
Mississippi	2	Sherman	Belleville
	8	Cady	Jackson
	16	Ransom	Natchez
	17	Elliot	Vicksburg
	22	Edwards	Vicksburg
	25	Greenville	Greenville
	28	Ullman	Chatham
	32	Douglass	Warrenton
	33	Lynch	Port Gibson
	38	Duncansby	Duncansby
	42	Osterhause	Edwards
	44	Ebenezer	Ebenezer
	46	Allen	Glen Allen
	47	Vandergriff	Summit
	50	Leland	Leland
	55	Smith	Horn Lake
Missouri	42	Candler	Macon
	295	Collie	Lexington
	343	R. G. Shaw	St. Louis
	363	Capitol City	Jefferson City
	418	Clay Shaw	Sedalia
	452	Tipton	Tipton
	459	Whaling	St. Joseph
	539	Perril	Moberly
New Jersey	51	Robeson	Camden
	53	Delany	Atlantic City
	56	Hamilton	Trenton
	65	Tucker	Newark
	80	Shaw	Moorestown
	95	Birney	Red Bank
	105	Hunter	Princeton
	119	Callioux	Asbury Park
New York	207	Garrison	New York
	234	Andrew	New York
	255	Stevens	New York
	620	Beecher	Brooklyn
North Carolina	15	Abbot	Wilmington
	20	Fletcher	Elizabeth City
	22	Beecher	Newbern
	33	Flusser	Washington
	42	Harrel	Edentown

STATE	POST NO.	NAME	LOCATION
Ohio	244	Anderson	Washington Courthouse
	390	Stevens	Cleveland
	450	Brown	Oxford
	500	Daniel	Xenia
	580	Shaw	Cincinnati
	588	Wright	Chillicothe
	615	Delany	Dayton
	633	Brown	Springfield
	657	Steele	Columbus
	675	Allen	Wilmington
	713	Jackson	Ripley
	716	Wyatt	Circleville
Pennsylvania	27	Jackson	Philadelphia
	80	Bryan	Philadelphia
	80	Shaw	West Chester
	103	Sumner	Philadelphia
	130	Smith	West Chester
	138	Temple	Kennett Square/ Avondale
	194	Brown	Chester
	206	Shaw	Pittsburgh
	365	Dawson	Uniontown
	369	Small	York
	390	Fribley	Williamsport
	412	McCorkey	Delta/Peach Bottom
	440	Thompson	Carlisle
	444	Keith	Wilkes-Barre
	487	Roberts	Christiana
	494	Delany	Chambersburg
	520	Stevens	Harrisburg
	535	Jones	Brownsville
	577	Atchenson	Washington
	593	Elliot	Uniontown
	607	Benn	Lancaster
Rhode Island	13	Ives	Providence
South Carolina	9	Hunter	Beaufort
	12	Lincoln	Hilton Head
	13	Reed	Charleston

STATE	POST NO.	NAME	LOCATION
Tennessee	4	Lincoln	Nashville
	10	Lathrop	Pulaski
	22	Chickamauga	Chattanooga
	26	Giddings	Athens
	66	Johnsonville	Clarksville
	67	Jonesborough	Jonesborough
	80	Young	Knoxville
	86	Brown	Memphis
	102	Blaine	Columbia
Virginia	2	Callioux	Norfolk
	4	Dahlgren	Norfolk
	5	Shaw	Norfolk
	7	Fellows	Portsmouth
	8	Lincoln	Princess Anne County
	9	Garfield	Hampton
	11	Custer	Richmond
	12	Draper	Deer Creek
	18	Grant	Eastville
	19	Sherman	Savageville
	21	Burnside	Franktown
	24	Moore	Shoulders Hill
	27	Tracy	Berkely
	28	Holloway	Capeville
	36	Carter	Mappsville
	54	Steadman	Petersburg

Appendix II

Integrated GAR Posts

The following is a list of the integrated posts I was able to identify for this study (others may have existed, but these are the ones I found). This list is incomplete because, as was the case with all-black posts, GAR members never described a post as interracial. Unlike the concept of a "Colored" post, the notion of an interracial post did not exist in these men's minds. Occasionally a white veteran might report that there were black veterans in his local post. Black and white newspapers provide limited evidence of integration in local posts; racial exclusivity, not inclusivity, appears to have been newsworthy. State muster rolls and death records were the best source for indentifying integrated posts.

This list is neither comprehensive nor necessarily error free. It relies on the GAR having accurately recorded information, such as the unit a veteran had served in during the war. In addition, the spellings of post names and their locations are not always correct in GAR records. Unfortunately, the men recording this information were not as careful as we would like them to have been.

Identifying integrated posts and their locations is an ongoing process. I intend to include this list and any necessary corrections to my website devoted to African Americans in the GAR (www.blackgar.com). If readers know of any integrated posts that I have not listed here, please contact me at bagannon@mail.ucf.edu. I would be grateful for any information related to these groups.

★

STATE	POST NO.	NAME	LOCATION
California	80	Corinth	Marysville
Colorado	4	Lincoln	Denver
	5	Lyon	Boulder
	7	Thomas	Fort Collins
	8	Upton	Pueblo
	14	Denver	Denver
	22	Colorado Springs	Colorado Springs
	41	Kilpatrick	La Junta
	42	Veteran	Denver
	46	Farragut	Denver
	48	Colorado City	Colorado City
	52	Stevens	Minneapolis
	77	Laird	Steamboat Springs
	85	Washington	Denver
Connecticut	1	Sedgewick	Norwich
	2	Lyon	Hartford
	3	Howe	Bridgeport
	4	Drake	South Manchester
	5	Doolittle	Cheshire
	8	Merriam	Meridian
	9	Taintor	Colchester
	11	Stanley	New Britain
	12	Buckingham	Norwalk
	13	Thompson	Bristol
	17	Foote	New Haven
	19	Sedgewick	Brooklyn
	24	Lombard	Greenwich
	26	Kellogg	Birmingham/Derby
	27	McGregor	Danielsonville
	30	Long	Willimantic
	36	Dutton	Wallingford
	39	Van Horn	Milford
	43	Isbell	Naugatuck
	47	Perkins	New London
	50	Tyler	Hartford
	52	Merwin	New Haven
	53	Mansfield	Middletown
	55	Williams	Mystic
	59	Gregory	Sharon
	60	Cowles	Canaan
	62	Burnside .	Unionville
	65	Rodman	East Hartford
	71	Burpee	Rockville

STATE	POST NO.	NAME	LOCATION
Connecticut (cont.)	72	Chapman	Westbrook
	75	Redshaw	Anosonia
	77	Kilborn	Central Village
Dakota	47	Sturgis	Fort Meade
Illinois	1	Nevius	Rockford
	6	Bartleson	Joliet
	45	Shields	Galesburg
	48	Batavia	Batavia
	49	Veteran	Elgin
	67	Bryner	Peoria
	68	Streator	Streator
	70	Lott	Gibson City
	71	Estill	Petersburg
	75	Weider	Fairbury
	103	McDonough	Macomb
	105	Dickey	Pontiac
	106	Loomis	Du Quoin
	123	Duvall	Mason City
	128	Worthen	Murphysboro
	129	Black Eagle	Urbana
	138	Hall	Shelbyville
	140	Nodine	Champaign
	141	Dunham	Decatur
	157	Lowry	Clinton
	174	Van Vleck	Bushnell
	176	Washington Alexander	Bethany
	182	Myers	Lincoln
	209	Driskell	Paris
	219	Cowens	Pinckneyville
	243	Buford	Rock Island
	296	Carmi	Carmi
	301	Colby	Greenville
	312	Graham	Moline
	326	Atlanta	Atlanta
	327	Wright	Toulon
	330	McClanahan	Monmouth
	439	Cobden	Cobden
	442	Carlin	Carrolton
	443	Hecker	Belleville
	444	Meade	Chicago
	454	Newell	Harrisburg
	461	Edwardsville	Edwardsville
	468	Naper/Napier	Downer's Grove

STATE	POST NO.	NAME	LOCATION
Illinois (cont.)	534	Hubbard	Collinsville
	600	Crabtree	Walnut Hill
	613	Vlerebome	Buffalo
	623	Jones	Vernon
	628	Shepherd	Quincy
	724	Harvey	Harvey
	771	Cain	Carrier's Mills
	786	Hovey	Normal
	792	Lawton	Danville
Indiana	1	Morton	Terre Haute
	6	Emmett	Wabash
	7	McPherson	Crawfordsville
	8	Auten	South Bend
	15	Morgan/Merchant	Petersburg
	16	Davis	Vincennes
	18	Dumont	Shelbyville
	30	Harrison	Kokomo
	36	McKeehan	North Vernon
	37	Elmer	Elkhart
	40	Bass	Fort Wayne
	55	Meredith	Richmond
	56	Reyburn	Peru
	78	Williams	Muncie
	81	Wolfe	Rushville
	85	Slocum	Bloomington
	89	Huff	Lawrenceburg/Aurora
	90	Howell	Goshen
	92	Dunbar	Greenfield
	103	Smith	Sheridan
	119	Rader	Middletown
	126	Connersville	Connersville
	127	Wadsworth	Franklin
	128	Houghton	Mishawaka
	131	Coulter	Russiaville
	133	Lookout	Noblesville
	148	Leonard	New Castle
	154	Bailey	Portland
	164	Ogden	Danville
	179	Cambridge City	Cambridge City
	198	Shiloh Field	Elkhart
	230	Henry	Pendleton
	238	Hackleman	Hackleman
	240	Fairfax	Westfield
	244	May	Anderson

STATE	POST NO.	NAME	LOCATION
Indiana (cont.)	247	Newland	Bedford
	259	Burch	Arthur
	271	Wayne	Fort Wayne
	359	Miller	Windfall
	360	Rayl	Spiceland
	410	Leslie	Seelyville
	445	Rotramel	Carlisle
	515	Thomas	Paris
	520	Cockrum	Oakland City
	546	Bennett	Marion
Iowa	1	Wentz	Davenport
	6	Rice	Atlantic
	7	Kinsman	Des Moines
	8	Iowa City	Iowa City
	11	Warren	Clarinda
	12	Crocker	Des Moines
	15	Kerney	Glenwood
	19	Strong	Fairfield
	20	McFarland	Mt. Pleasant
	22	Smith/Hancock	Sioux City
	39	Myers	Greenfield
	40	Kearney	Oskaloosa
	44	Davis	Carroll
	45	Mills	Adel
	46	Warner	Fayette
	57	Garfield	Red Oak
	67	Miller	Boonsboro
	70	Lookout	Dubuque
	79	Harper	Keosauqua
	88	Baker	Clinton
	107	Winslow	Agency
	108	White	Washington
	110	Beaver	Tipton
	122	Bashore	Centerville
	134	Griffith	Oelwein
	141	Payne	Iowa Falls
	186	Kellogg	Seymour
	231	Norman	Muscataine
	235	Cook	Cedar Rapids
	236	Fort Donelson	Fort Dodge
	254	King	Farmington
	276	Center	Randalia
	312	Walton	Garden Grove
	314	Hancock	Belle Plaine

STATE	POST NO.	NAME	LOCATION
Iowa (cont.)	337	Orman	Albia
	343	Dilman	Toledo
	345	Abbott	West Point
	438	Phelps	Manilla
	448	Cantrill	Gravity
	452	Sheridan	Marshalltown
	459	Bonney	Denmark
	497	Tuttle	South Ottumwa
	510	Bryant	Castana
Kansas	1	Lincoln	Topeka
	7	Wadsworth	Council Grove
	8	Larned	Larned
	14	Mead	Sterling
	17	Hooker	Hutchinson
	18	Thomas	Ottawa
	22	Ellsworth	Ellsworth
	25	Garfield	Wichita
	36	Kilpatrick	Newton
	38	Morton	Wamego
	52	Thomas	Great Bend
	53	Henderson	Frankfort
	54	Blair	Galena
	55	Plumb	Emporia
	59	Dix	Columbus
	69	Mitchell	Osborne
	75	Earl	Eskridge
	76	Stockton	Stockton
	79	Brownlow	Severy
	80	Alta Vista	Alta Vista
	88	Sheridan	Clay Center
	100	Gove	Manhattan
	104	Curtis	Spring Hill
	116	Wilderness	Delphos
	117	McCaslin	Paola
	118	Pea Ridge	Chetopa
	123	Baxter Springs	Baxter Springs
	127	Logan	Salina
	132	Junction City	Junction City
	142	Hackleman	Cherryville
	145	Humphrey	Neodosha
	147	Beloit	Beloit
	155	Williams	Oskaloosa
	158	Arkansas City	Arkansas City
	171	Ellis	Ellis

STATE	POST NO.	NAME	LOCATION
Kansas (cont.)	188	Centralia	Centralia
	195	Wier	Pardee
	197	Trego	Wakeeney
	198	Ransom	Oberlin
	244	Eggleston	Wichita
	279	McLouth	McLouth
	281	McFarland	Muscotah
	286	Cedron	Cedron
	316	Butterfield	Greensburg
	322	Ossawatomie	Ossawatomie
	328	Hale	Blue Rapids
	331	Harker	Lurray
	347	Willis	Skiddy
	352	Tucker	Garden Plain
	371	Mission Ridge	De Soto
	375	Ward	White Water
	380	Brennan	Leavenworth
	394	Lewis	Dodge City
	397	Morton	Beaumont
	405	Oakley	Oakley
	415	Dighton	Dighton
	449	Woodsdale	Woodsdale
	453	Black Eagle	Horton
	464	Hancock	Emporia
	467	Bugh	Nashville
	473	Butler	Sharon Springs
	483	Chevington	Goddard
Kentucky	171	West	Berea
Massachusetts	1	Rodman	New Bedford
	2	Dahlgren	South Boston
	4	Grant	Melrose
	5	Lander	Lynn
	9	Reno	Hudson
	10	Ward	Worcester
	11	Lincoln	Charlestown
	13	Webster	Brockton
	14	Phillips	Hopkinton
	16	Wilcox	Springfield
	19	Sumner	Fitchburg
	22	Fletcher	Milford
	24	Sprague	Grafton
	25	Legge	Uxbridge
	30	Smart	Cambridgeport

STATE	POST NO.	NAME	LOCATION
Massachusetts (cont.)	34	Sheridan	Salem
	35	Winthrop	Chelsea
	36	Gould	Arlington
	39	Needham	Lawrence
	41	Lyon	Westfield
	42	Butler	Lowell
	46	Borden	Fall River
	47	How	Haverhill
	52	Randall	Eastondale
	53	Stevens	Leominster
	56	Beck	Cambridge
	57	Davis	East Cambridge
	59	Pratt	Sterling
	62	Ward	Newton
	63	Wadsworth	Natick
	66	Lawrence	Medford
	68	Stone	Cambridge/Dorchester
	70	Custer	Millbury
	71	Kilpatrick	Holyoke
	72	St. John Chambre	Stoughton
	73	McPherson	Abington
	74	Hartstuff	Rockland
	76	Collingwood	Plymouth
	78	Russel	Whitman
	79	Sanford	North Adams
	80	Briscoe	Westborough
	81	Patten	Watertown
	83	Wilder	Hanover
	86	Baker	Northhampton
	89	Chipman Jr.	Beverly
	91	Carpenter	Foxborough
	92	Washburn	Brighton
	94	Revere	Canton
	99	Bartlett	Andover
	112	Robinson	Norwell
	120	Garfield	Andover
	121	Ingraham	Hyde Park
	124	Dimick	East Bridgewater
	125	Rockwell	Pittsfield
	128	Appelton	Ipswich
	130	Sargent	West Medway
	132	Chapman	Sandwich
	139	Kingsley	Somerville
	140	Smith	Athol
	144	Carroll	Dedham

STATE	POST NO.	NAME	LOCATION
Massachusetts (cont.)	147	Stanton	Amherst
	149	Stearns	Charleston
	156	Perkins	Everett
	159	Hawes	East Boston
	165	Wadsworth	Duxbury
	166	Strong	Easthampton
	168	Ammidown	Southbridge
	171	Johnson	Northfield
	173	Johnson	Sturbridge
	178	Nichols	Otis
	187	Hancock	Dalton
	190	Pierce	New Bedford
	191	Gettysburg	Boston
	195	Parker	East Pepperell
	198	Mount Miller	Plainfield
	199	Eaton	Revere
	205	Bridgewater	Bridgewater
	207	Gardner	Nantucket
	209	Hopkins	Williamstown
	210	Barnard	Sheffield
Michigan	38	Granger	East Saginaw
	45	Woodbury	Adrian
	137	Welch	Ann Arbor
	157	Anderson	Cassopolis
	351	Allen	Covert
Minnesota	13	Gorman	Duluth
	21	Ackers	St. Paul
	35	Dagget	Litchfield
Missouri	7	Custer	St. Joseph
	22	Dix	Kirksville
	104	Nichols	Gallatin
Nebraska	7	Custer	Omaha
	25	Farragut	Lincoln
	34	Sheridan	Schuyler
	47	Heckathorn	Tecumseh
	110	Omaha	Omaha
	180	Steadman	Ansley
New York	41	Sydney	Ithaca
	45	Crocker	Auburn
	83	Smith	Norwich

STATE	POST NO.	NAME	LOCATION
New York (cont.)	160	Knowlton	Cazenovia
	175	Lockwood	Port Byron
	217	Birney	Sandy Creek
	230	Robinson	Genoa
	285	Brown	Jamestown
	300	Terry	Amsterdam
	323	Spratt	Watertown
	496	Burnett	Tarrytown
	514	Watson	Catskill
	558	Charette	Warrensburg
	587	Collin	Sandy Hill
Ohio	1	McCoy	Columbus
	5	Veteran	Dayton
	10	Trescott	Salem
	12	Buckley	Akron
	14	Ford	East Toledo
	15	Forsyth	Toledo
	21	Hooker	Mount Vernon
	27	Norris	Fostoria
	29	Tod	Youngstown
	32	Rawson	Fremont
	36	Harmon	Warren
	50	Price	Westerville
	54	Stoker	Findlay
	65	Allen	Elyria
	81	Hazlett	Zanesville
	98	Brand	Urbana
	99	Spangler	Bellaire
	126	Cadot	Galliopolis
	140	Rochester	Logan
	141	Memorial	Cleveland
	153	Fowler	Berlin Heights
	158	Alexander	Piqua
	159	Coleman	Troy
	164	Bailey	Portsmouth
	165	Lambert	Ironton
	183	Douglas	Millbury
	202	Armstrong	Lima
	238	Baxter	Lyons
	276	Kelley	Corning
	280	Barnes	Waverly
	283	Stanley	Forrest
	293	Briney	North Lewisburg
	313	Devol	Carbon Hill

STATE	POST NO.	NAME	LOCATION
Ohio (cont.)	315	Bethel	Flushing
	353	Stevens	Morrow
	364	Lincoln	Oberlin
	365	Smith	Jackson
	403	Austin	Cleveland
	406	Bostwick	Mount Sterling
	415	Cass	Dresden
	422	Welch	Uhrichsville
	425	Livingston	Richwood
	441	Reynolds	Bellefontaine
	513	Crosby	Broughton
	537	Banner	Springsboro
	560	Lewis	Wilkesville
	570	Kimball	Milford Centre
	572	Reed	Palestine
	616	Taylor	Somerton
	621	Andrew Linberry	Melrose
	626	Sisson	Bidwell
	643	Logwood	Middleport
	683	Merchant	Paulding
	692	Climer	Omega
	695	Toland	Sandusky
	715	Volunteer	Toledo
	742	Grosevnor	Broadwell
Ontario, Canada	652	Hamlin	London
Pennsylvania	16	McLean	Reading
	44	Simpson	Huntington
	61	Chapman	Mauch Chunk
	62	Potts	Altoona
	64	Reno	Williamsport
	84	Thomas	Lancaster
	87	Young	Allentown
	95	Gregg	Bellefonte
	100	New Castle	New Castle
	139	Griffin	Scranton
	140	Lincoln	Shamokin
	141	Melvin	Bradford
	151	Patterson	Pittsburgh
	153	Espy	Pittsburgh
	156	Croll	Kittaning
	167	Evans	Oil City
	168	Billingsley	California
	169	Mercer	Mercer

STATE	POST NO.	NAME	LOCATION
Pennsylvania (cont.)	172	Jones	Tyrone
	176	Hulings	Lewistown
	178	Bayard	Belle Vernon
	182	Taylor	Bethlehem
	208	Stanton	New Brighton
	242	Brady	Brookville
	300	Heintzelman	Manheim
	331	Pieffer	Meadville
	349	Keenan	Jersey Shore
	405	Reynolds	Lancaster
	453	Four Brothers	Montrose
	468	Ward	Altoona
	478	Nissley	Mount Joy
	507	Elden	Bendersville
	541	Jones	Southfield
	544	Gaston	Gastonville
	571	Hess	Safe Harbor
	599	Reed	Coatesville
Rhode Island	5	Lawton	Newport
	16	Baker	Wickford
	18	Budlong	Westerley
	24	Tobin	Warrenburg
Tennessee	13	Lane	Bull's Gap
	25	Garfield	Athens
	26	Patton	Johnson City
	35	Jonesborough	Jonesborough
	39	Mcteer	Ellijoy
	40	Cove	Oak Grove
	46	McGuire	New Market
	47	Dyer	Rutledge
	58	Catlett	Sevierville
	78	Fisher	Knoxville
	91	McConnel	Maryville
	96	Stokes	New Middleton

Notes

INTRODUCTION

1. "A Scene to Stir the Heart" and "Keystone Veterans," *Washington Post*, September 21, 1892.

2. Logan, *Betrayal of the Negro*. The original title of Logan's work was *The Negro in American Life and Thought: The Nadir, 1877–1901*. There have been a number of studies on the coming of Jim Crow and the black apocalypse. Some of the more important works are Woodward, *Strange Career of Jim Crow*; Rabinowitz, *Race Relations in the Urban South*; Jones, *Labor of Love, Labor of Sorrow*; Gilmore, *Gender and Jim Crow*; Hale, *Making Whiteness*; Litwack, *Trouble in Mind*; and Hahn, *Nation under Our Feet*. Black men and women in the North seemed to be underrepresented in these studies, which may explain why so little was known about African American men and women in the GAR who were one part of a vibrant African American community in the postbellum North.

3. For more on the American veteran, see *Encyclopedia of the Veteran in America*. For more on the American Legion, see Pencak, *For God and Country*.

4. McConnell, *Glorious Contentment*; Shaffer, *After the Glory*, 7. The segregated paradigm began with the first examination of black participation in this organization by Wallace Davies, who, as part of a larger study of patriotic organizations, examined what he termed the "Problem of Race Segregation." Davies asserts that controversies involving black members in this group demonstrate that "while some members in the North did deprecate racial discrimination, many others, from above the Mason-Dixon line as well as below, obviously felt that the time had come to accept segregation," even in the GAR. See Davies, "Problem of Race Segregation," 371; and Davies, *Patriotism on Parade*.

5. McConnell, *Glorious Contentment*, 215; Shaffer, *After the Glory*, 189. For an excellent explanation of the difference between History and Memory, see Thelan, "Memory and History."

6. Blight, *Race and Reunion*, 5, 198. For more on the Lost Cause, see Foster, *Ghosts of the Confederacy*; Charles Reagan Wilson, *Baptized in Blood*; Bellows, *God and General Longstreet*; and Gallagher and Nolan, *Myth of the Lost Cause*. Of particular note in this essay collection is Alan Nolan's contribution, "The Anatomy of a Myth," which includes

★

an uncompromising assessment of the Lost Cause and its relationship to the facts of Civil War history.

7. Delbanco, *Portable Abraham Lincoln*, 321. For more on the horrific nature of the Civil War and how this affected postwar American society, see Faust, *This Republic of Suffering*. For a discussion of how the American prewar culture of death affected attitudes toward this carnage, see Schantz, *Awaiting the Heavenly Country*. A new examination of Civil War combat argues that rifled muskets were not more deadly than smooth-bore muskets, their predecessors. See Hess, *Rifle Musket in Civil War Combat*. The dead on both sides are included in this comparison since dividing the dead might require splitting the Union once again. If the dead of the Union army were compared to the population of the entire nation, the magnitude of Civil War losses would be understated. The other alternative would have been to compare the northern dead with the population of the United States in former Union states. The latter approach is methodologically suspect since many of the African Americans who died for the North came from the South, as did many loyal whites from areas like East Tennessee. There is an ongoing debate over whether the Civil War was a "total war" or a limited war. I tend to believe it was somewhere in between because, as Mark Neely argues, nineteenth-century Americans had certain notions of restraint based on how they believed civilized men should behave, which, in some instances, limited wartime destruction. Moreover, casualties in the Civil War were horrific for soldiers but not for civilians. In twentieth-century total wars World War I and World War II, more civilians died than soldiers. See Neely, *Civil War and the Limits of Destruction*. For more on the total war debate, see Williams, *Lincoln and His Generals*; Doughty and Gruber et al., *American Civil War*; Sutherland, *Emergence of Total War*; Neely, "Was the Civil War a Total War?"; Royster, *Destructive War*; and Grimsley, *Hard Hand of War*.

8. For a memoir of one soldier who was shot in the groin and lived for decades in pain afterward, see Roy, *Fallen Soldier*. Traditional wartime studies of comradeship, which evoke images of men and women at war fighting side by side, are not useful in examining race relations in the GAR. This organization prospered thirty or even forty years after veterans left their units; to these men, the war was a Memory. However, there have been a number of fine studies on this subject of wartime comradeship. Among the more notable works on soldier motivation are Linderman, *Embattled Courage*; Hess, *Liberty, Virtue, and Progress* and *Union Soldier in Battle*; Mitchell, *Civil War Soldiers*; and McPherson, *For Cause and Comrades*. For an excellent summary of the scholarship on Civil War soldiers, see Mitchell, "Not the General but the Soldier."

9. Chandra Manning has found some of the wartime antecedents of Union soldiers' postwar antislavery sentiment. See Manning, *What This Cruel War Was Over*. John R. Neff came up with his own appellation for the northern cause; he argues that there was a "Cause Victorious"—the northern notion of what they fought for and won—as evinced by the rituals and rhetoric of the postwar commemorations honoring the northern dead and by other observances. Neff emphasizes the idea of Union and American nationalism. My contention is that there was a "Won Cause" of Union *and* Liberty, which linked the triumph of Union and American nationalism to the end of slavery and the establishment of American liberty. See Neff, *Honoring the Civil War Dead*.

10. State encampment records include the text of veterans' long speeches in which

they asserted their understanding of what they had fought for. The New York GAR identified the source of these detailed records as a stenographer who made an official record of the annual meeting. See New York, *Twenty-seventh*, 1893, 68. Copies of many extant state GAR encampment records are in the Library of Congress.

11. For a comprehensive guide to black newspapers, see Danky and Hady, *African-American Newspapers and Periodicals*.

12. *The Oxford English Dictionary*, 2nd ed., s.v. "sentimentalism." Interest in the First World War and Memory has produced a number of fine studies on the birth of modernism. For the most important works in this field, see Fussell, *Great War*; Eksteins, *Rites of Spring*; Hynes, *War Imagined*; and Winter, *Sites of Memory, Sites of Mourning*. David Blight, in his examination of race and Civil War Memory, argues that sentimentalism itself had a great deal to do with the triumph of the Lost Cause. Even when he cites examples of nineteenth-century Americans recognizing black service in a war against slavery, he seems somewhat dismissive if they used sentimental language. For example, he quotes a poem written by Kate Sherwood, former president of the Woman's Relief Corps, "The Black Regiment at Port Hudson," in which she praises black military service "under the guns at Port Hudson," where black soldiers earned the "right to be men; to stand forth / Clean-limbed in the light of freedom." Blight agrees that "the special heroism of black soldiers animates Sherwood's message, even through the sentimental trappings" (Blight, *Race and Reunion*, 4, 95, 97, 237 [quote on 192]).

CHAPTER ONE

1. Pennsylvania, *Thirty-fifth and Thirty-sixth*, 1885, 295; Pennsylvania, *Thirty-fourth and Thirty-fifth* (semiannual), 1884, 260; "Geo. F. Smith Post," *West Chester Daily Local News*, May 31, 1893. When GAR encampments are cited, the entry will include the state, the meeting number, and the year the meeting took place. National encampments will be cited similarly. Meetings of the Woman's Relief Corps will be cited in the same fashion, but the author will be WRC. Hector spoke at many different types of GAR gatherings. For example, he was the 1885 Memorial Day speaker at a predominantly white post in Manheim, Pennsylvania. See "The Day in Manheim," *Lancaster Daily Examiner*, June 1, 1885. In other nineteenth-century social organizations, African Americans were formally excluded from membership. In her examination of nineteenth-century fraternal organizations Mary Clawson explains that "racial exclusion was a hallmark of mainstream American fraternalism throughout its history. This was accomplished not simply on a de facto basis, but by formally requiring that prospective members *must be* white." See Clawson, *Constructing Brotherhood*, 131–32 (italics in the original).

2. Three studies present differing views of the relationship between military necessity and the Emancipation Proclamation. See Franklin, *Emancipation Proclamation*; Berry, *Military Necessity and Civil Rights Policy*; and LaWanda Cox, *Lincoln and Black Freedom*. See also Guelzo, *Lincoln's Emancipation Proclamation*.

3. Millet and Maslowski, *For the Common Defense*, 196, 205; Cowley and Parker, *Reader's Companion*, 184; Tomblin, *Bluejackets and Contrabands*, 189.

4. A number of works written in the second half of the twentieth century chronicle the black military experience in the Civil War: Quarles, *Negro in the Civil War*; Cornish,

Sable Arm; Berlin, Reidy, and Rowland, *Black Military Experience* and *Freedom's Soldiers*; Glatthaar, *Forged in Battle*; Trudeau, *Like Men of War*; John David Smith, *Black Soldiers in Blue*; and Keith P. Wilson, *Campfires of Freedom*.

5. In his recent study of African Americans in the Union navy, Steven Ramold found that "while scholarship has revealed the intense racism and stereotyping that black soldiers overcame to serve in the Union Army, the Union Navy accepted African Americans with very little discord. Compared with the Army, the Union Navy compiled a highly credible record of race relations during the Civil War" (*Slaves, Sailors, Citizens*, 5). See also Tomblin, *Bluejackets and Contrabands*. For a broader study of the Union navy, see Bennett, *Union Jacks*. Addressing the invisibility of black sailors required the efforts of a number of researchers led by Joseph R. Reidy. Howard University partnered with the National Park Service and the Department of the Navy to create the Civil War Sailor database that documents the 18,000 African Americans who served in the Union navy. See United States, National Park Service, "Civil War Soldiers and Sailors System."

6. Joseph T. Wilson, *Black Phalanx*, 212–13, 217–18. Black and white veterans frequently invoke "manhood" when describing their wartime experiences. For a discussion of this idea as it relates to African American veterans, see Shaffer, *After the Glory*. For more on Port Hudson, see Hewitt, *Port Hudson*; Cunningham, *Port Hudson Campaign*; and Hollandsworth, *Louisiana Native Guards*.

7. George Washington Williams, *History of the Negro Troops*, 192, 199. For more on Williams, see Franklin, *George Washington Williams*. For more on the Fifty-fourth Massachusetts Infantry, see Burchard, *One Gallant Rush*; Emilio, *Brave Black Regiment*; Duncan, *Blue-eyed Child of Fortune* and *Where Death and Glory Meet*; Gooding, *On the Altar of Freedom*; and Blatt, Brown, and Yacovone, *Hope and Glory*.

8. Joseph T. Wilson, *Black Phalanx*, 270, 273. For more on the Thirty-fifth USCT, see Reid, *Freedom for Themselves*.

9. Fox, *Regimental Losses*, 53, 56, 421–23. Other states formed black regiments, but they ultimately became Federal units. Initially, the state organized the First Michigan Colored, later designated the 102nd USCT. Veterans frequently refer to Fox's Fighting Regiments; for example, see Connecticut, *History of the Organization of Admiral Foote Post, No. 17*, 25.

10. George Washington Williams, *History of the Negro Troops*, 231. For a biography of a black soldier who won the Medal of Honor during the Petersburg campaign, see Claxton and Puls, *Uncommon Valor*. For more on the campaigns around Petersburg, see Green, *Final Battles of the Petersburg Campaign*.

11. Fox, *Regimental Losses*, 54–55.

12. Dearing, *Veterans in Politics*, 117, and McConnell, *Glorious Contentment*, 30–33. Dearing also discussed black veterans in the GAR, focusing on controversies related to their membership in this group (see Dearing, *Veterans in Politics*, 411–19). Scholars who have studied the GAR in two states found that it was not a subsidiary of the Republican Party. In Minnesota, the GAR elected Democrats to departmental offices. The New York GAR was also willing to work with that state's Democratic Party if this alliance served its interests. See Heck, *Civil War Veteran*, 147; and Lankevich, "Grand Army of the Republic," 161–90.

13. McConnell, *Glorious Contentment*, xiv, 206; Dearing, *Veterans in Politics*, vii; Shaffer, *After the Glory*, 196.

14. New York, *Sixth*, 1872, 11 (emphasis in original); Indiana, *Thirty-ninth*, 1918, 69 (emphasis in original); Missouri, *Second*, 1883, 21; Arkansas, *Twenty-third*, 1905, 3–4.

15. Pennsylvania, *Thirty-fourth and Thirty-fifth* (semiannual), 1884, 43–44; Pennsylvania, *Fifty-second and Fifty-third* (semiannual), 1893, 160. For an example of another state's rules, see Illinois, *Twenty-sixth*, 1891, 209.

16. Missouri, *Tenth*, 1891, 119, 134–35; New Jersey, *Thirty-fifth*, 1902, 30–31; Massachusetts, *Thirty-sixth*, 1902, 55.

17. Massachusetts, *Forty-first*, 1907, 109–11; New York, *Twenty-sixth*, 1892, 256–57; Illinois, *Thirty-fifth*, 1901, 162.

18. Pennsylvania, *Forty-second* (*annual*), 1908, 211–12; New York, *Twenty-third*, 1889, 226–27; New York, *Twenty-fourth*, 1890, 249.

19. New York, *Twenty-third*, 1889, 227; New York, *Twenty-first*, 1887, 86; New Jersey, *Twenty-first*, 1888, 91.

20. For Andrew James as representative, see Pennsylvania, *Thirty-Fifth* (annual), 1901, 5; and Pennsylvania, *Thirty-ninth* (annual), 1905, 4–5, 273; for Price as delegate, see "G.A.R. Notes," *Philadelphia Inquirer*, February 9, 1884; and Pennsylvania, *Thirty-fourth and Thirty-fifth* (semiannual), 1884, 224. For the election of African Americans as representatives in various states, see Massachusetts, *Twenty-fourth*, 1890, 27; and Massachusetts, *Thirtieth*, 1896, 188. See also New Jersey, *Twenty-fifth*, 1892, 124; Potomac, *Forty-third*, 1911, 25, 78; and Rhode Island, *Thirty-ninth*, 1906, 61. Black Rhode Islanders often sat on the Council of Administration. See Rhode Island, *Twenty-sixth*, 1893, 46; Rhode Island, *Twenty-ninth*, 1896, 54–55. In many instances, African Americans served as alternate delegates. For example, Comrade Carter of Post 50, the all-black unit in Chicago, was an alternate in 1890. See Illinois, *Twenty-fourth*, 1890, 158.

21. Illinois, *Fifty-seventh*, 1923, 129, 143; Ohio, *Twenty-second*, 1888, 288; Pennsylvania, *Forty-second and Forty-third* (*semiannual*), 1888, 159, 288; Indiana, *Twenty-second*, 1901, 135, 200–201, 226; Indiana, *Twenty-third*, 1902, 134–35. A letter to state officials in Ohio claimed that "many members left because Negroes were elected to departmental offices" (Noyes, "History of the Grand Army of the Republic," 39), supporting the notion that when the GAR granted political equality to its black members, it did so realizing that not all of its white members approved.

22. Massachusetts, *Thirty-seventh*, 1903; Massachusetts, *Thirty-eighth*, 1904; and Massachusetts, *Thirty-ninth*, 1905, 52, 106. The vote for Wolff was 500 to 15; see "All Except 15 Vote for Wolff," *Boston Globe*, February 15, 1905.

CHAPTER TWO

1. Tennessee, *Eighth*, 1891, 101.

2. Davies, "Problem of Race Segregation," 354–67; Dearing, *Veterans in Politics*, 411–19; McConnell, *Glorious Contentment*, 213–15; Shaffer, *After the Glory*, 143–55.

3. Texas, *Seventh*, 1892, 72; Texas, *Eighth*, 1893, 21, 25; Alabama, *Third*, 1891, 7.

4. *Twenty-ninth National*, 1895, 82b, c, i; *Thirtieth National*, 1896, 64. Extant Texas records did not note any change in the state's racial policy; so few records of the GAR in Alabama have survived that it is difficult to determine the ultimate fate of black veterans in the state.

5. Georgia (including South Carolina), *First* (Provisional), 1889, 13; Georgia, *First*,

1890, 8, 12, 15–17. In the North, most posts were under the authority of a department that encompassed a single state; for example, the Department of Indiana comprised the state of Indiana. In the South, where the GAR was smaller, departments sometimes covered two states; for example, the Department of Georgia included South Carolina.

6. Georgia, *First*, 1890, 9; Georgia, *Roster and History*, 1894. On the Georgia controversy, see Dearing, *Veterans in Politics*, 414; McConnell, *Glorious Contentment*, 215–16; and Davies, "Problem of Race Segregation," 358. Another controversy in Arkansas was taken out of context by previous studies. Many accounts of African American GAR members in this state include a statement from an Arkansas official who complained that officials created black posts and "received money from these deluded creatures for dues year after year, and never place[d] one cent to their credit" (Arkansas, *Sixteenth*, 1898, 4–5), suggesting that exploiting black veterans was routine there. On the contrary, the official was referring to an embezzlement scheme that affected all members of the Arkansas GAR, black and white. One official involved in this scheme was court-martialed; the other died before legal action could be initiated. See Arkansas, *Sixteenth*, 1898, 4–5, 16; Arkansas, *Seventeenth*, 1899, 36; and Arkansas, *Nineteenth*, 1901, 18. For previous accounts of this incident, see Dearing, *Veterans in Politics*, 419; and Shaffer, *After the Glory*, 152.

7. *Twenty-fifth National*, 1891, 256, 257, 258. Previous studies have given the lion's share of their attention to those who advocated segregation. Since these individuals appeared to be fringe elements in the GAR, I have not quoted their views of black members. Suffice it to say, they questioned the value of black soldiers' military service and invoked the usual excuses for racial separation, including the notion that black veterans wanted their own department. See Davies, "Problem of Race Segregation," 356–63; McConnell, *Glorious Contentment*, 216–17; and Shaffer, *After the Glory*, 146–50.

8. *Twenty-fifth National*, 1891, 250, 255.

9. "Black and Whites Equal in the Eyes of the G.A.R," *New York Herald Tribune*, August 7, 1891. Even before this vote was taken, speakers supporting segregation were hissed from the galleries. In my examination of GAR records, I found no other instances of a speaker being treated in such a disrespectful manner.

10. See Shaffer, "Marching On," 259. Pictures in encampment records confirm that the position of junior vice-commander in Kentucky was usually held by an African American. See Kentucky, *Thirty-third*, 1915, 83; and Kentucky, *Thirty-fourth*, 1916, 18. Similarly in Delaware, members of the all-black post in Wilmington served as junior vice-commander of the state GAR. Three African American veterans who held this position died in 1915. See Delaware, *Thirty-fifth*, 1915, unpaged. For Georgia and South Carolina, see Georgia, *Fourth*, 1892, 58; Georgia, *Tenth*, 1898, 29; and Georgia, *Thirteenth*, 1901, 28. For black Marylanders' electoral successes, see Maryland, *Twentieth*, 1896, 40; and Maryland, *Twenty-fourth*, 1900, 62. See "The G.A.R. in Virginia," *New York Freeman*, March 19, 1887, for Virginia officeholders. One of the African Americans who served as the junior vice-commander in Maryland was John H. Murphy, editor of the *Baltimore Afro-American*. See Farrar, *Baltimore Afro-American*.

11. Shaffer, *After the Glory*, 149; *Twenty-fifth National*, 1891, 257. For number of members and delegates sent to the annual encampment for all-black posts, Post Nos. 8, 9, 12, 13, compared to the entire department, see Georgia, *Seventh*, 1895, 7–9, 20. Not all white

posts sent delegates; for example, the Blue Ridge Post of Jasper, Georgia, failed to send a representative to the encampment in 1894. See Georgia, *Sixth*, 1894, 6.

CHAPTER THREE

1. Pennsylvania, Shaw Post, *Minutes*, vol. 1, December 1881–June 1885, 41, 48, 64, 65, 69, 83, 91; vol. 2, August 1885–December 1887, 24; vol. 3, January 1897–November 1904, 3, 29, 46, 72, 76; Pennsylvania, Hull Post, *Minutes*, vol. 2, 255, 259; vol. 4, 372–73; vol. 5, 328. Citations to Shaw Post and other Pittsburgh GAR post records represent examples of these posts' interactions and are not a complete record of all such events described in these meeting minutes.

2. Pennsylvania, Shaw Post, *Minutes*, vol. 1, 23, 71; vol. 2, 8; vol. 3, 80, 157. For a detailed description of a "campfire," see McConnell, *Glorious Contentment*, 175–77, 179–80.

3. Pennsylvania, Shaw Post, *Minutes*, vol. 1, 33, 62–63, 66, 96; vol. 2, 91; vol. 3, 54, 64, 71, 94, 97, 103.

4. "Mounds and Memories," *Pittsburgh Press*, May 29, 1892, 7; "A Combined Observance," *Pittsburgh Press*, May 29, 1898, 11; Pennsylvania, Shaw Post, *Minutes*, vol. 3, 201, 211; vol. 1, 65.

5. Pennsylvania, Shaw Post, *War Sketches*. African American veterans remembered that they showed no quarter to southern troops because Confederate forces gave them no quarter; black soldiers were often murdered after they surrendered. The most notorious example of this occurred after the surrender of Fort Pillow in the western theater. Black and white soldiers were slain after they surrendered to troops under the command of Nathan Bedford Forrest. See Cimprich, *Fort Pillow*; and Ward, *River Run Red*. For more on the murder of African American soldiers and retaliation for these actions, see Urwin, *Black Flag over Dixie*; and Burkhardt, *Confederate Rage, Yankee Wrath*.

6. Pennsylvania, *Thirty-eighth and Thirty-ninth* (semiannual), 1886, 121. A black newspaper might discuss the activities of a post, and state records would confirm the post's identity. For example, an African American newspaper discussed the activities of the John Brown Post, and an examination of the death records for the GAR in the state of Illinois confirmed the racial composition of this organization. See *Western Appeal*, July 23, 1887; May 26, 1888, 1; Illinois, *Thirty-Third*, 1898, 223; and Illinois, *Thirty-Fourth*, 1899, 135.

7. Du Bois, *Autobiography*, 95.

8. Tennessee, *Tenth*, 1892, 35, 66; Massachusetts, *Twenty-seventh*, 1893, 25; Pennsylvania, *Fifty-second and Fifty-third* (semiannual), 1893, 160. I was able to identify only one all-black post in Delaware, the Sumner Post in Wilmington, because Delaware GAR records singled out this post for recognition. See Delaware, *Twenty-fourth*, 1904, 14. An article describing the parade at the 1892 national encampment of the GAR claimed that Arkansas had sixteen African American posts; my research uncovered only a handful. See "One Colored Post from Arkansas," *Washington Post*, September 21, 1892.

9. U.S. Census Bureau, *Report on the Population of the United States*, part 2. GAR records suggest that, in general, a post needed at least fifteen members to survive. Once membership fell below this number, the post usually folded. Since some veterans did

not join the GAR—at its height, only one-third of all former soldiers belonged to this group—approximately three times fifteen, or about forty-five veterans living in an area, were required to sustain an all-black post.

10. Illinois, *Thirty Seventh*, 1903, 113; McConnell, *Glorious Contentment*, 71. In freedom, African Americans established not only their own churches but also their own denominations—for example, the African Methodist Episcopal (AME) Church and the AME Zion Church. For more on the development of autonomous black social organizations and churches, see Nash, *Forging Freedom*; and Horton and Horton, *In Hope of Liberty*. In slavery, they could not create their own institutions, but they did use religion as a form of autonomy and a means of resistance. See Raboteau, *Slave Religion*, and Genovese, *Roll, Jordan, Roll: The World the Slaves Made* (to which the title of this section pays homage). For more on the black church, see Lincoln and Mamiya, *Black Church in the African-American Experience*; and Frazier, *Negro Church*.

11. Indiana, *Thirtieth*, 1909, 95; New York, *Twenty-first*, 1887, 119; New York, *Thirty-first*, 1897, 81, 297; Pennsylvania, Shaw Post, *Minutes*, vol. 1, 85; Iowa, Pratt Post, *Minute Book*, 7–8.

12. New York, *Thirtieth*, 1896, 161; Massachusetts, *Thirty-first*, 1897, 179; New Jersey, *Thirty-second*, 1899, 21, 27, 28.

13. Pennsylvania, *Fifty-first and Fifty-second* (semiannual), 1892, 181–98; Tennessee, *Tenth*, 1893, 66–69. The Bryan Post probably owned its meeting place, and this likely represented much of its property holdings. In addition, black posts in Tennessee may have owned their own meeting halls if they were unable to use white-owned facilities.

14. "True Blue," *The Sun*, May 29, 1889; Potomac, *Seventeenth*, 1885, 27; Maryland, "Inspection Report," *Eighth*, 1884; Kentucky, *Thirteenth*, 1895, 50–54; New Jersey, *Nineteenth*, 1886, 52. The price Williamsport GAR members paid for a uniform was typical. While members of the O. P. Morton Post may have taken care to wear the uniform correctly, they were not as careful with GAR rules. This post lost its charter when members admitted to allowing men to join who had not served in the Union army. Racism likely played no role in this decision; the Sumner Post, another all-black post, was part of the investigating committee. Allowing nonveterans to join a GAR post would have resulted in expulsion for any post, regardless of its racial composition. See Potomac, *Thirty-third*, 1901, 22–25.

15. GAR, *Services for the Use of the Grand Army of the Republic*; Illinois, *Twenty-eighth*, 1893, 147; "G.A.R. Notes," *Philadelphia Inquirer*, June 23, 30, 1883; Tennessee, "Inspection Report," *Tenth*, 1893; *Thirty-first National*, 1897, 66. The GAR rituals were considered secret, and in that way they were similar to those of the Masons and other fraternal groups. For more on Masonry in America, see Dumenil, *Freemasonry and American Culture*; Bullock, *Revolutionary Brotherhood*; and Muraskin, *Middle-Class Blacks in a White Society*.

16. Maryland, *Eleventh*, 1887, 38–39; Maryland, *Fifteenth*, 1891, 33; Tennessee, *Fourteenth*, 1897, 13; Ohio, *Charters*; Illinois, "Inspection Report," *Twenty-fifth*, 1891.

17. Pennsylvania, Shaw Post, *Minutes*, vols. 1–3; 2000 and 2005 Research History Class, *William A. Anderson Post 244*, 69–100; Iowa, Pratt Post, *Minute Book*.

18. Pennsylvania, *Fifty-eighth*, 1924; Pennsylvania, *Sixtieth*, 1926; Pennsylvania, *Sixty-first*, 1927; Pennsylvania, *Sixty-fourth*, 1930; Pennsylvania, *Sixty-fifth*, 1931; Indiana, *Twenty-second*, 1900, 150; Tennessee, *Tenth*, 1893, 12; Tennessee, *Thirteenth*, 1896, 39;

between Illinois, *Sixty-seventh*, 1833, and Illinois, *Sixty-ninth*, 1935, the John Brown Post failed; Maryland, *Eighteenth*, 1893, 49; Maryland, *Fifty-third*, 1929, 6; Florida, *Ninth*, 1893, 17; Florida, *Nineteenth*, 1903, 13. The GAR's longevity in Christiana reflected the legacy of antebellum radicalism of this city. When slave catchers came to this town to transport runaways back to slavery, they faced armed opposition. See Slaughter, *Bloody Dawn*.

19. Georgia, *Roster and History*, 1894, 25–26.

20. Delaware, *Twenty-fourth*, 1904, 27.

21. "Grand Army Notes," *New York Age*, January 28, 1888; January 29, 1887; "Grand Army Notes," *New York Freeman*, September 15, 1885; January 15, 1886.

22. "John H. Walker's Funeral," *New York Age*, January 26, 1889; "Celebration at Bethel," *New York Age*, November 26, 1887.

23. "A Grand Army Post Fair," *New York Age*, April 15, 1890; "A Faithless Wooer," *New York Freeman*, February 14, 1885; "Race Doings at the Hub," *New York Freeman*, April 16, 1887. These examples represented only some of the interactions between black and white posts outside New York City.

CHAPTER FOUR

1. "Grand Army Notes," *New York Freeman*, March 26, 1887.

2. African American WRC units were similar to black women's groups affiliated with fraternal groups or African American women's clubs. For more on this subject, see Joe Trotter, "African American Fraternal Organizations in American History." African American women's clubs of the late nineteenth and early twentieth centuries involved middle-class women and, like the WRC, provided charity to impoverished members of their community. However, these clubs also promoted racial uplift and had a conscious political agenda to advance African Americans' civil, economic, and social status. The African American women in the ladies' auxiliary of the GAR seemed to be from disparate class backgrounds and included less-educated women who may not have been part of the women's club movement. See Lerner, "Early Community Work of Black Club Women"; Knupfer and Silk, *Toward a Tenderer Humanity*; and Hendricks, *Gender, Race, and Politics in the Midwest*.

3. Davies, *Patriotism on Parade*, 37–38; O'Leary, *To Die For*. The LGAR prided itself on its independence. A New Jersey LGAR official commented to members of a New Jersey encampment, "We are not auxiliary to any post[. W]e are an independent organization. . . . We consider ourselves equal to you, and we are working side by side with you" (New Jersey, *Forty-fifth*, 1912, 15).

4. Davies, "Problem of Race Segregation," 367–71; O'Leary, *To Die For*, 82–90.

5. WRC, *Services and Activities*, 131–35, 412–16. This volume includes histories of the different departments and detached units of the WRC and is an invaluable record of WRC activities. It appears to have been overlooked in previous studies of this organization.

6. Ibid., 131, 414–16. Maryland was an unusual case. According to previous studies, Maryland segregated black corps in 1900. Sources chronicling the organization after this date, however, describe an interracial organization. State records list only one detached corps in the early twentieth century; this unit associated with a white post in Baltimore.

The Maryland GAR commander in 1916 thanked the WRC for its efforts. He wanted it clearly understood that he "included all our corps, white and colored" (Maryland, *Fortieth*, 1916, 13). A brief history of the Maryland WRC written in 1933 listed, in order of seniority, black and white corps together, with no indication that some of these were all-black corps. Of the six corps that still survived in this border state, two were composed of African American women. The WRC in Maryland may have received permission to segregate, but they appeared to have decided against instituting a formal color line in their group. See WRC, *Services and Activities*, 138.

7. "To the Editor of the Freeman," *New York Freeman*, March 6, 1886; WRC, Kansas, *Thirty-ninth*, 1923, 30; WRC, Indiana, *Tenth*, 1893, Inspection Records; WRC, Illinois, *Fifth*, 1888, 47; WRC, Illinois, *Sixth*, 20, 21; and WRC, Illinois, *Second*, 14.

8. Pennsylvania, Shaw Post, *Minutes*, vol. 3, 28, 43, 211. Encampment records include inspection reports which list all posts and whether they affiliate with a women's group. See Pennsylvania, *Fifty-fourth and Fifty-fifth* (semiannual), 1894, 186, 188–202 (27, 80, 103, 130, 138, 194, 206, 365, 369, 390, 412, 440, 444, 487, 520, 535, 577, 593, and 607); New Jersey, *Twenty-ninth*, 1896, 58–62 (51, 56, 65, 95, 105); and Tennessee, *Tenth*, 1893, 66–69 (4, 10, 22, 26, 66, 67, 80, 86, 102). Theda Skocpol et al. studied black fraternal organizations and found that, as with the WRC, black women seemed more likely than white women to be involved with these women's organizations (Skocpol, Liazos, and Ganz, *What a Mighty Power We Can Be*). There has been a great deal written about the relationships of white and black women in slavery and freedom. While many different views on this issue exist, I tend to agree with those who believe there was very little sisterhood between black women who were owned and the white women who may have owned them. See Fox-Genovese, *Within the Plantation Household*; and Glymph, *Out of the House of Bondage*.

9. WRC, *Seventh National*, 1891, 43; Georgia, *Ninth*, 1897; WRC, *Synopsis of Proceedings of the Woman's Relief Corps in New Jersey, 1885–1894*, 44, 45, 56; Committee on United States Colored Troops, *Souvenir Handbook and Guide*.

10. The following are examples of the New York *Freeman* and *Age*'s coverage of men's and women's groups in New York City: "Grand Army Notes," *New York Freeman*, February 14, 1885; December 12, 1885; January 1, 1887; June 13, 1885; and March 28, 1885. The following are the examples cited of men's and women's groups outside of New York: "Trenton Tips," *New York Age*, April 18, 1891; "Red Bank Etchings," *New York Age*, March 13, 1888; "To the Editor of the Freeman," *New York Freeman*, March 6, 1886; and "The G.A.R. in Norfolk," *New York Freeman*, March 28, 1885.

11. "Public Installation," *The Bee*, February 11, 1902; "R. G. Shaw Installation" and "G.A.R. Notes," *Republican Courier*, January 27, 1900; "To the Public," *Leavenworth Advocate*, June 8, 1889.

12. WRC, Connecticut, *Seventh*, 1889, 23–24; *Eighth National*, 1890, 26; *Ninth National*, 1891, 139. See O' Leary, *To Die For*, for a national focus. Francesca Morgan also focuses on the national WRC and nationalism and acknowledges the importance of the interracial nature of the WRC. See Morgan, *Women and Patriotism in Jim Crow America*.

13. WRC, Illinois, *Sixth*, 1889, 53; WRC, Kansas, *Thirty-ninth*, 1923, 30; "G.A.R. Notes," *New York Age*, April 12, 1890.

14. "G.A.R. Notes," *New York Freeman*, March 28, 1885; "Funeral of John H. Gall,"

New York Age, September 15, 1888; and "Grand Army Notes," *New York Age*, March 29, 1890. One of the members of the Bell Post's ladies' auxiliary was Susie King Taylor, who wrote an account of her wartime service as a nurse. See Taylor, *A Black Woman's Civil War Memoirs*.

15. "Flag Presentation," *New York Age*, May 21, 1891; "Grand Army Notes," *New York Age*, April 30, 1887; February 11, 1888; Pennsylvania, Shaw Post, *Minutes*, vol. 1, 30.

16. "The First Full Dress Reception (advertisement)," *New York Age*, December 28, 1889; "Grand Army Notes," *New York Freeman*, February 14, 1885; January 15, 1887; "Congregational Chats," *Western Appeal*, July 21, 1888; "Oxford," *Cleveland Gazette*, February 13, 1886; "Providence Driftings," *New York Freeman*, January 17, 1885. These are just a few examples of the types of events held by black posts and their affiliates. Many more are documented in nineteenth-century newspapers that served the black community.

17. Pennsylvania, Shaw Post, *War Sketches*, preface.

CHAPTER FIVE

1. New York, *Thirty-second*, 1898, 127, 157–62; Richings, *Evidence of the Progress*, 45–47. Mrs. Scott also spoke to the national encampment in Buffalo.

2. Black veterans' and their associates' service in this battle for Memory epitomizes a tradition in African American history, the "site of Memory." In *History and Memory in African-American Culture*, Geneviève Fabre, Robert O'Meally, and their colleagues apply the theories of French historian Pierre Nora concerning sites of Memory, or *lieux de mémoire*, to explain important phenomena in black history. Among the sites of Memory cataloged by these scholars are events such as antebellum emancipation celebrations; cultural developments, such as the blues; books, such as Ralph Ellison's *Invisible Man*; and even an entertainer who lived in France for much of her life, Josephine Baker. These scholars contend that Nora's theories are particularly useful as the means to include the common man and woman, those "'black and unknown bards,' historians without portfolio, who inscribed their world with landmarks made significant because men and women remembered them so complexly and so well that somehow traces of their memory survive to become history" (Fabre and O'Meally, *History and Memory in African-American Culture*, 8–15).

3. Levine, *Martin R. Delany*; Trefousse, *Thaddeus Stevens*; "Hawkins Boston Budget," *New York Age*, June 6, 1891; Glen B. Knight, "The Grand Army of the Republic in Lancaster County"; "Colored Veterans Organizing," *Wilkes-Barre Record*, June 26, 1884; and "Theodore W. Pratt," Lee County Post, No. 413, *Membership Cards*. For rules on GAR naming practices, see GAR, *Grand Army Blue Book*, 1884, 3.

4. Potomac, *Thirty-fourth*, 1902, 57.

5. Tennessee, *Descriptive Records*; "Providence People," *New York Age*, June 1, 1889; Maryland, *Nineteenth*, 1895, 38.

6. Pennsylvania, Shaw Post, *War Sketches*, preface; Nulty, *Confederate Florida*, 142–43, 185, 190; "G.A.R. Notes," *Philadelphia Inquirer*, June 16, 1883.

7. *New York Age*, April 20, 1905; "Grand Army Notes," *New York Freemen*, February 12, 1887; February 19, 1887.

8. "At the Grave of Thaddeus Stevens," *Daily Examiner*, May 31, 1886; "Our Fallen

Braves," *Daily Examiner*, May 28, 1890; "Ready for Memorial Day," *Daily Examiner*, May 26, 1891.

9. "Lawlessness in Kentucky," *New York Freeman*, September 5, 1885; "Grand Reunion," *Leavenworth Advocate*, January 18, 1891; "Grand Army Notes," *New York Age*, February 5, 1888. The Fort Wagner engagement took place in 1863, not 1864.

10. Pennsylvania, Shaw Post, *Minutes*, vol. 1, 8–9; "Grand Army Notes," *New York Freeman*, January 24, 1885; "Grand Army Celebration," *New York Age*, April 11, 1891; Palmer, *Colored Soldiers*. For the text of "The Black Regiment," see Guthrie, *Camp-fires of the Afro-American*, 26.

11. "Grand Army Notes," *New York Freeman*, May 27, 1887; May 21, 1887; "Topeka, Kansas," *Leavenworth Advocate*, April 11, 1890.

12. "Blood Thirsty Kentucky," *New York Freeman*, August 8, 1885; "Locals," *Kansas Blackman*, May 4, 1894; "Delaware Justice," *New York Freeman*, November 27, 1886; "Providence Letter," *New York Globe*, January 6, 1883. For a description of GAR camp-fires, see McConnell, *Glorious Contentment*, 175–77.

13. "Keith Post," *New York Freeman*, May 30, 1885; "A Bad Candidate," *New York Freeman*, October 17, 1885; "A Worthy General," *New York Freeman*, January 30, 1886.

14. "Pittsburgh Notes," *New York Freeman*, September 26, 1885; "A Virginia Celebration," *New York Age*, January 7, 1888; "Emancipation Celebration," *New York Freeman*, January 9, 1886; "Emancipation Celebration," *New York Age*, August 17, 1889; "Grand Army Notes," *New York Freeman*, February 19, 1887; "Richmond Colored Troops," *New York Freeman*, March 28, 1885; "The Fifteenth Amendment Celebration," *New York Age*, April 7, 1888. Accounts of the Garrison Post's celebration do not include a description of the composition and purpose of the Women's Vigilance Committee, but I have assumed that it was an African American women's group affiliated with the post.

15. "G.A.R. Notes," *New York Freeman*, April 18, 25, 1885; May 2, 1885; "General Ulysses S. Grant," *New York Freeman*, July 25, 1885; "Newarker Indignant," *New York Freeman*, August 15, 1885; "The Soldiers and Sailors," *New York Freeman*, April 30, 1887; "General Grant—The Dying Chief," *New York Freeman*, April 11, 1885. For more on Grant, including a detailed study of the response to his death, see Waugh, *U.S. Grant*.

16. Pennsylvania, *Eighteenth and Nineteenth* (semiannual), 1877, 15; "Delaware Doings," *New York Freeman*, September 17, 1887; "Bicentennial Celebration," *Public Ledger*, October 28, 1882; "Indignant Excursionists," *New York Freeman*, July 11, 1885; Illinois, *Fourteenth*, 1880, 59; Maryland, *Twentieth*, 1896, 32; and "The Battle of Antietam," *New York Freeman*, September 25, 1886. The inclusion of black Americans in these celebrations stands in stark contrast to social practices in antebellum Pennsylvania. Susan G. Davis's study of parades in Jacksonian-era Philadelphia demonstrates that African Americans were neither welcome in mixed-race processions nor allowed to organize their own parades. When African Americans marched, white Philadelphians rioted and attacked them and their property. See Davis, *Parades and Power*, 4, 46–47; and Shane White, " 'It Was a Proud Day.' "

17. GAR, *Unofficial Proceedings, Twenty-fourth National*, 1890, 117, 122, 124; GAR, *Unofficial Proceedings, Thirty-eighth National*, 1894, 50, 54; Kansas, *Twenty-fifth*, 1906, 160; Indiana, *Twenty-second*, 1901, 213.

18. "Heroes March to Old Tunes of War Days" and "Appearance of Parade," *Philadelphia Inquirer*, September 21, 1892.

19. "Buffalo, New York, 1897, GAR Arch Erected by the Colored Citizens," *American and Foreign Views* (Philadelphia: Griffith and Griffith, 1897).

20. Dickerson, *Relationship of the Colored Man to the Republic*, 6–7.

21. New York, *Twenty-fifth*, 1891, 231–32; Missouri, *Ninth*, 1890, 119, 120, 121, 135, 139.

22. New York, *Twenty-third*, 1889, 83–84, 240; New Jersey, *Forty-first*, 1908, 9–10, 29–30.

23. Pennsylvania, *Forty-sixth and Forty-seventh* (semiannual), 1890, 46–47.

24. Maryland, *Thirty-eighth*, 1914, 50; Pennsylvania, *Forty-second and Forty-third* (semiannual), 1888, 285–86.

25. New York, *Twenty-fifth*, 1891; Illinois, *Twenty-second*, 1888, 101; *Twenty-third*, 1889, 156; WRC, New Jersey, *Ninth*, 1892, 103.

26. Pennsylvania, *Thirty-sixth and Thirty-seventh* (semiannual), 1884, 295; New Jersey, *Twenty-Third*, 1890, 148; Massachusetts, *Thirty-ninth*, 1905, 111.

27. "At the Bethel A.M.E. Church," *West Chester Daily Local News*, May 31, 1884.

CHAPTER SIX

1. Beath, *History*, 90. For a discussion of the political uses of Emancipation Day by black southerners and Confederate Memorial Day by white southerners, see Blair, *Cities of the Dead*. For more on African American commemorations, see Clark, *Defining Moments*. While the dearth of sources often limits the scholar's ability to reconstruct the activities of nineteenth-century African Americans such as the members of the black GAR circle, a plethora of evidence facilitates re-creating their Memorial Day activities. Much of this information has come from mainstream newspapers whose editors deemed most Memorial Day events, including commemorations involving African American posts, as newsworthy.

2. "Grand Army Notes," *New York Freeman*, May 29, 1886; "Delaware Doings," *New York Freeman*, May 28, 1887; "Chestertown," *African-American Ledger*, May 30, 1896; "Sermon to the Colored Post," *Evening Sentinel*, May 29, 1899; "A Colored Preachers Eloquence," *Wilkes-Barre Record*, May 25, 1886; Pennsylvania, Shaw Post, *Minutes*, vol. 3, 70, 185, 271; Rhode Island, *Thirty-third*, 1900, 19–20.

3. "Memorial Day Observance," *Harrisburg Patriot*, May 30, 1898; "Where Sleep the Brave," *Washington Reporter*, May 30, 1892; "Grand Army Notes," *New York Age*, May 26, 1888; "New Jersey Matters," *Philadelphia Public Ledger*, June 1, 1891; "Gone but Not Forgotten," *Chambersburg Public Opinion* (Pennsylvania), June 3, 1892.

4. "Memorial Day," *York Gazette*, June 3, 1884; "How Sleep the Brave," *Washington Reporter*, May 31, 1895; "Memorial Day," *Philadelphia Public Ledger*, May 31, 1890.

5. "Elizabeth City, N.C.," *New York Age*, June 13, 1891; "Memorial Day," *Kent News* (Maryland), June 1, 1889; and *Salisbury Advertiser* (Maryland), June 1, 1889.

6. Georgia, *Roster and History*, 1894, 4; Georgia, *Fourth*, 1892, 1.

7. Georgia, *Tenth*, 1898, 21; Georgia, *Eleventh*, 1899, 18.

8. "Memorial Day Services," *New York Age*, May 23, 1907; "Memorial Day," *Philadelphia Public Ledger*, May 31, 1890; "All About Steeltown," *Harrisburg Patriot*, May 30, 1891.

9. WRC, Illinois, *Fourth*, 21; WRC, Illinois, *Fifth*, 1888, 40; WRC, Illinois, *Sixth*, 1889, 59, 64; "Sacred Concert in New Bedford," *New York Age*, June 9, 1910; Savage, *Standing Soldiers, Kneeling Slaves*, 187.

10. "Afternoon Exercise," *Daily Examiner*, May 30, 1896; "Pleasure at the Hub," *New York Freeman*, May 16, 1885.

11. "At Bethel A.M.E. Church," *West Chester Daily Local News*, May 31, 1887.

12. George Washington Williams, *Advent of the Colored Soldier*, 6; Palmer, *Colored Soldiers*, 4; "A Rhode Island Memorial," *New York Age*, June 9, 1888.

13. "Memorial Day," *Daily Evening Sentinel*, May 25, 1887; "Memorial Day Sermon," *Lancaster Daily Examiner*, May 27, 1895; "Will Attend Two Services," *Washington Reporter*, May 25, 1895; and "Memorial Day," *Washington Daily Reporter*, May 29, 1893.

14. "Memorial Day," *Daily Evening Sentinel*, May 31, 1887; "Covered with Flowers," *Gate City*, May 31, 1891; Rhode Island, *Twenty-fourth*, 1891, 124; "New Bedford News," *New York Age*, June 15, 1886; New Jersey, *Nineteenth*, 1886, 52.

15. Tennessee, *Seventeenth*, 1900, 5, 17; Maryland, *Fifteenth*, 1891, 14; Maryland, *Thirty-eighth*, 1914, 77; "The Nation's Dead in Antietam National Cemetery," *Hagerstown Herald and Torchlight*, May 30, 1889; "Local Affairs," *Hagerstown Herald and Torchlight*, May 30, 1890.

16. "At Allegheny Cemetery," *Pittsburgh Press*, May 30, 1898.

17. "New Jersey," *Philadelphia Inquirer*, May 31, 1887; Mulderink, "'We Want a Country,'" 377; "To Honor the Heroes," *Gate City*, May 30, 1895.

18. "Editorial Note," *Genius of Liberty*, June 2, 1898; "GAR Program," *Genius of Liberty*, May 25, 1899; "Memorial Day," *Republican Standard*, May 29, 1890; "The Dead Defenders," *Republican Standard*, June 1, 1893. The newspapers characterized the members of the Uniontown post as "colored Grand Army boys." This word "boy" was not a racial slight in this context. Grand Army men, white or black, often called themselves "boys" because when they served in the military most of them were very young.

CHAPTER SEVEN

1. "R. A. Pinn," *Cleveland Gazette*, December 4, 1886; "Where's Your Humanity?" *Cleveland Gazette*, June 7, 1885 (emphasis in original); "Death of a Colored Soldier," *Cleveland Gazette*, August 22, 1885; "Pinn" and "A Negro Soldier Recognized by his White Comrades," *Cleveland Gazette*, January 30, 1886.

2. "The Prudence Crandall Fund," *New York Freeman*, April 17, 1886; "Tarrytown on the Hudson," *New York Age*, January 17, 1890; New York, *Twenty-sixth*, 1892, 24, 185. The four predominantly black regiments in the U.S. Army in the postwar era were: the Ninth and Tenth Cavalry and the Twenty-fourth and the Twenty-fifth Infantry. See Dobak and Phillips, *Black Regulars*; Nankivell, *History of the Twenty-fifth Regiment*; and Christian, *Black Soldiers in Jim Crow Texas*. The African American cavalry units are better known today. See Leckie, *Buffalo Soldiers*. For previous studies of the GAR, see McConnell, *Glorious Contentment*, 71, 213; Shaffer, *After the Glory*, 153–56.

3. New York, *Twenty-sixth*, 1892, 24, 185; Michigan, *Fifteenth*, 1893, 43–47; Indiana, *Eighteenth*, *Twenty-third*, *Twenty-fourth*, and *Twenty-sixth*.

4. U.S. Census Bureau, *Report on Population of the United States at the Eleventh Census*, part 2, 815; California, Corinth Post, No. 80, Marysville, *Register of the Department of California*; Colorado and Wyoming, *Complete Records of the Members of the Grand Army of the Republic*. Integrated posts in Nebraska were identified by an examination

of Sherard, "Nebraska Civil War Grand Army of the Republic Members Index"; and Northcott, *Iowa, Kansas, and Nebraska Civil War Veterans.*

5. Virginia and North Carolina, *Encampments*, 1889–1894; Georgia and South Carolina, *Roster and History.*

6. Kentucky, *Twenty-sixth*, 1908, 42; Tennessee, *Descriptive Records*, vols. 1 and 2. Levant Dodge was a professor at Berea College, an integrated institution. He was the Kentucky department commander for two years, 1907–9, and was elected national junior vice-commander in chief in 1915. See Kentucky, *Thirty-second*, 1914, 48; and Kentucky, *Thirty-fourth*, 1916, preface.

7. Kansas, *Roster*; Sons of Union Veterans of the Civil War (Missouri), *Roster*; Kansas, *Fourth*, 36. For more on the Civil War in Kansas and Missouri, see Fellman, *Inside War*; and Castel, *Civil War Kansas.*

8. Fox, *Regimental Losses*, 422; Sargent, *GAR Massachusetts.*

9. "Happenings in New Haven," *New York Age*, December 31, 1887; Connecticut, *GAR Members List*; Fox, *Regimental Losses*, 179; Connecticut, Taylor Post, *Vitae.*

10. Voegli, *Free but Not Equal*. See also Litwack, *North of Slavery*. For Massachusetts death records, see Massachusetts, *Proceedings of the Encampments, Eighteenth [1885] to the Thirty-fifth [1901]*; and Sargent, *GAR Massachusetts*, for the list of most of the members of the GAR in this state. For Indiana deaths, see Northcott, *Indiana Civil War Veterans*. For deaths in Illinois, see Northcott and Brooks, *Grand Army of the Republic*. Sometimes, integrated posts formed in the Midwest even after white veterans initially rejected their black comrades. In Murphysboro, Illinois, an all-black post formed because white veterans refused to admit African Americans. But just as the black post was about to fold, the local white post unanimously voted to merge with the black post and welcomed African American members into their group. For an extremely well-done study on the Murphysboro GAR, see Jones et al., *Forgotten Soldiers.*

11. U.S. Census Bureau, *Report on Population of the United States*, part 2, 815; Iowa, *Muster Rolls*, vols. 1, 2, 3; "Just Recognition," *Iowa Bystander*, August 31, 1894.

12. New York, *Proceedings Twenty-second* (1888) to *Thirty-third* (1899); New Jersey, *Twenty-second* (1889) to *Forty-fifth* (1912). Anecdotal evidence suggests the presence of integrated posts in New York. For example, on the New York encampment floor, Comrade Griffith endorsed a black veteran for state chaplain, explaining that he had served as commander for a post of "230 odd members[;] within that little circle we have had ten or fifteen colored comrades" (New York, *Twenty-third*, 1889, 224).

13. I reached this conclusion after I reviewed a number of Pennsylvania encampments, including all available death records published from 1899 (*Thirty-Third*) until 1930 (*Sixty-fourth*). For the specific years cited, see *Fortieth*, 1906, and *Forty-third*, 1909. For the formation of an all-black post in Pennsylvania, see *Thirty-sixth and Thirty-seventh* (semiannual), 1885, 260–61. For nine years of Ohio death records, see *Twentieth*, 1886, to *Twenty-ninth*, 1895. Robert Pinn described the makeup of GAR posts in Cleveland. See "R. A. Pinn," *Cleveland Gazette*, December 4, 1886.

14. Hunt, *Good Men Who Won the War*. Russel Beatie is writing a multivolume history of the Army of the Potomac, but the best completed study of this army is Bruce Catton's magisterial trilogy, *Mr. Lincoln's Army*; *Glory Road*; and *A Stillness at Appo-*

mattox. For more on the western war, see Daniel, *Days of Glory*, a study on the largest Union army in that theater.

15. Massachusetts, *Sixteenth*, 1882, 20 (emphasis in original); New York, *Twenty-first*, 1887, 81; Beath, *History*; GAR, *Grand Army Blue Book*, 1886, 22. The Shaw Post recovered temporarily, though it ultimately failed. At least one member of the Shaw Post joined another integrated New Bedford post, Post 190, one of the last posts formed in this state. See Sargent, *GAR Massachusetts*, rosters of Post 146 (Shaw) and 190.

16. GAR, *Grand Army Blue Book*, 1884, 21; GAR, *Grand Army Blue Book*, 1904, 33.

17. New York, *Encampment*, 1884, 25; Massachusetts, *Eighteenth*, 1884, 88; Massachusetts, *Nineteenth*, 1885, 94; Massachusetts, *Twenty-fifth*, 1891, 110; Sargent, *GAR Massachusetts*; New York, *Encampment*, 1884, 25. According to a history of the African American community in Elgin, Illinois, "there was some amazement" when John C. Hall, barber and veteran of the Twenty-ninth USCT, "was accepted as a member of the local post of the Grand Army of the Republic and a white applicant rejected" (Alft, *Elgin's Black Heritage*, 29).

18. "Again the Color Line," *New York Freeman*, reprinted from the *Waterbury* [Conn.] *American*, November 6, 1886; "The Old Soldier," *Leavenworth Advocate*, September 21, 1889; *Detroit Plaindealer*, November 30, 1889. The article in the *Leavenworth Advocate* did not identify the location of Moberly. An examination of Missouri GAR records suggests that it was the Moberly Post in this nearby state. The black post in Moberly, the Perril Post, no. 539, may have formed because of racial exclusion. The *Detroit Plaindealer* placed this untitled piece in the section of the paper featuring news from other African American newspapers and did not attribute the story.

19. *Times-Democrat*, December 10, 1889; Connecticut, Lyon Post, *Minute Books*, September 17, 1889; October 1, 1889; October 15, 1889; Connecticut, Taylor Post, *Descriptive Book*. A comparison of the African American members of both posts revealed that at least three of the Lyon Post's black members later belonged to the Taylor Post. See Connecticut, *GAR Members List*.

20. Connecticut, Lyon Post, *Minute Books*, October 29, 1889; November 19, 1889; December 3, 1889; January 21, 1890; April 1, 1890; *Detroit Plaindealer*, December 20, 1889. Forbes was listed in post records as a journalist, and he may have reported the circumstances of Hamilton's rejection to the press. Since members pledged never to divulge GAR proceedings, he may have been charged for reporting Hamilton's story to outsiders. Green listed his occupation as "pressman," so he may have also worked for a newspaper. See Connecticut, Lyon Post, *Roster*. Court-martials were rare in GAR posts. Stuart McConnell examined the records of the thirty-six posts in Philadelphia and found that these units averaged only two convictions each between 1875 and 1900. See McConnell, *Glorious Contentment*, 41.

21. Connecticut, Taylor Post, *Minutes* and *Muster Roll*; untitled, *Detroit Plaindealer*, December 20, 1890.

22. "Color Line Drawn Again," *New York Freeman*, September 17, 1887; "Wm. H. Dupree of Massachusetts," *New York Freeman*, March 14, 1885. It has been virtually impossible to delineate the role of other African Americans in the GAR circle who were associated with a predominantly white post. Black post members and their associates themselves are only visible because of their membership in or affiliation with African American units. A pamphlet describing the post's trip to the national encampment

listed Mrs. Dupree as a member of the WRC. Since Dupree was not a common name, we can assume that this was William Dupree's wife. See Massachusetts, *Historical Souvenir*.

23. Letter from John Will, adjutant, Crocker Post, Des Moines, Iowa, to the assistant adjutant general, Department of Iowa, September 30, 1887; Iowa, Crocker Post, *Minutes*, vol. 1, 225–27; vol. 2, 4–5, 83. Bruce was not the first African American veteran to apply for membership in the Crocker Post; two black veterans had already joined this group. J. A. Palmer of the Fifty-fourth Massachusetts joined in 1883, and Henry Harrison of the Sixtieth USCT joined in 1886. These men may have been more acceptable since they had served in a famous unit and Iowa's own black regiment, respectively. See Iowa, Crocker Post, *Minutes*, vol. 1, 86, 193, and *Descriptive Book*. To re-create the day-to-day operations of mixed-race organizations I focused on the meeting minutes of three integrated units: the Crocker Post in Des Moines, Iowa; the Taylor Post in Hartford, Connecticut; and the Welch Post in Ann Arbor, Michigan.

24. Michigan, Welch Post, *Record Book*, vol. 1, 40–43, 88.

CHAPTER EIGHT

1. "Obituary Notes," *New York Times*, January 31, 1915. Before her death, Nichols was featured on the front page of the *Saturday Globe*, a national newspaper, which described the attention she received at the GAR's national encampment in 1900. See "A Colored Woman Veteran," *Saturday Globe*, September 1, 1900. For the story of the *Saturday Globe*, see Frasca, *Rise and Fall of the Saturday Globe*.

2. Blight, *Race and Reunion*, 195.

3. Dearing, *Veterans in Politics*, 117; Elgin Historical Society, *Obituaries*, 118, 215.

4. Michigan, Welch Post, *Record Book*, vol. 2, 324; Connecticut, Taylor Post, *Scrapbook*, 1907–1924; and *Descriptive Book*; Iowa, Crocker Post, *Minutes*, vol. 1, 87.

5. Michigan, Welch Post, *Record Book*, vol. 3, 90; Connecticut, Taylor Post, *Minutes*, vol. 4, 39; Iowa, Polk County Posts, *Membership Cards*; Connecticut, Admiral Foote Post, *Descriptive Book*; Illinois, Veterans Post, *Muster Roll*. GAR posts tended to attract a cross-section of society; even elite posts, such as Post 2 in Philadelphia, had a number of skilled and unskilled workers in their ranks. No other organization with pretensions of elitism would have welcomed any of these men. See McConnell, *Glorious Contentment*, 58–59.

6. Ohio, Tod Post, *Descriptive Book*; Connecticut, Taylor Post, *Descriptive Book*; Iowa, Crocker Post, *Descriptive Book*; Tennessee, *Descriptive Records*, vol. 1. This mix was not representative of the black population as a whole since most African Americans in this era worked in agriculture. It might be a fair representation of black veterans who were more prosperous than their nonveteran counterparts and more likely to pursue high-status occupations. See Shaffer, *After the Glory*, 45–59.

7. Illinois, Veterans Post, *Muster Roll*; Iowa, Crocker Post, *Descriptive Book*. The 1890 census report includes a summary of the population of veterans in cities with populations of over twenty-five thousand, which included Des Moines but not Elgin. Since approximately 10 percent of all white veterans were foreign-born in this Iowa city, the Crocker Post's membership reflected the makeup of this city's veteran population. See U.S. Census Bureau, *Report on the Population of the United States*, part 2, 815–16.

8. Connecticut, Admiral Foote Post and Merwin Post, *Descriptive Book*; Connecticut, *GAR Members List*.

9. Connecticut, *Twenty-fifth*, 1892, 56; Connecticut, *Encampment*, 1886, 30.

10. Iowa, Crocker Post, *Descriptive Book*; Kansas, *Roster*, 1895, 80; Kansas, *Twenty-fifth*, 1906, 167; Massachusetts, *Forty-fifth*, 1911, 84. (The Major How Post is spelled with no "e.")

11. Iowa, Torrence Post, *Bylaws and Roster*, 3, 34; Veterans Post, *Muster Roll*; Tennessee, *Descriptive Records*, vols. 1 and 2.

12. "Massachusetts," *Grand Army Record* 2, no. 11 (October 1887): 8; Ohio, Tod Post, *Personnel War Sketches*.

13. Connecticut, Taylor Post, *Vitae*; Iowa, Crocker Post, *Descriptive Book*.

14. Many of the members of the Griffin Post had served in the Fifty-second Pennsylvania. Another unit heavily represented was the Second Pennsylvania Heavy Artillery. The Ezra Griffin Camp of the Sons of Union Veterans provided me with a roster of this post. I discovered the Cazenovia, New York, post when I was contacted by the PBS show *The History Detectives*; the staff was investigating an integrated post there. The 114th New York was designated one of Fox's fighting three hundred regiments. See Ancestry.com, *1890 Veterans Schedules*, Cazenovia, New York, to identify the regiments of local veterans. I consulted Dyer's *Compendium of the War of the Rebellion* for the service of Civil War regiments.

15. Tennessee, *Thirty-third*, 1916, 24; Tennessee, *Descriptive Records*, vols. 1 and 2; *Cleveland Gazette*, December 12, 1885; Ohio, *Charters*; Iowa, *Muster Rolls*, vols. 1–3. The GAR post in Covert was only one part of an integrated northern community. See Anna-Lisa Cox, *Stronger Kinship*.

16. Michigan, Welch Post, *Record Book*, vol. 2, 47, 130, 196, 541; Connecticut, Taylor Post, *Minutes*, vol. 3, 267–68; vol. 4, 21, 105, 115.

17. Massachusetts, *Thirty-seventh*, 1904, 28; Massachusetts, *Thirty-first*, 1897, 22; Massachusetts, *Thirty-fifth*, 1902, 26; Connecticut, *Twenty-seventh* 1894, 13; Kentucky, *Twenty-sixth*, 1908, 42. Adelle Logan Alexander chronicles the life of her great-grandfather in *Homeland and Waterways*. Singleton wrote a brief memoir of his life as a slave and a free man in the 1920s. See Singleton, *Recollections*. For more on William Benjamin Gould and his GAR involvement, see the book by his great-grandson, Gould, *Diary of a Contraband*, 45–46, 90, 163, 289, 294–97. It is difficult to determine how many black veterans from integrated posts held high office because lists of post officers do not mention race. Had the GAR listed the wartime units and ranks of these officers, then racial identification would be simple. In some cases, observers noted the fact that African American veterans achieved such rank. Posts also elected representatives to the state, and Bond and Singleton acted as delegates. If a black veteran was a post commander, he also attended state encampments as a delegate.

18. Iowa, Crocker Post, *Minutes*, vol. 2, 36; Michigan, Welch Post, *Record Book*, vol. 2, 9, 47, 81, 282, 560, 571; Connecticut, Taylor Post, *Minutes*, vol. 4, 3, 69, 103; Illinois, Veterans Post, *Muster Roll*. Professionals and white-collar veterans dominated post leadership roles, though a surprising number of skilled craftsmen achieved high post office as well. Laborers, janitors, and other unskilled veterans did not hold high office. See McConnell, *Glorious Contentment*, 58–59, 63–64, 66.

19. "General Butler in Line," *Washington Post*, September 21, 1892; "Just Recogni-

tion," *Iowa Bystander*, August 31, 1894; Connecticut, Taylor Post, *Minutes*, vol. 4, 39; Tennessee, *Nineteenth*, 1902, 20, 32–33. John Talley was the department color-bearer in 1904, 1906, and 1908. Black veterans occupied this position in 1902 and 1903 but they belonged to all-black posts. Tennessee was obviously pleased with the notoriety its "Colored Comrades" afforded it. See Tennessee, *Encampments*, 1902, 1903, 1904, 1906, and 1908.

20. Michigan, Welch Post, *Record Book*, vol. 2, 44, 608; Iowa, Crocker Post, *Minutes*, vol. 2, 191; vol. 4, 137; Connecticut, Taylor Post, *Minutes*, vol. 4, 95; Connecticut, Long Post, *Ledger*, 96–103.

21. Salvatore, *We All Got History*.

22. Michigan, Welch Post, *Record Book*, vol. 2, 275; Connecticut, Taylor Post, *Minutes*, vol. 4, 213.

23. Michigan, Welch Post, *Record Book*, vol. 2, 146–47, 148, 516, 545, 569.

24. Civil War Pension File of Lucy Nichols (Higgs), National Archives, Washington, D.C.

25. "Back in the Old Days"; "Once Upon a Time"; and Yuoule, *History of Clinton County Iowa*, in Elizabeth Fairfax File, Clinton County Historical Society.

26. Tappan, *Passing of the Grand Army*; Kimball, *Brinley Hall Album*, 167–79.

27. "A Brave Soldier," *Youngstown Daily Vindicator*, January 25, 1898; "Oscar Boggess," *Youngstown Daily Vindicator*, October 10, 1907; "Gallant," *Youngstown Daily Vindicator*, October 26, 1906. At least two other monuments included black and white Civil War soldiers and sailors in the United States. The best known is the monument to the Fifty-fourth Massachusetts in Boston; lesser known is Brooklyn's Civil War memorial. In his study of Civil War memorialization, Kirk Savage argues that these monuments were atypical, "extremely ambitious projects in urban areas [and] . . . in both cases the size and sculptural programs left some room for black representation." In contrast, he argues, in local small-town monuments, the "'representative' soldier . . . always took the image of the white majority." See Savage, *Standing Soldiers*, 185, 191–92. Given the small black population in small towns in the North, a white soldier represents the supra-majority of all soldiers from that area. In fact, many towns likely sent no black soldiers to war.

28. Massachusetts, *Twenty-eighth*, 1894, 166.

29. Robinson, *Decoration Day*, 5.

CHAPTER NINE

1. O'Reilly, *Baked Meats of the Funeral*, 205–6. While other, slightly different versions of this poem exist, I chose this version because it was in a collection published during Halpine's life and presumably with his editorial approval. For more on Halpine, see Roosevelt, *Poetical Works of Charles G. Halpine*.

2. O'Reilly, *Baked Meats of the Funeral*, 59–60; *Decoration Day*, 1882, 51; Maryland, *Eighteenth*, 1894, 28; Massachusetts, *Twenty-first*, 1887, 33.

3. Massachusetts, *Fifty-first*, 1917, 123–24. See also Pennsylvania, Shaw Post, *Minutes*, vol. 1, 41.

4. Pennsylvania, *Forty-eighth*, 1914, 32; Pennsylvania, *Forty-Ninth*, 1915, 36–37; *Twenty-first National*, 1887, 251; New York, *Encampments* (annual and semiannual),

1884–85, 58; Beath, *History*. For a study highlighting the contributions of foreign-born USCT officers, see Ofele, *German-Speaking Officers*.

5. "To Do or Die," *National Tribune*, July 5, 1894; "The Crater, Awful Fight in the Exploded Mine Before Petersburg," *National Tribune*, November 6, 1884; "The Colored Troops, Organization and Service in the Army of the Cumberland," *National Tribune*, July 14, 28, 1887; August 4, 11, 1887. The newspaper accounts of the Thirtieth USCT's travails, which included the description of the attack on Petersburg, were published in Bowley, *Honor in Command*. For more on the Memory of white and black soldiers, see Fleche, "'Shoulder to Shoulder as Comrades Tried.'"

6. Pennsylvania, Shaw Post, *War Sketches*; Connecticut, Taylor Post, *Vitae*; Ohio, Tod Post, *War Sketches*. The *Vitae* of Taylor Post members contain the information transcribed in the personal war sketches.

7. Ohio, Tod Post, *War Sketches*; Michigan, Welch Post, *War Sketches*; "At the Bethel A.M.E. Church," *West Chester Daily Local News*, May 31, 1886.

8. Pennsylvania, Shaw Post, *War Sketches*; Connecticut, Taylor Post, *Vitae*.

9. Niven, *Connecticut for the Union*; Connecticut, *Encampment*, 1883, 73. Only three Connecticut regiments fought at Gettysburg, and all three were transferred with the Eleventh and Twelfth Corps to the West. See Hewett, *Supplemental to the Official Records*, part 2, vol. 3, serial 15–16. Ironically, Niven makes no mention of the wartime activities of the Twenty-ninth Connecticut, the state's all-black regiment. For information on this unit, see Newton, *Out of the Briars*.

10. Michigan, Welch Post, *War Sketches*; Connecticut, Taylor Post, *Vitae*. Ironically, I was unable to locate any personal war sketches written by African American soldiers who fought at Port Hudson. Perhaps most of these soldiers were born in the Deep South and did not join the northern posts whose records I examined.

11. *Twenty-ninth National*, 1895, 354; Ohio, *Twenty-sixth*, 1892, 132.

12. *Grand Army Record*, vol. 3, no. 2, December 1887, 6; Matthews, *Poems of American Patriotism*, 218–21; Blight, *Race and Reunion*, 192; *Twenty-first National*, 1887, 253.

13. Ohio, *Twenty-sixth*, 1892, 7; Illinois, *Twenty-ninth*, 1895, 224; Indiana, *Twelfth*, 1891, 82.

14. Pennsylvania, *Encampments*, 1867–72, appendix, 8; Delaware, *Twenty-fourth*, 1904, 27–28; "In War and in Peace," *West Chester Daily News*, May 31, 1900.

15. Indiana, *Twenty-fifth*, 1904, 6.

16. Kansas, *Twenty-fifth*, 1906, 117.

17. Schacter, *Seven Sins of Memory*, 162, 174. For a study of the biochemical basis of trauma and Memory, see Hu et al., "Emotion Enhances Learning." For an explanation of this study for the general reader, see Johns Hopkins Medical Institutions, "Why Emotionally Charged Events Are So Memorable."

18. Pennsylvania, Shaw Post, *Vitae*; Ohio, Tod Post, *War Sketches*; Connecticut, Taylor Post, *Vitae*.

19. Ohio, Tod Post, *War Sketches*; Pennsylvania, Shaw Post, *War Sketches*.

20. Connecticut, Taylor Post, *Vitae* and *Minutes*, vol. 1, 121; Pennsylvania, Shaw Post, *War Sketches*.

21. Connecticut, Taylor Post, *Vitae*; Pennsylvania, Childs Post, *War Sketches*; Michigan, Welch Post, *War Sketches*.

22. Pennsylvania, Shaw Post, *War Sketches*; Connecticut, Taylor Post, *Vitae*; Pennsylvania, Childs Post, *War Sketches*.

23. A number of studies have examined Andersonville prison and the experience of the prisoners in that camp. Some modern studies argued that conditions at this prison were the product of circumstances beyond the control of the Confederate commander, Henry Wirz, the only southern officer tried and executed for war crimes after Appomattox. See William Marvel, *Andersonville*. James M. Gillispie (*Andersonvilles of the North*) examined northern prisons that have been compared to Andersonville and argues that while conditions were terrible in these institutions, it was a sin of omission and not commission. Charles Sanders (*While in the Hands of the Enemy*) argues that the cruelty in Civil War prisons was intentional.

24. Taylor Post, *Minutes*, vol. 4, 179; Connecticut, *Twenty-second*, 1889, 121; Taylor Post, *Vitae*; Tod Post, *War Sketches*; Welch Post, *War Sketches*.

25. Ohio, Tod Post, *War Sketches*; Michigan, Welch Post, *War Sketches*. Bell Wiley (*Life of Billy Yank*) estimates that the standard load carried by a soldier, which included forty—not sixty—rounds, and not including his overcoat, weighed forty or fifty pounds.

26. Michigan, Welch Post, *War Sketches*; Ohio, Tod Post, *War Sketches*.

27. Iowa, Crocker Post, *Minutes*, vol. 1, 1877–88, 39; Michigan, Welch Post, *War Sketches*; Pennsylvania, Shaw Post, *War Sketches*; Ohio, Tod Post, *War Sketches*. Nesbitt, who stated, "I was a Slave and was owned by William Nesbitt of Gordon County, Georgia," was the only member of the Shaw Post to record his prewar status as a slave.

CHAPTER TEN

1. "Corporal James Tanner," *Grand Army Record* 1, no. 9 (July 1886); New York, *Twenty-seventh*, 1893, 106; Thomas, *Robert E. Lee*, 271.

2. Dearing, *Veterans in Politics*, vii; McMurry, "Bureau of Pensions," 343–47. Dearing was not the first to decry costly veterans' pensions. In his study of Revolutionary War soldiers, John Resch states: "Opponents denounced the [Revolutionary War pension] bill for breaching the Founders' republican principle that pension establishments were aristocratic and vice-ridden institutions that undermined civic virtue" (Resch, *Suffering Soldiers*, ix). Similar language was used in a study of all pensions ever awarded to American soldiers written almost one hundred years after the Revolutionary War pension was approved. The author—who, ironically, published this study under the auspices of the Carnegie Institute for Peace—argued that "the most serious evils that have risen have been in connection with the [Civil War] service pension system" (Glasson, *Federal Military Pensions*, 147). Theda Skocpol examined soldiers' pensions and determined that while some Progressive Era reformers hoped to "transform Civil War pensions into more universally publicly funded benefits for all workingmen and the[ir] families, . . . many elite and middle-class Americans viewed Civil War pensions as a prime example of government profligacy and electorally rooted political corruption" (Skocpol, *Protecting Soldiers and Mothers*, 2).

3. Illinois, *Forty-seventh*, 1913, 90; Palmer, *Colored Soldiers*, 2.

4. Pennsylvania, *Fifty-second and Fifty-third* (semiannual), 1893, 150; Ohio, *Twenty-first*, 1887, 245; Massachusetts, *Early History*, 329.

5. Fussell, *Great War*; Silber, *Romance of Reunion*.

6. G. Edward White, *Oliver Wendell Holmes, Jr.*

7. U.S. Department of the Interior, *Report of the Secretary of the Interior*, 68–69. Veterans still suffering from wartime illnesses could move to an extensive system of soldiers' homes. Patrick Kelly (*Creating a National Home*, 125) found that from 1865 until 1900, nearly one hundred thousand veterans stayed in one of the regionally based National Homes. The GAR, particularly at the grassroots post level, was concerned with veterans who did not go to the soldiers' homes, including those who resisted being institutionalized in a military setting and those who refused to abandon their families. The national GAR fought for pensions to help these men, and local posts cared for them when necessary.

8. Connecticut, Taylor Post, *Scrapbook*, 1911; New Jersey, *Twenty-seventh*, 1894, 39; Massachusetts, *Twenty-eighth*, 1894, 166.

9. Pennsylvania, Childs Post, *War Sketches*; New York, *Twenty-sixth*, 1892, 145.

10. Iowa, *Fourteenth*, 1888, 48; "In War and in Peace," *West Chester Daily News*, May 31, 1900; "Death of a Colored Soldier," *Cleveland Gazette*, August 22, 1885; "Death of a Veteran," *New York Age*, August 4, 1888.

11. For an example of an all-black GAR post's charitable efforts, see Pennsylvania, Shaw Post, *Minutes*, vol. 1, 33, 62–63, 66, 96; vol. 2, 91; vol. 3, 19, 64, 71, 94, 97, 103. A record of the death of Comrade Jacobs and the post's efforts to support his widow are found in Michigan, Welch Post, *Record Book*, vol. 2, 146–48, 516, 545, 569. Veterans who were suffering from illnesses that were not related to their wartime service still would have received their comrades' assistance.

12. Kelly, *Creating a National Home*, 31–47, 62–67; Connecticut, *Seventh Annual*, 1889, 23–24. Cecilia O'Leary argues that while the WRC "narrowly focused on charitable work at the outset," these units "had transformed themselves into a significant nationalist force by the end of the nineteenth century" (O'Leary, *To Die For*, 70). The change in role may be due to the fact that by the time of the Spanish-American War, there were fewer and fewer soldiers to care for and many of the women of the WRC were from the successor generation; a middle-aged woman during this period would have been a child during the war. Theda Skocpol traced the origins of certain government programs for women—for example, mother's pensions—to the expansion of women's voluntary organizations like the WRC in the nineteenth and early twentieth centuries (see Skocpol, *Protecting Soldiers and Mothers*, 20, 323–40, 424–79). On how benevolent movements were shaped by more than notions of gender roles in this era, see Ginzberg, *Women and the Work of Benevolence*.

13. Iowa, *Fifteenth*, 1889, 157; New Jersey, *Twenty-fourth*, 1891, 80. Theda Skocpol argues that the pensions passed in 1890 "cannot be set aside as mere unavoidable concomitants of the human damage inflicted by the original human conflict, [because] the extension of Civil War benefits came after claims directly due to wartime casualties had peaked and were in decline" (Skocpol, *Protecting Soldiers and Mothers*, 7). The GAR argued that the granting of service-based pensions was a response to a decline in the number of veterans' pensions being approved. Soldiers found it difficult to prove a service-related disability that was aggravated by their advancing age, years after the war's end. Eric T. Dean (*Shook Over Hell*) documented PTSD in Civil War veterans using the records of an Indiana insane asylum as one way of challenging the notion that

Vietnam veterans were somehow the only American veterans to experience this disorder. For a discussion of contemporary nineteenth-century theory that rooted mental illness in physical ailments, see Dean, *Shook Over Hell*, 144–47. Even before doctors understood PTSD, they studied the effect of wartime service on the cardiac and nervous systems of soldiers. Based on studies of soldiers' experiences in the Civil War through World War I, medical professionals identified what they considered illnesses related to military service: "Soldier Hearts," "Irritable Heart," or "DaCostas Syndrome." Soldiers experienced heart palpitations, shortness of breath, and chest pain that medical professionals initially diagnosed as caused by the physical strain of military service. While some of these soldiers may have had cardiac disease, many medical professionals today believe that these symptoms were caused by post-traumatic stress disorder. In a 1918 article on this syndrome, the authors noted that in some cases these attacks occurred in individuals "with a history of shell shock or severe physical or mental stress immediately preceding the onset." Another article in the same medical journal admitted that "some even believe that the 'irritable heart' represents merely the cardiac difficulties of soldiers suffering from war neuroses" (Fraser and Wilson, "Sympathetic Nervous System"; Oppenheimer and Rothschild, "Psychoneurotic Factor"). See also Wooley, *Irritable Heart*.

14. Pizarro, Silver, and Prause, "Physical and Mental Health Costs."

15. Civil War Pension File of Lucy Nichols (Higgs), National Archives, Washington, D.C. There is much outstanding literature on the effect of the Vietnam War on nurses. See, for example, Van Deventer, *Home before Morning*. For an excellent oral history on women who served in various capacities in Vietnam, see Walker, *Piece of My Heart*.

16. Shay, *Achilles in Vietnam* and *Odysseus in America*.

17. Kansas, *Fifth*, 1886, 27; Pennsylvania, Childs Post, *War Sketches*; Michigan, Welch Post, *Record Book*, vol. 3, 15; Michigan, Welch Post, *War Sketches*.

18. For a description of the successful reintegration of World War II veterans into society, see Gambone, *Greatest Generation Comes Home*. For a discussion of the troubled homecoming of World War II veterans, see Childers, *Soldier from the War Returning*.

19. Ohio, *Twenty-ninth*, 1891, 151–52; Ohio, *Twentieth*, 1882, 126; and "A Romance of the Rebellion," *Grand Army Record* 1, no. 7 (May 1886): 4. Veterans clearly would agree with Nina Silber about the "sentimental rubric [which] took hold of the reunion process" (Silber, *Romance of Reunion*, 3). Scholars have noted the reunions held by veterans and have accused—and that is the proper term—northern veterans of reconciling with their former enemies. David Blight condemns their reconciliation efforts out of hand because he believes that they were part of the greater failure of postwar American society to protect black civil rights. According to Blight, "As American society slid into a racial nightmare, most veterans on both sides were having an 'adorable reunion'" based on a shared nonideological "soldier's faith" and "the soldierly virtue of devotion, whatever the cause." Blight found this notion of a "soldier's faith" in a speech by Civil War veteran Oliver Wendell Holmes, who described it as the willingness to "throw away his life in obedience to a blindly accepted duty, in a cause which he little understands." This speech was not made to Holmes's fellow veterans, who had their own notions of what they died for, but rather to the Harvard class of 1895 as part of a larger campaign to encourage manliness among American youth at century's end. See Blight, *Race and*

Reunion, 86, 208–10. Holmes's idea that soldiers' dying and, more importantly, suffering were noble regardless of their cause would not have been a welcome sentiment at a GAR meeting. Nina Silber, who is more skeptical about the Grand Army of the Republic's participation in this national lovefest, argues that reconciliation challenged northern soldiers' masculinity. According to Silber, "As late as the 1890s, one could hear the voices of the Grand Army of the Republic members who objected to bonding with their enemies, at least the type of bonding that might deny the Union veteran the chance to reflect on his manly accomplishments" (Silber, *Romance of Reunion*, 11). John Neff (*Honoring the Civil War Dead*) found the same reluctant reunionism.

20. Illinois, *Forty-eighth*, 1914, 141; West Virginia, *Third*, 1885, 6; New York, *Twenty-fourth*, 1890, 75.

21. Texas, *Twenty-eighth*, 1913, 8; New Jersey, *Thirty-sixth*, 1903, 61.

CHAPTER ELEVEN

1. Ohio, *Twenty-ninth*, 1895, 205; Kansas, *Twenty-fifth*, 1906, 117.

2. For the text of Webster's famous speech, see Safire, *Lend Me Your Ears*, 241–52. My research supports the views of Earl J. Hess, who found that a significant percentage of veterans who wrote of their wartime experiences argued that they had fought both to free the slaves and to preserve the Union. See Hess, *Union Soldier in Battle*, 158–90.

3. Kentucky, *Twentieth*, 1902, 68; Kentucky, *Twenty-first*, 1903, 40; Missouri, *Eighteenth*, 1898, 94; New Jersey, *Thirtieth*, 1896, 11; "False School History," *Grand Army Record* 10, no. 11 (November 1895): 84.

4. Indiana, *Eighteenth*, 1897, 165; Missouri, *Eighteenth*, 1898, 94 (emphasis in original).

5. Kansas, *Fifteenth*, 1896, 68; New York, *Thirty-second*, 1898, 73; Massachusetts, *Thirty-second*, 1898, 176.

6. Potomac, *Thirty-fourth*, 1902, 50; Massachusetts, *Thirty-first*, 1897, 53. These are representative comments of northern veterans describing their opposition to some aspects of reunion with their former enemies, particularly if reunion included forgetting their Won Cause. Many GAR members expressed these sentiments. The sheer vitriol of these men against the Confederacy and its Lost Cause, particularly southerners' efforts to shape Civil War Memory, is astonishing and represents one of the most surprising findings of this study.

7. Ohio, *Twenty-first*, 1891; George Washington Williams, *Advent of the Colored Soldier*, 3–4 (emphasis in original); New York, *Twenty-ninth*, 1895, 95; New Jersey, *Nineteenth*, 1886, 131.

8. Connecticut, *Encampment*, 1886, 95; Ohio, *Twenty-sixth*, 1892, 131.

9. "In Bethel A.M.E. Church," *West Chester Daily Local News*, May 31, 1897; George Washington Williams, *Advent of the Colored Soldier*, 4–5 (emphasis in original); "In War and in Peace," *West Chester Daily Local News*, May 31, 1900. Everyone, with the exception of the Confederate legislature, understood the relationship between black military service and freedom; in 1865, it voted to arm slaves but not free them. Davis, encouraged by Lee, freed by executive order those who agreed to serve. See Durden, *Gray and the Black*; and Levine, *Confederate Emancipation*.

10. New York, *Thirty-third*, 1899, 67; Moore, *Problem of the Rebellion*, 19, 22, 25; Delaware, *History of the Grand Army of the Republic*, 89.

11. Ohio, *Twenty-fifth*, 1891, 67; Tennessee, *Nineteenth*, 1902, 60; Illinois, *Thirtieth*, 1896, 118.

12. Massachusetts, *Forty-ninth*, 1915, 50; Indiana, *Thirty-seventh*, 117; New York, *Twenty-third*, 1889, 57.

13. Pennsylvania, *Thirty-fifth*, 1901, 61; Ohio, *Twenty-first*, 1887, 162; Massachusetts, *Eighth*, 1874, 157–58; Massachusetts, *Forty-seventh*, 1913, 172. Mayor John Francis Fitzgerald was the father of Rose Kennedy and grandfather of John Fitzgerald Kennedy, the thirty-fifth president of the United States. See Goodwin, *Fitzgeralds and the Kennedys*. James Wolff, the Massachusetts state commander, expressed his "personal regard and personal respect" for Mayor Fitzgerald. When Fitzgerald was a Democratic congressmen, Wolff explained, he rose "up in justice and fair play, and rebuke[d] the men who were falsifying the record" of African Americans. In contrast, Wolff said, Republicans "permitted abuses to be heaped on my race" (Massachusetts, *Fortieth*, 1906, 124).

14. Massachusetts, *Thirty-seventh*, 1903, 141; Pennsylvania, *Fourteenth and Fifteenth* (semiannual), 1874, 51; *Decoration Day*, 1882, 92; Moore, "Problem of the Rebellion," 6, 8.

15. Pennsylvania, *Forty and Forty-first*, 1887, 299; Rhode Island, *Twenty-seventh*, 16; New York, *Thirty-second*, 1898, 159.

16. Illinois, *Thirty-eighth*, 1904, 160; Illinois, *Thirty-fifth*, 1901, 178; Illinois, *Forty-ninth*, 1915, 88; Kansas, *Twentieth*, 1901, 53; Arkansas, *Twenty-first*, 1903, 42; Ohio, *Twenty-second*, 1888, 163. Northern soldiers' wartime letters demonstrate their understanding that they fought for both Union and liberty. James McPherson argues that while initially soldiers rarely believed they were fighting for black freedom alone, they realized over the long years of this conflict that the "abolition of slavery was inseparably linked to the goal of preserving the Union." See McPherson, *For Cause and Comrades*, 117.

17. New York, *Decoration Day*, 1882, 95; Indiana, *Thirty-ninth*, 1918, 137.

18. Dickerson, *Relationship of the Colored Man to the Republic*, 5–6; George Washington Williams, *Advent of the Colored Soldier*, 9; "Grand Army Notes," *New York Age*, May 26, 1888.

19. Massachusetts, *Thirtieth*, 1896, 93; Tennessee, *Eleventh*, 1894, 19; Pennsylvania, *Fifty-second and Fifty-third* (semiannual), 1893, 150; Illinois, *Twenty-eighth*, 1894, 111; Illinois, *Thirty-sixth*, 1902, 180.

20. Ohio, *Twenty-second*, 1888, 98–99.

21. Ibid.

22. WRC, Illinois, *Fourth*, 9; Massachusetts, *Twenty-eighth*, 1895, 219; Ohio, *Twenty-ninth*, 1895, 147; New York, *Sixteenth*, 1882, 77.

23. WRC, *Third National*, 1889, 188; "In War and In Peace," *West Chester Daily Local News*, May 31, 1900; Ohio, *Twenty-sixth*, 1892, 131.

24. Kansas, *Nineteenth*, 1900, 3; Illinois, *Eighteenth*, 1899, 152; George Washington Williams, *Advent of the Colored Soldier*, 10.

25. Massachusetts, *Forty-eighth*, 1914, 152–53; Pennsylvania, *Thirty-fifth*, 1901, 64; Ohio, *Twenty-fifth*, 1891, 62; Tennessee, *Eleventh*, 1894, 56; Illinois, *Thirty-eighth*, 1904, 104, 160.

26. Ohio, *Twenty-eighth*, 1894, 212; Pennsylvania, *Thirty-eighth*, 1904, 59; Massachusetts, *Thirty-sixth*, 1902, 183; Massachusetts, *Early History*, 335.

27. Illinois, *Forty-first*, 1907, 200–201; Massachusetts, *Thirty-seventh*, 1903, 141; Massachusetts, *Forty-sixth*, 1916, 133.

28. *Thirtieth National*, 1896, 8–9; "Our Soldiers Dead," *West Chester Daily Local News*, May 31, 1884; Connecticut, *Encampment*, 1888, 93; Holmes, *Essential Holmes*.

29. Ohio, *Twenty-eighth*, 1894, 221–22; Missouri, *Ninth*, 1890, 127.

30. Ohio, *Twenty-second*, 1888, 171–72. The transcript of this meeting notes that these remarks were greeted with "great applause." An Ohio newspaper, the *Youngstown Vindicator*, used a similar logic but came to a very different conclusion. In a comment on Memorial Day in 1881, the editor asserted, "If there is anything that will cause a man, or many men, to regret the late 'cruel war,' with its emancipation and the national debt as a 'national blessing,' it is to hear the doleful sounds of a hand organ . . . manipulated by a one-legged veteran with a one-armed collector as an accompaniment" (*Youngstown Vindicator*, May 27, 1881). The editor demanded that the cause be worthy of the sacrifice, and, in his eyes, black freedom was unworthy of white limbs.

31. Delbanco, *Portable Abraham Lincoln*, 321. For a detailed discussion of the religious context of this oration, see Ronald C. White, *Lincoln's Greatest Speech*.

32. Blight, *Race and Reunion*, 2; Massachusetts, *Thirty-seventh*, 1903, 145; Kansas, *Twenty-Seventh*, 1908, 14–15; "At Bethel A.M.E. Church," *West Chester Daily Local News*, May 31, 1887.

CHAPTER TWELVE

1. Harlan, *Some Memories of a Long Life*, 112–13.

2. Barth, *Prophets with Honor*, 202, 204. For more on Justice Harlan, see Przybyszewski, *Republic According to John Marshall Harlan*; and Beth, *John Marshall Harlan*. Two U.S. officers and one former Confederate civilian official were members of the Supreme Court that rolled back civil rights in 1883. Only one other justice on the 1895 Court was a veteran, and he had served in the Confederate army. See Cushman, *Supreme Court Justices*.

3. Blight, *Race and Reunion*, 2–5.

4. Anderson, *Imagined Communities*, 6–7.

5. New York, *Eighteenth*, 1884, 83.

6. New York, *Thirty-first*, 1897, 464; New York, *Twenty-fourth*, 1890, 224. Little was born in Albany, New York, served in the Fifty-fourth Massachusetts, and married a former slave from South Carolina. He was employed as a shopkeeper at the construction department of the Navy Yard. See "Appointments to Office," *New York Age*, June 15, 1889; and "A Brooklyn Wiseacre," *New York Age*, June 8, 1889.

7. New York, *Twenty-fourth*, 1890, 250–51.

8. Ibid., 252; "The Butler Bill Condemned," *New York Age*, March 22, 1890.

9. Minnesota, *Thirty-second*, 1899, 122, 123; Minnesota, *Thirty-fifth*, 1902, 163. GAR records do not identify the postmaster as a comrade. If he had been, it is very likely the speakers would have invoked this status to secure support for the resolution.

10. Illinois, *Thirty-eighth*, 1904, 161; Kansas, *Eighth*, 1889, 61–64.

11. Kentucky, *Seventeenth*, 1899, 51–52; Kansas, *Eighth*, 1889, 62.

12. New York, *Twenty-third*, 1889, 84.

13. New York, *Decoration Day*, 1883, 90; Missouri, *Sixteenth*, 1897, 81; Massachusetts, *Thirtieth*, 1896, 179. For more on manhood and black men's Civil War service, see Shaffer, *After the Glory*.

14. Donald Shaffer found two other instances in which the GAR at the state level fought efforts to disenfranchise black veterans. Not surprisingly, the GAR in Louisiana and Mississippi, states in which most GAR members were African Americans, made a stand against disenfranchisement. The Arkansas GAR also opposed efforts to limit black voting rights in that state. See Shaffer, *After the Glory*, 241.

15. Arkansas, *Twelfth and Thirteenth*, 1894–95, 20; New York, *Twentieth*, 1886, 129. It should be noted that Little's is the only such complaint that I found in the GAR records I examined. As discussed in Chapter 3, my research uncovered many examples of interracial gatherings, particularly involving New York City posts. Little may have complained because this exclusion was unusual and contrary to the customary treatment of black veterans. It may also be true that if black veterans were generally unwelcome in white posts in a certain area, no one would have complained to the state GAR.

16. New Jersey, *Twenty-ninth*, 1896, 27; Kentucky, *Twenty-sixth*, 1908, 42–44. Despite the racial attitudes of Kentucky GAR men, Dodge was not a pariah; in fact, he was so popular he was elected department commander for a number of years, a rare feat since almost all states elected a new commander each year.

17. Kentucky, *Thirty-second*, 1914, 39; Kentucky, *Fourteenth*, 1896, 58. In Maryland, black posts frequently marched together in state parades. While they were segregated, there are some indications that they chose to march this way. First, since the order in which posts marched was almost always determined by either post number or seniority (see Chapter 6), had African American veterans not chosen to march separately, they would not have been forced to do so. Second, since a black veteran from the senior post in this state provided the leadership for this section of the parade, the all-black posts' decision to march as a unit may have been an issue of autonomy for them. Finally, the Maryland GAR held a contest to decide which five posts had the highest number of uniformed members in a parade. Black posts took three of the five top spots, indicating the rank and file's enthusiasm for these parades. See Maryland, *Fourteenth*, 1890, 65; and Maryland, *Seventeenth*, 1893, 21, 49, 75.

18. Pennsylvania, *Forty-sixth and Forty-seventh*, 1890, 252; Massachusetts, *Fortieth*, 1906, 128.

19. Ohio, *Twenty-sixth*, 1892, 144–45; Ohio, *Twentieth*, 1886, 191; Kentucky, *Twentieth*, 1902, 69.

20. Foner, *Free Soil*, 261–300; Delbanco, *Portable Abraham Lincoln*, 115.

21. Arkansas, *Fifteenth*, 1897, 61–62; Kansas, *Seventh*, 1888, 3; Massachusetts, *Thirtieth*, 1896, 221–22; Massachusetts, *Thirty-first*, 1897, 202.

22. Ohio, *Twenty-ninth*, 1895, 204–5.

23. Indiana, *Twenty-fifth*, 1904, 121; Illinois, *Thirty-third*, 1899, 129.

24. Ohio, *Twenty-second*, 1888, 180–81; Kansas, *Twentieth*, 1901, 102.

25. Iowa, *Twenty-fifth*, 1899, 5; Kansas, *Eighteenth*, 1899, 122–23; Massachusetts, *Thirty-third*, 1899, 56.

26. Tennessee, *Twenty-fifth*, 1908, 21; Illinois, *Forty-second*, 1908, 124; Indiana, *Thirty-seventh*, 1916, 116.

27. Massachusetts, *Thirty-third*, 1899, 49; *Thirtieth National*, 1896, 4.

CHAPTER THIRTEEN

1. "Quiet Reverence at Memorial Day Observances," *Elgin Courier News*, May 30, 2000, 1, 4, and my own personal observation of Elgin's Memorial Day, May 2000.

2. Ibid.

3. Delaware, *Thirty-fifth*, 1915, unpaged in back of record; Pennsylvania, *Thirty-seventh*, 1903, 49; Massachusetts, *Forty-eighth*, 1913, 15, 81; Civil War Pension File of Lucy Nichols (Higgs), National Archives, Washington, D.C.

4. New York, *Thirtieth*, 1896, 87, 97; Potomac, *Twentieth*, 1888, 67; Ohio, *Twenty-sixth*, 1892, 126.

5. "Vast by Blood's Baptism," *Washington Post*, July 2, 1913, reprinted from *New York World*; editorial, *Frederick Daily News*, May 30, 1887; "A Sweet Duty," *Evening Penny Post*, May 30, 1885.

6. New Jersey, *Thirty-eighth Encampment*, 1905, 49.

7. "Memorial Day," *Lancaster Daily Examiner*, May 30, 1900.

8. "Beautiful Memorial Day," *Harrisburg Patriot*, May 31, 1898.

9. Link, *Papers of Woodrow Wilson*, 23; Blight, *Race and Reunion*, 11. Wilson was not only a politician but also a historian and, as such, had his own interpretation of the Civil War. In his study of American history from 1829 to 1909, he argued that the agitation against slavery was the central cause of the Civil War; therefore, he cannot be accused of aiding and abetting those who erased slavery from the historical narrative. To blame the agitation against slavery and not the institution itself is to remove the onus for initiating this conflict from southern states and to place it squarely on the shoulders of northern states. Wilson did remove black U.S. soldiers from his chronicle and, instead, discussed the Afro-Confederate soldiers who were recruited only near the end of the war. See Woodrow Wilson, *Division and Reunion*, 208–12, 247. The book was reprinted a number of times between 1893 and 1914, indicating its popularity.

10. Link, *Papers of Woodrow Wilson*, 23, 25–26.

11. "Gettysburg Cold to Veterans Address," *New York Times*, July 5, 1913. Wilson's speech may not have been well received because, at one point, he claimed that "we have harder things to do than were done in the heroic days of war." This would not likely have been a popular statement among the Civil War generation of either side. See Link, *Papers of Woodrow Wilson*, 24.

12. Editorial, *New York Age*, July 10, 1913; "Cleveland, Sixth City," *Cleveland Gazette*, July 19, 1913; "Harrisburg Veterans off for Gettysburg," *Harrisburg Patriot*, July 1, 1913. According to Jim Weeks (*Gettysburg*, 94–98), African American veterans were not excluded from Gettysburg. The all-black posts in Baltimore sponsored excursions to Gettysburg that involved thousands of African Americans in the years before World War I. The excursions were not welcomed by some Gettysburg residents, nor were they particularly popular with some elements of the African American elite, who argued that they were "a waste of valuable resources and . . . excuses for license."

13. "Colored Veterans in Camp," *Philadelphia Public Ledger*, July 3, 1913. For an expla-

nation of why the northern middle class embraced this idealized view of plantation life, see Silber, *Romance of Reunion*, 108–10.

14. "At Gettysburg," *Washington Post*, June 30, 1913; "Vast by Blood's Baptism," *Washington Post*, July 2, 1913, reprinted from *New York World*.

15. "Grey Men Totter to Bloody Angle," *Washington Post*, July 4, 1913; "On to Gettysburg after the Battle," *Washington Post*, June 22, 1913.

16. Ohio, *Nineteenth*, 1885, 116–17; *Twenty-first*, 1887, 61; Indiana, *Thirty-second*, 1911, 5.

17. "Grey Men Totter to Bloody Angle," *Washington Post*, July 4, 1913; Gallagher, *Causes Won, Lost, and Forgotten*. For an outstanding study of Pickett's Charge and how its Memory and meaning evolved, see Reardon, *Pickett's Charge in History and Memory*.

18. "College Boys in Gettysburg Train to Become Real Army Officers," *Washington Post*, July 13, 1913; "At Gettysburg," *Washington Post*, June 30, 1913.

19. Untitled, *Indianapolis Freeman*, July 19, 1913; "Harrisburg, PA," *New York Age*, July 10, 1913. I examined the black newspapers from 1913 that have been preserved by the Library of Congress, including the *New York Age*, the *St. Paul Appeal*, the *Indianapolis Freeman*, the *Chicago Broad Ax*, the *Savannah Tribune*, the *Cleveland Gazette*, and *The Bee*.

20. "Anniversary of the Battle of Gettysburg," *The Bee*, June 24, 1913. Another editorial addressed the relationship between the reunion at Gettysburg and attacks on black rights; see "The Farce Begins," *The Bee*, June 7, 1913.

21. "President Lincoln and President Wilson at Gettysburg," *New York Age*, July 17, 1913. Black veterans may have been correct when they reported problems between northerners and southerners at the reunion. An article carried by many major newspapers described a melee that ensued when a veteran was angered by an insult to Lincoln at a Gettysburg hotel. One headline read: "7 Stabbed When Veteran Resents Insult to Lincoln." The victims had come to the aid of the northern veteran who had objected to the insult. The man accused of this crime was a resident of Camden, New Jersey. He was identified as the "son of R. R. Henry of Tazewell, Va., a general in the Confederate Army." See "7 Stabbed When Veteran Resents Insult to Lincoln," *Harrisburg Patriot*, July 3, 1913.

22. "Anniversary of the Battle of Gettysburg," *The Bee*, June 24, 1913; "Boston, Mass.," *New York Age*, July 24, 1913; "Col. Robert Gould Shaw Remembered," *Indianapolis Freeman*, July 26, 1913. A number of African American newspapers printed invitations to the semicentennial of the Fort Wagner battle; for an example, see "Battle of Ft. Wagner," *Cleveland Gazette*, July 12, 1913. Another factor that might have affected this coverage is that the African American elite had never been of one mind on the use of Civil War Memory. Alexander Crummel, the African American intellectual, missionary, and nationalist, argued that African Americans should turn away from their past and focus on the present. In contrast, Frederick Douglass believed in the power of Memory to advance the interests of African Americans. See Blight, *Race and Reunion*, 316–19. For more on Crummel, see Moses, *Alexander Crummel*. For more on Douglass and Civil War Memory, see Blight, "'For Something Beyond the Battlefield'" and *Frederick Douglass' Civil War*.

23. "Decoration Day Appropriately Observed," *Savannah Tribune*, June 7, 1913; "Heroes Remembered!" *Indianapolis Freeman*, June 7, 1913; "Baltimore," *New York Age*, June 5, 1913; "Philadelphia," *New York Age*, June 6, 1912; June 5, 1913. For more on Afri-

can American Odd Fellows and other fraternal groups, see Skocpol, Liazos, and Ganz, *What a Mighty Power We Can Be*.

24. "10th Cavalry Enroute to Summer Camp," *New York Age*, July 3, 1913; "110,000 Available for Good Investment," *New York Age*, May 30, 1912.

25. "The Twenty-fifth Infantry at Schofield Barracks," *Indianapolis Freemen*, July 5, 1913. On black elites' devotion to race progress, see Gaines, *Uplifting the Race*.

26. "Our Brave Soldiers of the Regular Army," *New York Age*, January 16, 1913; "Still Being Persecuted by Roosevelt and Taft" and "The Brownsville Affray Illustrated," *Cleveland Gazette*, June 1, 1912; Weaver, *Brownsville Raid*; Lane, *Brownsville Affair*. Personal memory may have played a part in motivating the Brownsville soldiers' strongest supporter, Joseph Foraker, a U.S. senator and Union army veteran. Foraker's forceful advocacy of these men's cause is chronicled in Weaver, *Senator and the Sharecropper's Son*, and in Foraker's autobiography, *Notes of a Busy Life*, 231–328. The Brownsville Affair was not the only incident involving Buffalo Soldiers in Texas. In 1916, soldiers of the all-black Twenty-fifth Infantry rioted in Houston to protest racist attacks: of the 156 men court-martialed, 19 were executed. See Christian, *Black Soldiers*.

27. "First Company for New Regiment Formed," *New York Age*, July 3, 1913; "Rev. W. S. Braddan Preached the Annual Sermon for the Eighth Regiment Illinois National Guards," *Chicago Broad Ax*, May 31, 1913. See also Johnson, *African-American Soldiers in the National Guard*.

28. "White Officers for Regiment Is Planned," *New York Age*, October 30, 1913; "Against Negro Students," *The Bee*, May 31, 1913; untitled, *Indianapolis Freeman*, May 22, 1913. Three years after this letter was published, the National Defense Act of 1916 created units at black colleges and universities, including Wilberforce and Howard, that trained potential officers in the Student Army Training Corps, the predecessor of the Reserve Officers Training Corps. Fletcher (*Black Soldier and Officer*) chronicles the service of black regulars of all ranks at the turn of the century. For more information on Benjamin O. Davis Sr., see Fletcher, *America's First Black General*; on his son, Benjamin O. Davis Jr., see his autobiography *Benjamin O. Davis Jr.*

29. The black military experience in World War I is discussed in Barbeau and Henri, *Unknown Soldiers*; Bill Harris, *Hellfighters of Harlem*; Stephen L. Harris, *Harlem's Hellfighters*; and Roberts, *American Foreign Legion*; and Lentz-Smith, *Freedom Struggles*. A recent study compares the wartime experiences of the Harlem Hellfighters and the 77th Division, which was composed of New York immigrants—Italian, Jews, and Eastern Europeans—and discusses how, when the nation needed these marginalized groups to serve, it welcomed them into the national community. See Slotkin, *Lost Battalions*.

30. Millet and Maslowski, *For the Common Defense*, 653. It is believed that at least 377,000 French troops were killed, wounded, or missing at Verdun. See Archer et al., *World History of Warfare*, 488. I found at least two instances in which GAR organizations protested discrimination against black soldiers during World War I. The mixed-race Crocker Post in Des Moines expressed its outrage when black officer candidates were arrested after they refused to comply with segregated seating in a local theater. The post expressed its "deep disapproval of this shameful and unlawful treatment which humiliated these comrades." The bond of comradeship embraced a new generation. The Kentucky GAR declared that a "law which prevents colored men from enlisting in the name of Kentucky . . . [was] unjust" and petitioned the legislature to repeal it. See Iowa,

Crocker Post, *Meeting Book*, vol. 5, July 7, 1917, 217–18; and Kentucky, *Thirty-fifth*, 1917, 34. Relegating most black soldiers to support units in World War I may have affected their postwar relationships with white veterans; veterans who fought in that conflict refused to take a stand against segregation. The American Legion, organized in the immediate aftermath of the Great War, admitted black veterans but allowed southern organizations to segregate African American members. See Pencak, *For God and Country*, 68–69, 99.

31. The most comprehensive study of black soldiers in World War II is still the official history done by the U.S. Army. See Lee, *Employment of Negro Troops*. There are a number of more specialized studies of the black service members in World War II. See Sandler, *Segregated Skies*; Early, *One Woman's Army*; McGuire, *He, Too, Spoke for Democracy*; Motley, *Invisible Soldier*; Putney, *When the Nation Was in Need*; and Graham Smith, *When Jim Crow Met John Bull*.

32. For more on the desegregation of the armed forces, see Nichols, *Breakthrough on the Color Front*, and Dalfiume, *Desegregation of the United States Armed Forces*.

33. Bush, *Inaugural Addresses*.

EPILOGUE

1. Illinois, *Sixty-second*, 1928, 87–88; New York, *Sixty-sixth*, 1932, 49; Illinois, *Eightieth*, 1946, 140.

2. In the case of black GAR posts, sometimes the record-keeping ended before the posts closed; for example, as shown in the last available encampment record, the Shaw Post, the Christiana Post, and three other all-black organizations were still reporting to the Pennsylvania GAR. New York records list two African American posts—Numbers 207 and 255—as still intact as late as 1932. The Delany Post of Indianapolis was on the Indiana GAR rolls in 1935 but not 1936. See also Pennsylvania, *Sixty-fifth*, 1931; New York, *Sixty-sixth*, 1932; and Indiana, *Fifty-sixth* and *Fifty-Seventh*, 1935–36. The last meeting of the Taylor Post occurred on May 7, 1937; four members were present. The Welch Post records noted that when the last member of the post died in September 1937, "the Grand Army of the Republic for Ann Arbor passes out also." See Connecticut, Taylor Post, *Minutes*; and Michigan, Welch Post, *War Sketches*, 103.

3. WRC, Potomac, *Thirty-second*, 1920–21, 70; House of Representatives, Committee on Public Buildings and Grounds, 19; WRC, *Services and Activities*, 299; LGAR, Minnesota, Biddle Circle, *Records*, 1950–56. Citizens of Chestertown, Maryland, have bought the post hall built by the all-black Sumner Post and the Sumner Corps and are raising funds to restore it.

4. Singleton, *Recollections*, 31.

5. "GAR Marches . . . ," *Grand Rapids Herald*, September 11, 1935; Singleton, *Recollections*, 2; Shaffer, *After the Glory*, 196–97.

Bibliography

UNPUBLISHED PRIMARY SOURCES

Ann Arbor, Michigan
 University of Michigan, Bentley Historical Library, Michigan Historical Collections.
  Grand Army of the Republic. Department of Michigan. Welch Post. No. 137. *Record Book* and *War Sketches*.
Clinton, Iowa
 Clinton County Historical Society
  Elizabeth Fairfax File
Columbus, Ohio
 Ohio Historical Society Archives/Library Division
  Grand Army of the Republic. Department of Ohio Records. 1876–1936. *Charters.*
Des Moines, Iowa
 State Historical Society of Iowa, Civil War Collection
  Grand Army of the Republic. Department of Iowa. Crocker Post. No. 12. *Descriptive Book*; *Meeting Book*; *Minute Book*; *Muster Rolls*; and *Records.*
  ———. Lee County Post. No. 413. *Membership Cards.*
  ———. Polk County Posts. *Membership Cards.*
  ———. Pratt Post. No. 413. *Minute Book.* 1889–96.
  ———. Torrence Post. No. 2. *Descriptive Book.*
Elgin, Illinois
 Historical Society
  Grand Army of the Republic. Department of Illinois. Veterans Post. No. 49. *Muster Roll.*
Hartford, Connecticut
 Connecticut State Library, Connecticut State Archives, Record Group 113, Grand Army of the Republic, 1866–1956
  Grand Army of the Republic. Department of Connecticut. *Grand Army of the Republic Members List.*
  ———. Admiral Foote Post. No. 17. *Descriptive Book.*
  ———. Long Post. No. 30. *Ledger.*
  ———. Lyon Post. No. 2. *Minute Books* and *Roster.*

★

————. Merwin Post. No. 52. *Descriptive Book.*

————. Taylor Post. No. 50. *Descriptive Books; Minutes; Muster Roll; Scrapbook; Vitae;* and *Records.*

Knoxville, Tennessee

East Tennessee Historical Society, Calvin M. McClung Historical Collection

Grand Army of the Republic. Tennessee. *Descriptive Records.*

Pittsburgh, Pennsylvania

University of Pittsburgh, Archives of Industrial Society, Grand Army of the Republic Collection

Grand Army of the Republic. Department of Pennsylvania. Col. Robert Gould Shaw Post. No. 206. *Minutes; Records;* and *War Sketches.*

————. Col. James C. Hull Post. No. 157. *Minutes.*

————. Col. James Childs Post. No. 230. *War Sketches.*

St. Paul, Minnesota

Minnesota State Historical Society

Ladies of the Grand Army of the Republic. Department of Minnesota, Biddle Circle, No. 38. *Records.* 1950–56.

Washington, D.C.

National Archives

Civil War Pension File of Lucy Nichols (Higgs), Nurse, Medical Department, U.S. Volunteers

Youngstown, Ohio

Mahoning Valley Historical Society, The Arms Family Museum of Local History

Grand Army of the Republic. Department of Ohio. Tod Post. No. 29. *Descriptive Books; Records; Vitae;* and *War Sketches.*

PUBLISHED PRIMARY SOURCES

The national and state meetings of the Grand Army of the Republic (GAR) and the Woman's Relief Corps (WRC) represent one of the most important sources of information for this study. Records of these annual gatherings were published under various titles; in some years, a state might call the transcript of their meeting a journal, in others a proceeding. Regardless of their title, the national GAR and WRC and all subordinate state entities made some type of record of their annual meetings. To avoid confusion, all annual GAR meetings will be referred to as encampments and WRC meetings as conventions. The largest single collection of these published transcripts is housed at the Library of Congress in Washington, D.C.

National Records of the Grand Army of the Republic and the Woman's Relief Corps

Grand Army of the Republic. *Decisions and Opinions of the Commanders-in-Chief and Judge Advocates-General of the Grand Army of the Republic.* Indianapolis: Hasselman Journal Co., 1884.

————. *Decoration Day.* New York: George F. Nesbitt Printers, 1882.

————. *Grand Army Blue Book: Containing the Rules and Regulations of the Grand Army of the Republic.* Philadelphia: Burk and McFetridge, 1884.

———. *Grand Army Blue Book*. Philadelphia: Burk and McFetridge, 1886.

———. *Grand Army Blue Book*. Philadelphia: J. B. Lippincott, 1904.

———. *Journal of the National Encampment*. Publisher and place of publication varies. 1887–97.

———. *Manual for the Guidance of the Grand Army of the Republic*. Philadelphia, 1881.

———. *Services for the Use of the Grand Army of the Republic*. N.p.: 1892.

Woman's Relief Corps. *National Meeting*, 1887–1919.

———. *Services and Activities of the Departments of the National Woman's Relief Corps*. N.p., 1933.

State Records of the Grand Army of the Republic and the Woman's Relief Corps

Grand Army of the Republic. Department of Alabama. *Encampments*. 1889–91.

———. Arkansas. *Encampments*. 1883–1917.

———. California. *Register of the Department of California*. 1886.

———. Colorado and Wyoming. *Complete Roster of the Members of the Grand Army of the Republic*. Denver: Press of the Rocky Mountain Herald, 1895.

———. Connecticut. *Encampments*. 1882–94.

———. Connecticut. *History of the Organization of Admiral Foote Post, No. 17*. New Haven: Tuttle, Morehouse & Taylor, 1891.

———. Delaware. *Encampments*. 1881–1917.

———. Delaware. *History of the Grand Army of the Republic and of Delaware, and its Auxiliaries, Union Veteran Legion and National Guard of Delaware*. N.p., 1895.

———. Florida. *Encampments*. 1887–1903.

———. Georgia. *Encampments*. 1889–1900.

———. Georgia and South Carolina. *Roster and History of the Department of Georgia and South Carolina*. 1894.

———. Illinois. *Encampments*. 1873–1948.

———. Indiana. *Encampments*. 1880–1936.

———. Iowa. *Encampments*. 1886–1906.

———. Iowa. Torrence Post. *By-laws and Roster*. 1891.

———. Kansas. *Encampments*. 1882–1918.

———. Kansas. *Roster of the Members and Post of the Grand Army of the Republic*. 1894.

———. Kentucky. *Encampments*. 1892–1918.

———. Louisiana and Mississippi. *Encampments*. 1891–1903.

———. Michigan. *Encampments*. 1884–90.

———. Maryland. *Encampments*. 1882–1923, 1929.

———. Massachusetts. *Early History of the Department of Massachusetts, G.A.R., from 1866 to 1880*. 1895.

———. Massachusetts. *Encampments*. 1871–1906.

———. Massachusetts. *Historical Souvenir of Benjamin Stone Jr., Post, No. 68, Twenty-sixth National Encampment*. 1892.

———. Massachusetts. *Official Souvenir of the Twenty-eighth Annual Encampment of the Dept. of Massachusetts Grand Army of the Republic, and the Sixteenth Annual Convention of the Department of Massachusetts Woman's Relief Corps*. 1895.

———. Michigan. *Encampments*. 1884–90, 1904.

———. Minnesota. *Encampments*. 1899–1902.

———. Missouri. *Encampment*. 1881–99.

———. New Jersey. *Encampments*. 1885–1912.

———. New York. *Encampments*. 1872–99, 1908, 1910, 1932.

———. Ohio. *Encampments*. 1882–95.

———. Pennsylvania. *Encampments*. 1868–1931.

———. Potomac. [Washington, D.C.]. *Encampments*. 1885–1913, 1919–21.

———. Rhode Island. *Encampments*. 1885–1924.

———. Rhode Island. *Register of the Department of Rhode Island*. 1888.

———. Tennessee. *Encampments*. 1884–1917.

———. Texas. *Encampments*. 1890–1907, 1909–17.

———. Virginia and North Carolina. *Encampments*. 1874, 1889–94.

———. West Virginia. *Encampments*. 1884–95.

Woman's Relief Corps. Department of Connecticut. *Convention*. 1890.

———. Illinois. *Conventions*. 1884–91.

———. Indiana. *Convention*. 1893.

———. Kansas. *Conventions*. 1920–24.

———. Massachusetts. *History of the Department of Massachusetts Woman's Relief Corps, 1879–1995*. Boston: E. B. Atillings & Co., 1895.

———. New Jersey. *Synopsis of Proceedings of Conventions Department of New Jersey WRC*. Trenton: MacCrellish & Quigley, 1895.

———. Potomac. 1920–22.

PUBLISHED PRIMARY SOURCES

Beath, Robert. *History of the Grand Army of the Republic*. New York: Bryan Taylor and Co., 1888.

Bowley, Freeman S. *Honor in Command: Lt. Freeman S. Bowley's Civil War Service in the 30th United States Colored Infantry*. Edited by Keith P. Wilson. Gainesville: University Press of Florida, 2006.

Committee on United States Colored Troops. *Souvenir Handbook and Guide, Complimentary to the Colored Veterans, Grand Army of the Republic, 33rd Reunion and Encampment, Philadelphia*. Philadelphia: n.p., 1899.

Delbanco, Andrew. *The Portable Abraham Lincoln*. New York: Penguin, 1992.

Dickerson, Charles Hatfield. *Relationship of the Colored Man to the Republic*. N.p.: 1886.

Elgin Historical Society. *Obituaries of Members of Veterans Post No. 49*. Elgin, Ill.: n.p., 1997.

Foraker, Joseph. *Notes of a Busy Life*. Vol. 2. Cincinnati: Stewart and Kidd Company, 1916.

Fox, William F. *Regimental Losses in the American Civil War*. 1889. Reprint, New York: Morningside Press, 1974.

Guthrie, Jason M. *Camp-fires of the Afro-American; or, The Colored Man as a Patriot*. 1899. Reprint, New York: Johnson, 1970.

Harlan, Malvina Shanklin. *Some Memories of a Long Life, 1854–1911*. Edited by Linda Przybyszewski. New York: The Modern Library, 2002.

Hewett, Jane B., ed. *Supplemental to the Official Records of the Union and Confederate Armies*. Wilmington, N.C.: Broadfoot, 1994.

Holmes, Oliver W., Jr. *The Essential Holmes: Selections from the Letters, Speeches, Judicial Opinions, and Other Writings of Oliver Wendell Holmes, Jr.* Edited by Richard A. Posner. Chicago: University of Chicago Press, 1997.

Link, Arthur, ed. *The Papers of Woodrow Wilson*. Princeton: Princeton University Press, 1978.

Kimball, Edward P. *Brinley Hall Album and . . . Post 10 (Ward) Sketch Book*. Worcester, Mass.: Blanchard, 1896.

Matthews, Brander, ed. *Poems of American Patriotism*. 1881. Reprint, Freeport, N.Y.: Books for Libraries Press, 1970.

Moore, Henry D. *The Problem of the Rebellion, an Address Read at the Fred C. Jones Post*. N.p., 1898.

Newton, Alexander H. *Out of the Briars: An Autobiography and Sketch of the Twenty-ninth Regiment Volunteers*. 1910. Reprint, Miami: Mnemosyne Publishing Co., 1969.

Northcott, Dennis. *Indiana Civil War Veterans: Transcription of the Death Rolls of the Department of Indiana, Grand Army of the Republic, 1882-1948*. St. Louis, Mo.: n.p., 2005.

————. *Iowa, Kansas and Nebraska Civil War Veterans: Compilation of the Death Rolls of the Department of Iowa, Kansas, and Nebraska, Grand Army of the Republic, 1883-1948*. N.p., 2007.

Northcott, Dennis, and Thomas Brooks. *Grand Army of the Republic, Department of Illinois: Transcription of the Death Rolls, 1879-1947*. St. Louis, Mo.: n.p., 2003.

O'Reilly, Miles. [Charles Graham Halpine]. *Baked Meats of the Funeral: Collection of Essays, Poems. Speeches, Histories and Banquets*. New York: Carleton, 1866.

Palmer, William R. A. *Colored Soldiers in the Civil War*. N.p.: 1897.

Pollard, Edward A. *The Lost Cause: A New History of the War of the Confederates*. New York: E. B. Treat, 1867.

Richings, G. F. *Evidence of Progress among the Colored People*. Philadelphia: George S. Ferguson, 1896.

Robinson, Henry C. *Decoration Day Address of Henry C. Robinson to the Veterans of the Grand Army of the Republic in Hartford, May 30, 1885*. Hartford, Conn.: Lockwood and Brainard, 1885.

Roy, Andrew. *Fallen Soldier: Memoirs of a Civil War Casualty*. Edited by William J. Miller and Medical Commentary by Clyde B. Kernek, M.D. Montgomery, Ala.: Elliot and Clark Publishing, 1996.

Sargent, A. Dean. *Grand Army of the Republic: Civil War Veterans Department of Massachusetts, 1866-1947*. Bowie, Md.: Heritage Books, 2002.

Sherard, Gerald E. *Colorado Civil War Grand Army of the Republic Members*. Lakewood, Colo.: Sherard, 1994.

Singleton, William H. *Recollections of Slavery Days*. New York: Highland Democratic Company, 1922.

Sons of Union Veterans of the Civil War (Missouri). *Roster of the Department of Missouri Grand Army of the Republic 1895*. Springfield, Mo.: n.p., 1999.

Taylor, Susie K. *A Black Woman's Civil War Memoirs*. Edited by Patricia W. Romero, with a new introduction by Willie L. Rose. New York: Markus Wiener, 1991.

2000 and 2005 Research History Class. Washington High School. Washington Courthouse, Ohio. *William A. Anderson Post 244: Grand Army of the Republic, United States Colored Troops, Washington Court House, Ohio 1882–1912*. 2nd ed. N.p.: 2000 and 2005.

U.S. Census Bureau. *Report of the Population of the United States at the Eleventh Census: 1890*. Washington, D.C.: Government Printing Office, 1897.

U.S. Congress. House. Committee on Public Buildings and Grounds. *To Create a Commission to Secure Plans and Designs: Hearing before the Committee on Public Buildings and Grounds*. 70th Cong. 1st sess. February 1, 1928.

U.S. Department of the Interior. *Report of the Secretary of the Interior Being Part of the Messages and Documents Communicated to the Two Houses of Congress at the Beginning of the Second Session of the Fiftieth Congress*. Washington, D.C.: Government Printing Office, 1888.

Williams, George Washington. *The Advent of the Colored Soldier*. Boston: James H. Earle Publisher, 1874.

———. *A History of the Negro Troops in the War of the Rebellion 1861–1865*. 1886. Reprint, New York: Bergman, 1968.

Wilson, Joseph T. *The Black Phalanx: African-American Soldiers in the War of Independence, the War of 1812 and the Civil War*. 1890. Reprint, New York: Da Capo, 1994.

Wilson, Woodrow. *Division and Reunion*. 1893. Reprint, New York: Longmans, Green and Company, 1914.

NEWSPAPERS

African-American Ledger (Baltimore)

The Bee (Washington, D.C.)

Chester Times (Pennsylvania)

Cleveland Gazette

Daily Evening Sentinel (Carlisle, Pa.)

Daily Examiner (Lancaster, Pa.)

Daily Post (Pittsburgh)

Daily Sun and Banner (Williamsport, Pa.)

Detroit Plaindealer

The Elgin Courier News

Evening Penny Post (Pittsburgh)

Evening Sentinel (Carlisle, Pa.)

Frederick Daily News (Maryland)

Gate City (Keokuk, Ia.)

Genius of Liberty (Uniontown, Pa.)

Grand Army Record

Grand Rapids Herald (Michigan)

Hagerstown Herald and Torchlight (Maryland)

Harrisburg Patriot (Pennsylvania)

Indianapolis Freeman

Iowa Bystander

The Kansas Blackman (Topeka)

Lancaster Daily Examiner (Pennsylvania)

Leavenworth Advocate (Kansas)

National Tribune

New York Age

New York Freeman

New York Globe

New York Herald Tribune

New York Times

Philadelphia Inquirer

Philadelphia Public Ledger

Pittsburgh Press

Public Ledger (Philadelphia)

The Republican Courier (New Orleans)

The Republican Standard (Uniontown, Pa.)

Saturday Globe (Utica, N.Y.)

Savannah Tribune

The Sun (Williamsport, Pa.)
The Times-Democrat (New Orleans)
Washington Post
Washington Reporter (Pennsylvania)
West Chester Daily Local News
  (Pennsylvania)

Western Appeal (St.Paul/Chicago)
Wilkes-Barre Record (Pennsylvania)
York Gazette (Pennsylvania)
Youngstown Daily Vindicator (Ohio)

INTERNET

Ancestry.com. *1890 Veterans Schedules*. Provo, Utah: Ancestry.com Operations Inc, 2005. Original data in "Special Schedules of the Eleventh Census (1890) Enumerating Union Veterans and Widows of Union Veterans of the Civil War," ⟨http://www .archives.gov/publications/microfilm-catalogs/census/1790-1890/part-08.html#ss⟩. October 13, 2010.

Bush, George W. *Inaugural Addresses of the Presidents of the United States: From George Washington to George W. Bush*. Washington, D.C.: Government Printing Office, 1989. Updated, Bartleby.com, 2001, ⟨www.bartleby.com/124/pres66.htm⟩. September 29, 2010.

Johns Hopkins Medical Institutions. "Why Emotionally Charged Events Are So Memorable." *Science Daily*, October 7, 2007, ⟨http://www.sciencedaily.com/ releases/2007/10/071004121045.htm#⟩. September 29, 2010.

Sherard, Gerald. "Nebraska Civil War Grand Army of the Republic Members Index." Edited for Internet by John C. Clement. Western History and Genealogy. The Denver Public Library, ⟨http://history.denverlibrary.org/research/civil_war_gar_neb⟩. September 29, 2010.

United States. National Park Service. "Civil War Soldiers and Sailors System," ⟨http// www.itd.nps.gov/cwss⟩. September 29, 2010.

SECONDARY SOURCES

Books

Alexander, Adelle Logan. *Homeland and Waterways: The American Journey of the Bond Family*. New York: Pantheon Books, 1995.

Alft, E. C. *Elgin's Black Heritage*. Elgin, Ill.: City of Elgin, 1996.

Anderson, Benedict. *Imagined Communities: Reflections on the Origin and Spread of Nationalism*. 2nd ed. London: Verso, 2006.

Archer, Christon I., John R. Ferris, Holger H. Herwig, and Timothy H. E. Travers. *World History of Warfare*. Lincoln: University of Nebraska Press, 2002.

Barbeau, Arthur E., and Florette Henri. *The Unknown Soldiers: Black American Troops in World War I*. Philadelphia: Temple University Press, 1974.

Barth, Alan. *Prophets with Honor: Great Dissents and Dissenters in the Supreme Court*. New York: Knopf, 1974.

Bennett, Michael. *Union Jacks: Yankee Sailors in the Civil War*. Chapel Hill: University of North Carolina Press, 2004.

Berlin, Ira, Joseph P. Reidy, and Leslie S. Rowland. *The Black Military Experience*. 2d ser. Vol. 1 of *Freedom: A Documentary History of Emancipation, 1861–1867*. New York: Cambridge University Press, 1982.

———. *Freedom's Soldiers: The Black Military Experience in the Civil War*. New York: Cambridge University Press, 1998.

Berry, Mary Frances. *Military Necessity and Civil Rights Policy, Black Citizenship and the Constitution, 1861–1868*. Port Washington, N.Y.: Kennikat Press, 1977.

Beth, Loren P. *John Marshall Harlan: The Last Whig Justice*. Lexington: University of Kentucky Press, 1992.

Blair, William A. *Cities of the Dead: Contesting the Memory of the Civil War in the South, 1865–1914*. Chapel Hill: University of North Carolina Press, 2004.

Blatt, Martin H., Thomas J. Brown, and Donald Yacovone, eds. *Hope and Glory: Essays on the Legacy of the 54th Massachusetts Regiment*. Amherst: University of Massachusetts Press, 2000.

Blight, David W. *Frederick Douglass' Civil War: Keeping Faith in the Jubilee*. Baton Rouge: Louisiana State University Press, 1991.

———. *Race and Reunion: The Civil War in American Memory*. Cambridge: Harvard University Press (Belknap), 2001.

Brown, Christopher Leslie, and Philip D. Morgan. *Arming Slaves: From Classical Times to the Modern Age*. New Haven: Yale University Press, 2006.

Buck, Paul H. *The Road to Reunion*. New York: Little, Brown and Company, 1937.

Bullock, Steven C. *Revolutionary Brotherhood: Freemasonry and the Transformation of the American Social Orders, 1730–1840*. Chapel Hill: University of North Carolina Press, 1998.

Burchard, Peter. *One Gallant Rush: Robert Gould Shaw and His Brave Black Regiment*. New York: St. Martin's Press, 1965.

Burkhardt, George S. *Confederate Rage, Yankee Wrath: No Quarter in the Civil War*. Carbondale: Southern Illinois University Press, 2007.

Castel, Albert. *Civil War Kansas: Reaping the Whirlwind*. Authorized ed. Lawrence: University Press of Kansas, 1997.

Catton, Bruce. *Glory Road*. Garden City, N.Y.: Doubleday, 1952.

———. *Mr. Lincoln's Army*. Garden City, N.Y.: Doubleday, 1951.

———. *A Stillness at Appomattox*. Garden City, N.Y.: Doubleday, 1953.

Childers, Thomas. *Soldier from the War Returning: The Greatest Generation's Troubled Homecoming from World War II*. Boston: Mariner Books, 2009.

Christian, Garna L. *Black Soldiers in Jim Crow Texas, 1899–1917*. College Station: Texas A&M University Press, 1995.

Cimprich, John. *Fort Pillow: A Civil War Massacre, and Public Memory*. Baton Rouge: Louisiana State University Press, 2005.

Clark, Kathleen. *Defining Moments: African American Commemoration and Political Culture in the American South, 1863–1913*. Chapel Hill: University of North Carolina Press, 2006.

Clawson, Mary L. *Constructing Brotherhood: Class, Gender, and Fraternalism*. Princeton: Princeton University Press, 1989.

Claxton, Melvin, and Mark Puls. *Uncommon Valor: A Story of Race, Patriotism, and Glory in the Final Battles of the Civil War*. Hoboken, N.J.: John Wiley and Sons, 2006.

Connelly, Thomas L., and Barbara L. Bellows. *God and General Longstreet: The Lost Cause and the Southern Mind*. Baton Rouge: Louisiana State University Press, 1982.

Cornish, Dudley Taylor. *The Sable Arm: Negro Troops in the Union Army 1861–1865*. Lawrence: University Press of Kansas, 1987.

Cox, Anna-Lisa. *A Stronger Kinship: One Town's Extraordinary Story of Hope and Faith*. Boston: Little, Brown and Company, 2006.

Cox, LaWanda. *Lincoln and Black Freedom: A Study in Presidential Leadership*. Columbia: University of South Carolina Press, 1981.

Cowley, Robert, and Geoffrey Parker, eds. *The Reader's Companion to Military History*. Boston: Houghton Mifflin, 1996.

Cunningham, Edward. *The Port Hudson Campaign, 1862–1863*. Baton Rouge: Louisiana State University Press, 1994.

Cushman, Claire, ed. *The Supreme Court Justices: Illustrated Biographies, 1789–1995*. Washington, D.C.: Congressional Quarterly, 1995.

Dalfiume, Richard M. *Desegregation of the United States Armed Forces: Fighting on Two Fronts, 1939–1953*. Columbia: University of Missouri Press, 1969.

Daniel, Larry J. *Days of Glory: The Army of the Cumberland, 1861–1865*. Baton Rouge: Louisiana State University Press, 2004.

Danky, James P., and Maureen E. Hady. *African-American Newspapers and Periodicals: A National Bibliography*. Cambridge: Harvard University Press, 1998.

Doughty, Robert, and Ira D. Gruber et al. *The American Civil War: The Emergence of Total Warfare*. Lexington, Mass.: Heath, 1996.

Davies, Wallace E. *Patriotism on Parade: The Story of Veterans and Hereditary Organizations in America, 1783–1900*. Cambridge: Harvard University Press, 1955.

Davis, Benjamin O., Jr. *Benjamin O. Davis Jr.: American*. Washington, D.C.: Smithsonian Institute Press, 1991.

Davis, Susan G. *Parades and Power: Street Theater in Nineteenth-Century Philadelphia*. Philadelphia: Temple University Press, 1986.

Dean, Eric T. *Shook Over Hell: Post Traumatic Stress, Vietnam, and the Civil War*. Cambridge: Harvard University Press, 1997.

Dearing, Mary R. *Veterans in Politics: The Story of the GAR*. Baton Rouge: Louisiana State University Press, 1952.

Dobak, William A., and Thomas D. Phillips. *The Black Regulars, 1866–1898*. Norman: University of Oklahoma Press, 2001.

Du Bois, W. E. B. *The Autobiography of W. E. B. Du Bois*. 2003. Reprint, New York: International Publishers, 1968.

Dumenil, Lynn. *Freemasonry and American Culture, 1880–1930*. Princeton: Princeton University Press, 1984.

Duncan, Russell, ed. *Blue-eyed Child of Fortune: The Civil War Letters of Colonel Robert Gould Shaw*. Athens: University of Georgia Press, 1992.

———. *Where Death and Glory Meet: Colonel Robert Gould Shaw and the 54th Massachusetts Infantry*. Athens: University of Georgia Press, 1999.

Durden, Robert F. *The Gray and the Black: The Confederate Debate on Emancipation.* Baton Rouge: Louisiana State University Press, 1972.

Dyer, Frederick H. *A Compendium of the War of the Rebellion.* 1908. Reprint, Dayton, Ohio: The Press of Morningside Bookshop, 1978.

Early, Charity Adams. *One Woman's Army: A Black Officer Remembers the WAC.* College Station: Texas A&M University Press, 1989.

Eksteins, Modris. *Rites of Spring: The Great War and the Birth of the Modern Age.* New York: Anchor Books, 1990.

Emilio, Luis F. *A Brave Black Regiment: History of the Fifty-fourth Regiment of Massachusetts Volunteer Infantry, 1863–1865.* Boston: The Boston Book Co., 1891.

Fabre, Geneviève, and Robert O'Meally, eds. *History and Memory in African-American Culture.* New York: Oxford University Press, 1994.

Farrar, Hayward. *The Baltimore Afro-American: 1892–1950.* Westport, Conn.: Greenwood Press, 1998.

Faust, Drew Gilpin. *This Republic of Suffering: Death and the American Civil War.* New York: Knopf, 2008.

Fellman. Michael. *Inside War: The Guerilla Conflict in Missouri During the American Civil War.* New York: Oxford University Press, 1989.

Fletcher, Marvin. *America's First Black General, Benjamin O. Davis, Sr., 1888–1970.* Lawrence: University Press of Kansas, 1989.

———. *The Black Soldier and Officer in the United States Army, 1891–1917.* Columbia: University of Missouri Press, 1974.

Foner, Eric. *Free Soil, Free Labor, Free Men: The Ideology of the Republican Party before the Civil War.* New York: Oxford University Press, 1970.

Foster, Gaines M. *Ghosts of the Confederacy: Defeat, the Lost Cause, and the Emergence of the New South, 1865–1913.* New York: Oxford University Press, 1986.

Fox-Genovese, Elizabeth. *Within the Plantation Household: Black and White Women in the Old South.* Chapel Hill: University of North Carolina Press, 1988.

Franklin, John Hope. *The Emancipation Proclamation.* Garden City, N.Y.: Doubleday, 1963.

———. *George Washington Williams: A Biography.* Chicago: University of Chicago Press, 1985.

Frasca, Ralph. *The Rise and Fall of the Saturday Globe.* Selinsgrove, Pa.: Susquehanna University Press, 1992.

Frazier, E. Franklin. *The Negro Church.* New York: Schocken Books, 1974.

Fussell, Paul. *The Great War and Modern Memory.* London: Oxford University Press, 1975.

Gaines, Kevin. *Uplifting the Race: Black Leadership, Politics and Culture in the Twentieth Century.* Chapel Hill: University of North Carolina Press, 1996.

Gallagher, Gary W. *Causes Won, Lost, and Forgotten: How Hollywood and Popular Art Shape What We Know about the Civil War.* Chapel Hill: University of North Carolina Press, 2008.

Gallagher, Gary W., and Alan T. Nolan, eds. *The Myth of the Lost Cause and Civil War History.* Bloomington: Indiana University Press, 2000.

Gambone, Michael T. *The Greatest Generation Comes Home: The Veteran in American Society.* College Station: Texas A&M University Press, 2005.

Genovese, Eugene. *Roll, Jordan, Roll: The World the Slaves Made.* New York: Vintage, 1976.

Gillispie, James M. *Andersonvilles of the North: The Myths and Realities of Northern Treatment of Civil War Confederate Prisoners.* Denton: University of North Texas Press, 2008.

Gilmore, Glenda Elizabeth. *Gender and Jim Crow: Women and the Politics of White Supremacy in North Carolina, 1896–1920.* Chapel Hill: The University of North Carolina Press, 1996.

Ginzberg, Lori D. *Women and the Work of Benevolence: Morality, Politics, and Class in the Nineteenth-Century United States.* New Haven: Yale University Press, 1992.

Glasson, William H. *Federal Military Pensions in the United States.* New York: Oxford University Press, 1918.

Glatthaar, Joseph. *Forged in Battle: The Civil War Alliance of Black Soldiers and White Officers.* New York: Meridian Books, 1991.

Glymph, Thavolia. *Out of the House of Bondage: The Transformation of the Plantation Household.* New York: Cambridge University Press, 2008.

Gooding, James Henry. *On the Altar of Freedom: A Black Soldier's Civil War Letters from the Front.* Edited by Virginia M. Adams. New York: Warner Books, 1992.

Goodwin, Doris Kearns. *The Fitzgeralds and the Kennedys: An American Saga.* New York: St. Martins Press, 1991.

Gould, William Benjamin, IV, ed. *Diary of a Civil War Contraband: The Civil War Passage of a Black Sailor.* Palo Alto: Stanford University Press, 2002.

Green, A. Wilson. *The Final Battles of the Petersburg Campaign, Breaking the Backbone of Rebellion.* Knoxville: University of Tennessee Press, 2008.

Grimsley, Mark. *The Hard Hand of War: Union Military Policy toward Civilians, 1861–1865.* Cambridge: Cambridge University Press, 1995.

Guelzo, Allen C. *Lincoln's Emancipation Proclamation: The End of Slavery in America.* New York: Simon and Schuster, 2004.

Hahn, Steven. *A Nation under Our Feet: Black Political Struggles in the Rural South from Slavery to the Great Migration.* Cambridge: Belknap Press of Harvard University Press, 2003.

Hale, Grace Elizabeth. *Making Whiteness: The Culture of Segregation in the South, 1890–1940.* New York: Pantheon, 1998.

Harris, Bill. *The Hellfighters of Harlem: African-American Soldiers Who Fought for the Right to Fight for Their Country.* New York: Carroll & Graf, 2002.

Harris, Stephen L. *Harlem's Hellfighters: The African-American 369th Infantry in World War I.* Washington, D.C.: Brasseys, 2003.

Heck, Fran H. *The Civil War Veteran in Minnesota Life and Politics.* Oxford, Ohio: Mississippi Valley Press, 1941.

Hendricks, Wanda A. *Gender, Race, and Politics in the Midwest: Black Club Women in Illinois.* Bloomington: Indiana University Press, 1998.

Hess, Earl J. *Liberty, Virtue, and Progress: Northerners and Their War for the Union.* New York: New York University Press, 1988.

———. *The Rifle Musket in Civil War Combat: Reality and Myth.* Lawrence: University Press of Kansas, 2008.

————. *The Union Soldier in Battle: Enduring the Ordeal of Battle.* Lawrence: University Press of Kansas, 1997.

Hewitt, Lawrence L. *Port Hudson: Confederate Bastion on the Mississippi.* Baton Rouge: Louisiana State University Press, 1994.

Hollandsworth, James G. *Louisiana Native Guards: The Black Military Experience During the Civil War.* Baton Rouge: Louisiana State University Press, 1998.

Horton, James, and Lois Horton. *Black Bostonians: Family Life and Community Struggle in the Antebellum North.* New York: Holmes and Meier, 1999.

————. *In Hope of Liberty: Culture, Community, and Protest Among Northern Free Blacks, 1700–1860.* New York: Oxford University Press, 1997.

Hunt, Robert. *The Good Men Who Won the War: Army of the Cumberland Veterans and Emancipation Memory.* Tuscaloosa: University of Alabama Press, 2010.

Hynes, Samuel. *A War Imagined: The Great War and English Culture.* London: Bodley Head, 1991.

Johnson, Charles, Jr. *African-American Soldiers in the National Guard: Recruitment and Deployment during Peacetime and War.* Westport, Conn.: Greenwood Press, 1992.

Jones, Jacqueline. *Labor of Love, Labor of Sorrow: Black Women, Work, and the Family, from Slavery to the Present.* New York: Basic Books, 1985.

Jones, P. M., and His 1993/1994-Murphysboro (Ill.) Middle School 6th Grade Class. *Forgotten Soldiers: Murphysboro's African-American Civil War Veterans.* N.p.: 1994.

Kelly, Patrick J. *Creating a National Home: Building the Veterans' Welfare State, 1860–1900.* Cambridge, Mass.: Harvard University Press, 1997.

Knupfer, Anne, and Leonard Silk. *Toward a Tenderer Humanity and a Nobler Womanhood: African American Women's Clubs in Turn-of-the-Century Chicago.* New York: New York University Press, 1997.

Lane, Ann J. *The Brownsville Affair: National Crisis and Black Reaction.* Port Washington, N.Y.: Kennikat Press, 1971.

Leckie, William. *The Buffalo Soldiers: A Narrative of the Negro Cavalry in the West.* Norman: University of Oklahoma Press, 1967.

Lee, Ulysses. *The Employment of Negro Troops.* Washington, D.C.: Center for Military History, 1965.

Lentz-Smith, Adriane. *Freedom Struggles: African Americans and World War I.* Cambridge, Mass.: Harvard University Press, 2009.

Levine, Bruce. *Confederate Emancipation: Southern Plans to Free and Arm Slaves during the Civil War.* New York: Oxford University Press, 2005.

Levine, Robert S. ed. *Martin R. Delany: A Documentary Reader.* Chapel Hill: University of North Carolina Press, 2003.

Lincoln, C. Eric, and Lawrence H. Mamiya. *The Black Church in the African-American Experience.* Durham, N.C.: Duke University Press, 1990.

Linderman, Gerald F. *Embattled Courage: The Experience of Combat in the Civil War.* New York: Free Press, 1987.

Litwack, Leon. *North of Slavery: The Negro in the Free States, 1790–1860.* Chicago: University of Chicago Press, 1961.

————. *Trouble in Mind: Black Southerners in the Age of Jim Crow.* New York: Knopf, 1998.

Logan, Rayford W. *The Betrayal of the Negro: From Rutherford B. Hayes to Woodrow Wilson*. 1954. Reprint, New York: Da Capo Press, 1997.

Manning, Chandra. *What This Cruel War Was Over: Soldiers, Slavery, and the Civil War*. New York: Knopf, 2007.

Marvel, William. *Andersonville: The Last Depot*. Chapel Hill: University of North Carolina Press, 1994.

McConnell, Stuart. *Glorious Contentment: The Grand Army of the Republic, 1865–1900*. Chapel Hill: University of North Carolina Press, 1992.

McGuire, Phillip. *He, Too, Spoke for Democracy: Judge Hastie, World War II, and the Black Soldier*. Westport, Conn.: Greenwood Press, 1988.

McPherson, James M. *For Cause and Comrades*. New York: Oxford University Press, 1997.

Millet, Allan R., and Peter Maslowski. *For the Common Defense: A Military History of the United States*. New York: Free Press, 1994.

Mitchell, Reid. *Civil War Soldiers*. New York: Viking Press, 1988.

Morgan, Francesca. *Women and Patriotism in Jim Crow America*. Chapel Hill: The University of North Carolina Press, 2005.

Moses, Wilson J. *Alexander Crummel: A Study of Civilization and Its Discontents*. New York: Oxford University Press, 1990.

Motely, Mary Penick. *The Invisible Soldier: The Experience of the Black Soldier, World War II*. Detroit: Wayne State University Press, 1975.

Muraskin, William A. *Middle-Class Blacks in a White Society: Prince Hall Freemasonry in America*. Berkeley: University of California Press, 1975.

Nankivell, John. *History of the Twenty-fifth Regiment, United States Infantry, 1869–1924*. 1927. Reprint, New York: Negro University Press, 1969.

Nash, Gary B. *Forging Freedom: The Formation of Philadelphia's Black Community, 1720–1840*. Cambridge: Harvard University Press, 1988.

Neff, John R. *Honoring the Civil War Dead: Commemoration and the Problem of Reconciliation*. Lawrence: University Press of Kansas, 2005.

Neely, Mark E. *The Civil War and the Limits of Destruction*. Cambridge, Mass.: Harvard University Press, 2007.

Nichols, Lee. *Breakthrough on the Color Front*. New York: Random House, 1954.

Niven, John. *Connecticut for the Union*. New Haven: Yale University Press, 1965.

Nora, Pierre. *Realms of Memory: Rethinking the French Past*. Translated by Arthur Goldhammer. New York: Columbia University Press, 1996.

Nulty, William H. *Confederate Florida: The Road to Olustee*. Tuscaloosa: University of Alabama Press, 1990.

Ochs, Stephen J. *A Black Patriot and a White Priest: Andre Cailloux and Claude Paschal Maistre in Civil War New Orleans*. Baton Rouge: Louisiana State University Press, 2006.

Ofele, Martin. *German-Speaking Officers of the U.S. Colored Troops, 1863–1867*. Gainesville: University of Florida Press, 2004.

O'Leary, Cecilia. *To Die For: The Paradox of American Patriotism*. Princeton: Princeton University Press, 1999.

Pencak, William. *For God and Country: The American Legion, 1919–1941*. Boston: Northeastern University Press, 1989.

————, ed. *Encyclopedia of the Veteran in America.* Santa Barbara, Calif.: ABC-CLIO, 2009.

Putney, Martha S. *When the Nation Was in Need: Blacks in the Women's Army Corps during World War II.* Metuchen, N.J.: Scarecrow Press, 1992.

Przybyszewski, Linda. *The Republic According to John Marshall Harlan.* Chapel Hill: University of North Carolina Press, 1999.

Quarles, Benjamin. *The Negro in the Civil War.* New York: Russell and Russell, 1953.

Rabinowitz, Howard N. *Race Relations in the Urban South, 1865–1900.* New York: Oxford University Press, 1978.

Raboteau, Albert. *Slave Religion: The "Invisible Institution" in the Antebellum South.* New York: Oxford University Press, 1978.

Ramold, Steven. *Slaves, Sailors, Citizens: African Americans in the Union Navy.* DeKalb: Northern Illinois University Press, 2002.

Reardon, Carol. *Pickett's Charge in History and Memory.* Chapel Hill: University of North Carolina Press, 1997.

Reid, Richard M. *Freedom for Themselves: North Carolina's Black Soldiers in the Civil War Era.* Chapel Hill: University of North Carolina Press, 2008.

Resch, John. *Suffering Soldiers: Revolutionary War Veterans, Moral Sentiment, and Political Culture in the Early Republic.* Amherst: University of Massachusetts Press, 1999.

Roberts, Frank. *The American Foreign Legion: Black Soldiers of the 93rd in World War I.* Annapolis, Md.: U.S. Naval Institute Press, 2004.

Roosevelt, Robert B., ed. *The Poetical Works of Charles G. Halpine (Miles O'Reilly).* New York: Harper Brothers, 1869.

Royster, Charles. *The Destructive War: William Tecumseh Sherman, Stonewall Jackson, and the Americans.* New York: Vantage, 1993.

Safire, William. *Lend Me Your Ears: Great Speeches in History.* New York: W. W. Norton, 2004.

Salvatore, Nick. *We All Got History: The Memory Book of Amos Webber.* New York: Times Books, 1996.

Sanders, Charles W. *While in the Hands of the Enemy: Military Prisons of the Civil War.* Baton Rouge: Louisiana State University Press, 2005.

Sandler, Stanley. *Segregated Skies: Black Combat Units of World War II.* Washington, D.C.: Smithsonian Institution, 1992.

Savage, Kirk. *Standing Soldiers, Kneeling Slaves: Race, War, and Monument in Nineteenth-Century America.* Princeton: Princeton University Press, 1997.

Schacter, Daniel L. *The Seven Sins of Memory: How the Mind Forgets and Remembers.* New York: Houghton Mifflin, 2001.

Schantz, Mark S. *Awaiting the Heavenly Country: The Civil War and America's Culture of Death.* New York: Cornell University Press, 2008.

Skocpol, Theda. *Protecting Soldiers and Mothers: The Political Origins of Social Policy in the United States.* New York: Belknap Press of Harvard University Press, 1995.

Skocpol, Theda, Ariane Liazos, and Marshall Ganz. *What a Mighty Power We Can Be: African-American Fraternal Groups and the Struggle for Racial Equality.* Princeton: Princeton University Press, 2006.

Shaffer, Donald R. *After the Glory: The Struggles of Black Civil War Veterans*. Lawrence: University Press of Kansas, 2004.

Shay, Jonathan. *Achilles in Vietnam: Combat Trauma and the Undoing of Character*. Touchstone: New York, 1995.

———. *Odysseus in America: Combat Trauma and the Trials of Homecoming*. New York: Scribner, 2002.

Silber, Nina. *The Romance of Reunion*. Chapel Hill: University of North Carolina Press, 1993.

Slaughter, Thomas P. *Bloody Dawn: The Christiana Riot and Racial Violence in the Antebellum North*. New York: Oxford University Press, 1994.

Slotkin, Richard. *Lost Battalions: The Great War and the Crisis of American Nationality*. New York: Henry Holt, 2005.

Smith, Graham. *When Jim Crow Met John Bull: Black American Soldiers in World War II Britain*. New York: St. Martin's Press, 1988.

Smith, John David, ed. *Black Soldiers in Blue: African American Troops in the Civil War Era*. Chapel Hill: University of North Carolina Press, 2002.

Sutherland, Daniel E. *The Emergence of Total War*. Ft. Worth, Tex.: Ryan Place Publishers, 1996.

Tappan, Franklin D. *The Passing of the Grand Army of the Republic*. Worcester, Mass.: Commonwealth Press, 1939.

Thomas, Emory. *Robert E. Lee: A Biography*. New York: W. W. Norton, 1997.

Tomblin, Barbara. *Bluejackets and Contrabands: African Americans and the Union Navy*. Lexington: University Press of Kentucky, 2009.

Trudeau, Noah. *Like Men of War: Black Troops in the Civil War 1862–1865*. New York: Little, Brown and Company, 1998.

Urwin, Gregory J. W., ed. *Black Flag over Dixie: Racial Atrocities and Reprisals in the Civil War*. Carbondale: Southern Illinois University Press, 2004.

Van Deventer, Lynda. *Home before Morning: The Story of an Army Nurse in Vietnam*. 1983. Reprint, Amherst: University of Massachusetts Press, 2001.

Voegli, Jacque. *Free but Not Equal: The Midwest Negro during the Civil War*. Chicago: University of Chicago Press, 1967.

Walker, Keith. *A Piece of My Heart: The Stories of 26 American Women Who Served in Vietnam*. New York: Presidio Press, 1997.

Ward, Andrew. *River Run Red: The Fort Pillow Massacre in the American Civil War*. New York: Penguin, 2006.

Waugh, Joan. *U.S. Grant: American Hero, American Myth*. Chapel Hill: University of North Carolina Press, 2009.

Weaver, John D. *The Brownsville Raid*. College Station: Texas A&M University Press, 1992.

———. *The Senator and the Sharecropper's Son: Exoneration of the Brownsville Soldiers*. College Station: Texas A&M University Press, 1997.

Weeks, Jim. *Gettysburg: Memory, Market, and American Shrine*. Princeton: Princeton University Press, 2003.

White, G. Edward. *Oliver Wendell Holmes, Jr*. New York: Oxford University Press, 2006.

White, Ronald C. *Lincoln's Greatest Speech: The Second Inaugural*. New York: Simon and Schuster, 2002.

Wiley, Bell. *Life of Billy Yank: The Common Soldier in the War for the Union.* Indianapolis: Bobbs-Merrill, 1952.

Williams, T. Harry. *Lincoln and His Generals.* New York: Knopf, 1952.

Wilson, Charles Reagan. *Baptized in Blood: The Religion of the Lost Cause, 1865–1920.* Athens: University of Georgia Press, 1980.

Wilson, Keith P. *Campfires of Freedom: The Camp Life of Black Soldiers during the Civil War.* Kent, Ohio: Kent State University Press, 2002.

Winter, Jay. *Sites of Memory, Sites of Mourning: The Great War in European Cultural History.* Cambridge: Cambridge University Press, 1995.

Woodward, C. Vann. *The Strange Career of Jim Crow.* New York: Oxford University Press, 1955.

Wooley, C. F. *The Irritable Heart of Soldiers and the Origins of Anglo-American Cardiology: The U.S. Civil War (1861) to World War I (1918).* Aldershot, U.K.: Ashgate, 2002.

Articles and Essays

Blight, David W. "'For Something beyond the Battlefield': Frederick Douglas and the Struggle for the Memory of the Civil War." *The Journal of American History* 75 (March 1989): 1156–78.

Davies, Wallace E. "The Problem of Race Segregation in the Grand Army of the Republic." *The Journal of Southern History* 13 (August 1947): 354–72.

Fleche, Andre M. "'Shoulder to Shoulder as Comrades Tried': Black and White Union Veterans and Civil War Memory." *Civil War History* 51 (June 2005): 175–201.

Fraser, Francis, and R. M. Wilson. "The Sympathetic Nervous System and the 'Irritable Heart of Soldiers.'" *The British Medical Journal* 2 (July 13, 1918): 27–29.

Gannon, Barbara A. "'Sites of Memory, Sites of Glory': African American GAR Posts in Pennsylvania." In *Making and Remaking Pennsylvania's Civil War*, edited by William A. Blair and William Pencak, 164–88. University Park: Pennsylvania State University Press, 2001.

Hu, Hailan, Eleonore Real, Kogo Takamiya, Myoung-Goo Kang, Joseph Ledoux, Richard L. Huganir, and Roberto Malinow. "Emotion Enhances Learning via Norepinephrine Regulation of AMPA-Receptor Trafficking." *Cell* 131 (October 2007): 160–73.

Knight, Glen B. "The Grand Army of the Republic in Lancaster Society." *Journal of the Historical Society of Lancaster* 97, no. 2 (1995): 98–132.

Lerner, Gerda. "Early Community Work of Black Club Women." *Journal of Negro History* 59 (April 1974): 158–67.

McMurry, Donald M. "The Bureau of Pensions during the Administration of President Harrison." *Mississippi Valley Historical Review* 13 (December 1926): 343–64.

Mitchell, Reid. "Not the General but the Soldier." In *Writing the Civil War: The Quest to Understand*, edited by James M. McPherson and William J. Cooper Jr., 81–95. Columbia: University of South Carolina Press, 1998.

Neely, Mark E., Jr. "Was the Civil War a Total War?" *Civil War History* 37 (March 1991): 5–28.

Oppenheimer B. S., and M. A. Rothschild. "The Psychoneurotic Factor in the 'Irritable Heart' of Soldiers." *The British Medical Journal* 2 (July 13, 1918): 29–31.

Pizarro, Judith, Roxanne Cohen Silver, and JoAnn Prause. "Physical and Mental Health Costs of Traumatic War Experiences among Civil War Veterans." *Archives of General Psychiatry* 63 (February 2006): 193–200.

Skocpol, Theda, and Jennifer Lynn Oser. "Organization Despite Adversity: The Organization Development of African-American Fraternal Associations." *Social Science History* 28 (Fall 2004): 367–437.

Thelan, David. "Memory and History." *Journal of American History* 75 (March 1989): 1117–29.

Trotter, Joe W. "African American Fraternal Organizations in American History: An Introduction." *Social Science History* 28 (Fall 2004): 355–66.

White, Shane. "'It Was a Proud Day': African Americans, Festivals, and Parades in the North, 1741–1834." *Journal of American History* 81 (June 1994): 13–50.

Dissertations

Lankevich, George. "The Grand Army of the Republic in New York State." Ph.D. diss., Columbia University, 1968.

Mulderlink, Earl F., III. "'We Want a Country': African-American Citizenship and Irish Life in New Bedford, Massachusetts, during the Civil War Era." Ph.D. diss., University of Wisconsin, 1995.

Noyes, Elmer E. "A History of the Grand Army of the Republic in Ohio." Ph.D. diss., Ohio State University, 1945.

Shaffer, Donald R. "Marching On: African-American Civil War Veterans in Postbellum America, 1865–1951." Ph.D. diss., University of Maryland, 1996.

Index

Numbers in italics indicate images.

★

Gallagher, Gary, 187

Gardiner, Washington, 158

Garrison Post (New York City), 55, 62, 64, 72, 75

Gelbert, Theodore, 127

George, Wallace, 104

Georgia and South Carolina GAR: black veterans joining, 30–31

Gettysburg, battle of, 16; excursions to site of, 248 (n. 12); fiftieth anniversary of, commemorated, 182–90, 191; seventy-fifth reunion of, 198–99

Gettysburg (dir., Maxwell), 118

Gibson (comrade, Ohio), 161

Gill Post (Evansville, Ind.), 43

Gleason (comrade, Georgia), 31

Glory (dir., Zwick), 11, 18, 118

Goodge, J. Edward, 126

Gould, William Benjamin, 107

Grand Army of the Republic: auxiliary groups of, 5, 47–48 (*see also* Ladies of the GAR; Woman's Relief Corps); blacks' autonomy in, 5; blacks serving as third in command in, 33, 25–26; blacks winning elective office in, 23–27; brotherhood of, based on memory and Memory, 166; cardinal principles of, 35–36; color-bearers in, 108–9; color-blind records of, 38; comrades of, sharing personal memories, 118–19; controversy in, when blacks were excluded, 28–34; Council of Administration, 25, 33; death of final member, 21, 199; defining itself as an interracial organization, 21–22; dues and fees paid to, 40–41; fighting the Lost Cause concept, 147; first post formed, 20–21; guard positions in, 107–8; interracial gatherings of, 46; living to see the atomic age, 196; local meetings of, 35–38; mourning rituals of, 109–10; naming and numbering of posts, 59–60; Norfolk reunion of, 37; numbers of veterans needed to support a post, 227–28 (n. 9); organization of, 3, 22–23, 37–38; origins and growth of, 2–3; as political inter-

est group, 21, 131–32; political life of, blacks participating in, 5, 15–16; posts in, wealth of, 41; poverty affecting participation in, 109; as precursor to other veterans' groups, 2; rejecting applicants (*see* Blackballing system); rejecting reunionism, 164; review of (1892), 1, 2; rituals of, 41–42; southern branches in, 28–34; state and local records of, 9–10; treatment of blacks in, accounts of, 3; two phases of its existence, 20–21; uninvolvement of, in protecting African Americans' rights, 164–65, 168–71, 193; uniqueness of, 15–16; white members of, remembering blacks' service, 5. *See also* African American GAR posts; Integrated GAR posts

Grant, Ulysses S., 64

Graveyards, Memorial Day decoration of, 73–74, 76

Green, A. J., 96

Griffin Post (Scranton, Pa.), 105

Gross, George, 121, 126

Guard positions, 107–8

Hacker, Newton, 151

Hall, Andrew, 122

Hall, Clay, 166

Halpine, Charles Graham, 117–18

Hamilton, Frank, 95–96, 102, 108

Hamilton, Julia West, 198

Hamilton, Matthew, 126

Hamilton, W. H. L., 135

Hamilton Post (Trenton, N.J.), 52–53

Harlan, John, 163–64

Harlan, Malvina Shanklin, 163

Harlem Hellfighters, 194

Harris, Edward F., *44*, 180

Harris, John L., 109

Harris, Maggie J., *53*

Harris, W. J., 108

Harrison, Henry, 104, 106

Harvey, Owen, 126

Hawley, George, 126

Hayes, Rutherford B., 155–56, 173

Hector, Jacob, 15, 31, 70, 71, 223 (n. 1)

Henderson (representative, Stevens Post, N.Y.), 61

Henry, C. W., 108

Hess, Earl J., 244 (n. 2)

Hinks, Edward, 134–35

History: distinguished from Memory, 3–4

Holmes, Oliver Wendell, 133, 160, 243–44 (n. 19)

Hood, Solomon, 124, 150, 157

Hull Post (Pittsburgh), 35

Hullett (comrade, Chicago), 23

Hunger during Civil War, soldiers' memory of, 129–30

Hunt, Robert, 93

Hunter, David, 16, 117

Hunter Post (Beaufort, S.C.), 74–75

Hurley, Robert, 24

Iliad, The, 138

"I'll Report to God the Reason Why" (poem), 122

Imprisonment, memories of, 127–29

Indiana, Twenty-third, 110–11

Indianapolis Freeman, 190, 192

Integrated GAR posts: African Americans' longevity in, 109; blacks holding elected offices in, 107–9; concerned for deceased comrades' families, 110; daily life in, significance of, 99–100, 107; decisions about, taking place at local level, 93–94; different regional approaches to, 87–93; difficulty in identifying, 86; distribution of, in different states, 85–88; economic diversity in, 101–3; forgotten in battle for Civil War Memory, 113–14; former enlisted comrades joining, 104; honoring their dead, 109–10; immigrants in, 103; intentional creation of, 105–7; language differences among, 103; percentage of black veterans in, 90; political partnership not a factor in, 100; race-based exclusion from, 94–98; significance of, 6–7; welcoming black veterans based on experience, 104–5; white members' experience affecting makeup of, 105

Integration of the military, 194–95

Iowa: integrated posts in, 90; Fifteenth Infantry, 102; Twenty-sixth Infantry, 111–12

Irritable Heart, 243 (n. 13)

Ives, Robert, 60

Ives Post (Providence, R.I.), 46, 55, 62–63, 64, 73, 77, 78

Jackson, Joseph, 126

Jackson, Thomas Jefferson, 104

Jackson Circle (New Bedford, Mass.), 76

Jackson Post (Philadelphia), 74

Jacobs, Stephen, 98, 110, 136

James, Andrew, 23, 24, 25

James, William, 126–27

Jim Crow, era of, 179

Johnson (comrade, Newark, N.J.), 25

Johnson (comrade, Washington, D.C.), 31

Johnson, Henry, 64

Johnson, Isaac, 105

Jones, Evan, 129–30

Jones, Moses, 103

Jones, Samuel, 180

Joselyn, Edward S., 100

Kansas: First Colored regiment, 89; integrated posts in, 88–89

Kay, Joseph W., 23

Keith Post (Wilkes-Barre, Pa.), 59, 63, 65

Kentucky GAR: endorsing segregation, 171–72; refusing to go on record against lynching, 168–69

Keyes, William, 103

Klein (immigrant comrade, New Haven, Conn.), 103

Ku Klux Klan, 168

Ladies of the GAR (LGAR), 47; circles of, 59; membership requirements of, 48

Lafayette (reverend/comrade, Pittsburgh), 36

Lafayette Post (New York), 45

Lattimer, George A., 102

Layton, Julia Mason, 197

Lee, Robert E., 93, 131, 147

charity as most important duty, 53–54; membership requirements of, 48; naming of units, 59; segregation of, 48–49; records of, emphasizing aid to widows and orphans, 136–37

Women: associated with GAR posts, 99

Women's auxiliaries, 36, 47, 197–98; African American, primary focus of, 50–51, 53; benevolence of, 136–37; correspondents reporting on, 52–53; forming during the Memorial Day period, 76; racial affiliations of, 50–51. *See also* Ladies of the GAR; Woman's Relief Corps

Women's clubs, 229 (n. 2)

Women's Vigilance Committee, 64

Won Cause: advocacy for, 145–46; coining of term, 146–47; consistency of belief in, 154; in GAR members' minds, 149–50; linked with African Americans' status, 166; meaning of, 7; prevailing, 195; rhetoric of, evolving, 175–77; victory of, 200

Wood, John M., 152

Wounds, memories of, 126–27

Youngstown Vindicator, 113, 246 (n. 30)

Youth groups, 55